PC VIRUSES
Detection, Analysis and Cure

DR. ALAN SOLOMON

PC VIRUSES

Detection, Analysis and Cure

Springer-Verlag
London   Berlin   Heidelberg   New York
Paris   Tokyo   Hong Kong
Barcelona   Budapest

Alan Solomon, PhD
S&S International Limited
Berkley Court, Mill Street
Berkhamsted, Hertfordshire HP4 2HB, UK

ISBN 3–540–19691–9 Springer-Verlag Berlin Heidelberg New York
ISBN 0–387–19691–9 Springer-Verlag New York Berlin Heidelberg

British Library Cataloguing in Publication Data
Solomon, Alan
PC viruses: detection, analysis and cure.
1. Computers. Viruses
I. Title
005.8
ISBN 3–540–19691–9

Library of Congress Cataloging-in-Publication Data
Solomon, Alan, 1948–
PC viruses: detection, analysis and cure / Alan Solomon.
p. cm.
ISBN 3–540–19691–9 (alk. paper). – ISBN 0–387–19691–9 (alk.
paper)
1. Computer viruses.   I. Title.
QA76.76.C68S65   1991   91-3608
005.8–dc20   CIP

Typeset by Saxon Printing Ltd., Saxon House, Derby
Printed by Page Bros (Norwich) Ltd., Mile Cross Lane, Norwich
34/3830 543210 Printed on acid-free paper.

Author's Note

The technical content of this book is based on
the material I developed for the manual that
accompanies my anti-virus software
Dr. Solomon's Anti-Virus Toolkit.

CONTENTS

1.	**Introduction**	1
1.1	Anti-virus Toolkits	5
1.2	Viruses in the Corporate Environment	6
1.3	Viruses in the Academic Environment	17
1.4	The Future	19
2.	**What is a Virus?**	23
2.1	Bugs, Clashes, Trojans and Viruses	25
2.2	How to Identify a Virus	33
2.3	False Alarms	36
3.	**The Types of Viruses and How They Operate**	39
3.1	Boot Sector Viruses	41
3.2	Partition Sector Viruses	41
3.3	File Viruses: Direct Action	42
3.4	File Viruses: Indirect Action	43
3.5	How do Viruses Spread?	43
3.6	Viruses on Networks	44
4.	**The Known PC Viruses: Recognition, Analysis and Cure**	47
4.1	Brain	50
4.2	Ashar	53
4.3	Italian	56
4.4	Stoned	59
4.5	Yale	62
4.6	Denzuk	63
4.7	Lehigh	67
4.8	405 Virus	69
4.9	Vienna Virus	70
4.10	Datacrime Virus	72
4.11	Cascade (1701) Virus	74
4.12	Jerusalem (1813) Virus	77
4.13	Fu Manchu Virus	80
4.14	Traceback Virus	83
4.15	Icelandic Virus	84
4.16	The SURIV Viruses	87
4.17	Datacrime II Virus	89
4.18	Ogre	91
4.19	Typo	94

4.20	Big Italian	96
4.21	Virus-B	99
4.22	Dark Avenger	100
4.23	Vacsina	102
4.24	Mix1	104
4.25	Fumble	106
4.26	Dbase	108
4.27	Virdem	110
4.28	Denzuk I	111
4.29	Yankee Doodle	115
4.30	Alabama	117
4.31	Ghostballs	120
4.32	765 Virus	122
4.33	Lisbon Virus	124
4.34	W13 Virus	125
4.35	Oropax	127
4.36	Twelve Tricks	129
4.37	Zero Bug	134
4.38	Sylvia	136
4.39	Tenbytes	138
4.40	Sunday	140
4.41	Stupid	142
4.42	Vcomm	143
4.43	More Versions of Cascade (1704)	145
4.44	Syslock	146
4.45	Saturday 14th	148
4.46	June 16th	150
4.47	Aids	151
4.48	4096	153
4.49	Chameleon	155
4.50	Eddie 2	158
4.51	Print Screen Virus	159
4.52	Taiwan	162
4.53	December 24th Virus	164
4.54	Number of the Beast	166
4.55	Devil's Dance	169
4.56	More Versions of Vienna	171
4.57	Pixel Virus	173
4.58	NJH	174
4.59	EDV	177
4.60	Eight Tunes	180
4.61	Dark Avenger 3	182
4.62	Virus-90	184
4.63	Zapper	186
4.64	Prudents	189
4.65	Kennedy	190
4.66	Solano	192
4.67	Vbasic	193
4.68	Casper	195
4.69	Luz Virus	197

4.70	Anarkia Virus	198
4.71	Thanksgiving	200
4.72	Joshi	203
4.73	VP Virus	207
4.74	Zerotime Virus	208
4.75	Virus-101	211
4.76	XA1 Virus	213
4.77	Hallochen	215
4.78	Jojo	217
4.79	Victor	219
4.80	PSQR Virus	221
4.81	Tiny Virus	223
4.82	The Swedish Disaster	224
4.83	V1024 Virus	227
4.84	Amoeba Virus	229
4.85	Shake Virus	232
4.86	Mendoza Virus	234
4.87	Jerspain Virus	236
4.88	Frere Virus	237
4.89	More Pixel Viruses	239
4.90	Form	240
4.91	SVIR Virus	243
4.92	Subliminal Virus	245
4.93	Liberty Virus	247
4.94	Fish Virus	249
4.95	Murphy Virus	252
4.96	The "Legendary" Agiplan	254
4.97	The Anticad Series of Viruses	258
5.	**Action Plan**s	265
5.1	Precautions	267
5.2	What To Do If You Are Hit: General Advice	268
5.3	Procedures for Eradicating a Virus	270
6.	**General Advice**	275
6.1	Some General Advice	277
6.2	The Anti-virus Service	278
6.3	Inoculated Blank Diskettes	278
6.4	Update Service	278
6.5	Further Reading	279
6.6	How It All Got Started in the UK	279
Glossary		283

Chapter 1
Introduction

"Hello? Could I speak to Dr Solomon? I think I've got a virus."

Polite disbelief.

"We're getting lots of floppy disks with the volume label "(c) Brain", and I think it's a virus."

Polite scepticism.

"I'll send you a few of them. Can you tell me what it is?"

And so it was that the first virus in the UK arrived through my door, in early 1988. What led up to this, and why did the user contact me?

S&S International was set up in 1983, when the IBM PC came to the UK. I looked at the computer, and decided it was a serious machine, at a time when very few other people did. We bought one, and started to work out how it functioned, with the aid of the rather fine documentation that was available. There weren't many computers around where you could get a manual giving you the source code to the BIOS.

After delving into it for some months, I emerged to find a major discussion going on, about a very important issue. How do you get a pound sign in a Lotus 1-2-3 spreadsheet? I had a look at the problem, and found a way to do it, and expected that at any time, everyone else would do the same. But this didn't happen, and I decided that perhaps I should offer it as a product. It was my first product; I called it "The Pound", sold it for £9.99, and it was an instant success. I added a few other utilities to it, such as a program to print wide spreadsheets sideways, a printer buffer, and a couple of other goodies. I had a few favourable reviews in magazines, and sales took off.

It was clear that I had found a market, so I wrote other such utilities for doing things that people needed, but which were not part of the system that they had, and sold them via mail order. Then, one day, Karen phoned up.

Karen had a computer, and she had an important database on it. Through no fault of her own, she was unable to do a backup, and when her disk became inaccessible, her database was gone too. When she phoned, she said that she had tried seventeen other people, and no one could even try to help her. I said I'd have a go, on a no-fix, no-fee basis. As it turned out, I was able to recover her database, and she was very pleased, and wrote a letter to a magazine saying so. Thus the first data recovery service in the world was born – people especially liked the no-fix, no-fee, because it meant that they had nothing to lose. The data recovery business gradually grew as word spread, and people came to us with all sorts of hard and floppy disk problems. It is usually the case that a £50 utility can't do as well as a human being when it comes to tricky problems like data recovery.

I had heard rumours of a virus, but that was far away in the US, and who knows what might really have been happening. For sure, I knew that people lost data for all sorts of standard reasons; no virus was needed to explain a hard disk that stopped spinning. But it was my involvement in disks and data recovery that gives the reason why a university in the Midlands contacted me when they thought they had a virus.

The story of the investigation of Brain is told elsewhere in this book. The idea of a self-replicating piece of code was absolutely fascinating to me, as it would be to most mathematicians. The next question was what to do about it. At the time, people were warning each other about COMMAND.COM, as the Lehigh virus was the only one that had been widely publicised. But this virus didn't attach to a file, let alone a particular file. Brain is a boot sector virus. I decided that if everyone was watching out for COMMAND.COM, a boot sector virus would be so unexpected, that it could infect quite widely before being publicised, and so I decided to warn people about this new phenomenon.

A virus is a program that copies itself. I realised that a successful virus could spread quite widely; that what was currently a very rare phenomenon would turn into an increasingly common one. It was clear that something should be done, but no one seemed to be doing anything. So, instead of complaining that no one else was doing anything, I decided that I would tackle the problem.

Because I was the first to warn people, I was immediately regarded as the virus expert, and so I was sent the first specimen of Italian virus, another boot sector virus, except this one infected hard disks whereas Brain only infected floppies. Next came Stoned, which originally arrived in the UK as source code, but was either assembled and escaped, or else it spread naturally from New Zealand to the UK. At this point, it looked as if boot sector viruses were going to be the main problem, and then the first file virus, Vienna, arrived. This was the virus that was listed in the Burger book; I was sent a copy by a researcher in Austria, as by that time, I was beginning to become well known internationally. In November 1988 I was sent the first specimen of Jerusalem, by an infected user in Spain, and the drip turned into a trickle.

Up to December 1988, I had been dealing with each outbreak by going to help the infected site, but in December, two things happened. One was the first ever seminar about computer viruses, which was attended by over 100 people. The second was an outbreak of Jerusalem in a major financial institution in the City of London, which consumed a lot of time in dealing with it as there were over 500 computers on the site. After that, it was clear that in the long run, I could not continue to help each infected site; I had to find a way that they could help themselves. That December and January, I wrote software to make this possible, and called it the "Anti-Virus Toolkit".

At first, only a few people wanted it. Then came Friday, January 13th, and the first media circus; in fact there were a few sites that discovered Jerusalem, including British Rail (they went public on it), a printer manufacturer, and a local education authority. We provided that early version of the Toolkit to help them clean up, and it worked. In February 1989, we had the manuals ready, and we started to send out copies; one every few days or so.

It was clear from the start that it would be necessary to upgrade the Toolkit as new viruses came out; at that time, I thought that it might be every few months, and there might be times when I could skip the upgrade, as there might be no new viruses. This didn't happen, of course – the trickle of viruses became a steady flow. Now we get deliveries of viruses from Bulgaria and elsewhere around the world in dozens.

The rest is really just more of the same. I was in this problem from the beginning, and I'll be in it at the end. The British Bulldog has a nose that slopes backwards from his jaws; that is so that he can breath without having to let go of his quarry.

1.1 Anti-virus Toolkits

If you just want to know about viruses, this book is all you need. But if you also want to do a clean-up, or protect against a possible future infection, you will need some software tools. There are several such kits of tools on the market; I am most familiar with the tools that are called "Dr Solomon's Anti-Virus Toolkit", since I wrote them. Many of the tools in this Toolkit are mentioned in this book. Other anti-virus products may have equivalents to the virus finder and other tools in the Toolkit; in that case you could use those instead.

The Anti-Virus Toolkit is available to readers of this book at a substantial saving over the normal price. Send the coupon at the back of the book to the appropriate address shown and a full copy of the Toolkit will be sent to you, on diskette, so that you can implement the anti-virus strategy that is most appropriate for you. Alternatively, if you want to know more about the Toolkit, contact S&S International on 0442 877877 (+44 442 877877 if dialling from outside the UK). Local language versions are available in many countries; we can put you in touch with your local supplier.

1.2 Viruses in the Corporate Environment

Corporate users are more at risk from viruses than small business users, as they tend to swap disks more. And just about every large corporate user has had at least one outbreak by now. What are the effects of this on the use of PCs, and what should be done?

The virus problem has been gradually growing, and it has been growing in three ways. First, the older viruses continue to spread (as they are designed to do); the commonest viruses are the older ones. Second, it has now become quite easy to get hold of a library of viruses if you are plugged into the right scene or know the right people. Indeed, there are bulletin boards that specialise in offering viruses to callers for download. Third, the number of viruses has grown considerably; they are numbered in hundreds rather than dozens.

First, how does a virus commonly come into a company and spread within it? The general assumption is that they are spread through the use of games, which has led to a number of companies banning the playing of games on company computers. Unfortunately, this does not actually address the virus problem.

In my experience, hardware engineers and their diagnostic disks have played a great part in the spreading of viruses. In addition, consultants who move from company to company, and also salesmen running demos from disks that they take from place to place, are part of the problem. The solution for these people is so simple; it is a pity that it is implemented so infrequently. The solution is the write-protect tab, which will mean that the engineer will not pick up anything unwanted from his customer, and therefore not pass anything on to the next one.

Certainly, any company wishing to keep viruses out should take a careful look at the practices of the hardware maintenance people. At the very least, all their diskettes should have a write-protect tab, and it would be even better if the diskettes were not writable (if 5¼-inch, without a notch, or if 3½-inch, without a tab). Non-writable disks give you an assurance that a removable tab cannot. In some companies, incoming engineers have to leave all diskettes behind, and have to use the company's own copies of the diagnostic software.

With a salesman's demos, the ideal is that he brings in a laptop and runs the demo on that. This solves several problems at once, including the salesman's problem of the time taken to install the demo, and the worry about whether it will work on a strange machine.

I could not argue with a ban on games-playing on company computers, but it is important to understand that this is not a security issue; it is a management issue, concerned with time-wasting. How do you define a game? What is a business simulation? What is a typing tutor that makes good use of colour and sound, and entertains a bit while it teaches?

A more sensible set of rules depends on the importance that you attach to remaining virus-free. Probably the most important rule is that every incoming diskette and file must be sheep-dipped using a virus checker such as FindVirus before it is used. This rule should be applied without exceptions, even including disks from IBM and similarly reputable companies, and even to the upgrades to the virus-checking program. It is easier to include everything than to start making complicated rules about what must be checked, and what need not be checked.

The second important rule is to say that all software must be acquired from a reputable source. This does not rule out shareware and bulletin board software, provided the source is reputable. For example, it would be silly to cut off the Novell Netwire source of information and drivers, and this is commonly accessed via a BBS. Reputable source is the key.

So what is a reputable source? That is difficult. Some companies have well-known names, and are reputable by virtue of that. Other smaller, less well-known companies are equally reputable. I would recommend that as a minimum, you must know the company address, phone number and a contact name for each source of software; a PO Box is not, of course, sufficient.

The most disreputable source of software is a colleague in the same office, or a good friend. Unless they are taking precautions, they could unwittingly pass on a virus, and be terribly apologetic afterwards. Another disreputable source is a disk that arrives through the post, unsolicited, from a company you've never heard of. This is the way that the Aids Information Diskette trojan was distributed.

For a higher level of prevention, some companies have adopted a rule that says that all software must be authorised; you may not run any software unless it has come from the authorisation centre, which is usually the PC Support staff. This doesn't mean that you can avoid having the sheep-dip, though, unless you also specify that incoming diskettes must go via that channel as well.

The next problem is enforcing these rules. Some companies have gone for a rather ill-considered Draconian system, with rules like: "Anyone who plays games or uses unauthorised software faces instant dismissal". This is worse than an over-reaction; it could actually lead to the opposite of the desired effect. Consider the following scenario.

James is a PC user, and he isn't really interested in playing games. But one day, as he boots up, he notices "Your PC is now Stoned", and he knows that this means that he has a virus. He isn't technically oriented, so he doesn't know that this is a boot sector virus, and could have come from any data disk. But he does know about the instant-dismissal rule, and he values his job. He decides that if he tells the powers-that-be about the virus, his job is at risk, so it would be far safer to deal with it himself. He obtains a copy of an anti-virus program, and runs it. Maybe the anti-virus program does the job; maybe it doesn't. Maybe the manual doesn't explain that he should check all his diskettes, or maybe he doesn't read the manual. A week later, he sees "Your PC is now Stoned", and knows it hasn't worked. So he formats the disk, and that doesn't fix it, because a high level format doesn't get rid of Stoned. Or he low level formats, but didn't boot from a clean DOS disk first, because why would he know that? All he knows is that he is still seeing "Your PC is now Stoned", and his job is at risk. He knows that he is going to have to report a virus on his computer, or does he, because in spite of the virus, everything seems to work fine. Maybe he'll just keep quiet about it. Or, in a flash of inspiration, he suddenly realises that his job is only at risk, because his is the only computer with the virus – if only a few others were infected …

The wrong set of rules can create a pressure that is in the opposite of the desired direction. You must not have an instant-dismissal rule (which is not a plausible threat anyway); instead a graduated system of penalties.

If management takes data security seriously, then so will the staff. If management takes it seriously, then data security should be part of the job description, insofar as it is relevant to the job. Then, if an employee breaches data security, this failure to do his job properly should be reflected in his next salary review – in other words, you make a credible threat to a place that can hurt, the wallet.

A minor security breach, such as failing to take a proper backup, should lead to a reminder about the importance of backups. Persistent failure to take backups should lead to a good talking-to, and a warning. Likewise, a failure to sheep-dip an incoming diskette should be treated as a minor breach of the rules.

If there is a rule against running unauthorised software, and someone breaks that rule, it is a bit more serious, and the first such breach should lead to a telling-off, or it should affect the next salary review. If there is a more serious offence against data security (for example, if the local area network (LAN) supervisor fails to do backups, or a user has committed a considerable act of piracy, or is giving out software that has come from an unauthorised source), a more severe penalty is in order; perhaps he should be dropped a grade in seniority.

If someone reports a breach of data security, even if they committed the breach themselves, they should be praised. It is very easy to run some unauthorised program, and then realise afterwards that that is what you have done. But if this is then reported, little or no harm is done, and the user should feel that self-reporting will not lead to any penalties being applied. But conversely, if there is a breach of data security and it is not reported, or even worse, covered up, that could lead to the maximum penalty of dismissal.

The practice of how you apply these principles will vary – the important thing is to have a graduated system of penalties, with the most severe being reserved for the cover-up. You can see how such a system would prevent the scenario described above – the user would have reported the virus as soon as he saw it.

1.2.1 Damage Done by Viruses

Damage done by viruses falls into various classes: direct, indirect, and unrelated. Probably the greatest damage is the unrelated damage caused by the very existence of viruses, but let's go through them in order.

First, direct damage. A virus is just a program that copies itself, so it is limited in what it can do, to what is possible in software. But that is quite sufficient. It is possible to damage hardware by using software; if you park a hard disk using the wrong park program, it can lead to permanent damage. If a stepper-motor drive is parked at a track that doesn't exist, the software repeatedly bangs the heads against the stop, which can lead to them going off- track. I have seen a number of drives that have suffered this way. If a park program can do this, so could a virus.

In practice, though, there are no viruses that aim to damage hardware, and even if there were, this would not be a great concern, as hardware is easily replaceable.

The next possibility is damage to software; a virus that targets a particular package and modifies it could lead to unreliable computing. The nearest I have seen to that is the following viruses:

- Anticad, which looks for a file called ACAD.EXE, and if this is run, triggers a damaging trojan.
- AntiPascal, which looks for .PAS and .BAK files, and aims to erase them.
- Omicron, which patches COMMAND.COM.

The third, and most worrying, category is damage to data. There are several viruses that aim to do sudden and irreversible damage to the data on the hard disk, such as Ogre which, when it triggers, encrypts the data on the drive, and Datacrime, which does a low level format of track zero, making the disk inaccessible.

An even more worrying prospect, though, is subtle damage. The first virus aiming at this was Dark Avenger, which every now and then writes a sector of rubbish to a random sector on the hard disk: this could be into empty disk space, or into the middle of a database, or into a directory or the file allocation table (FAT). If this is undiscovered for some time, the backups will contain these partially overwritten files, too. The Dbase virus is so called because it aims at .DBF files. It keeps a list in a hidden file called BUGS.DAT of each .DBF file that it has treated – treatment consists of swapping each pair of consecutive bytes. If the virus is in memory, then when the database is read from disk, it unswaps the bytes, so that the data appears normal, and then swaps them back when the disk is rewritten.

The Syslock virus is another subtle one. It gradually works its way down the disk, 100 sectors at a time, changing each instance of the word "Microsoft" to "Macrosoft". This is a fairly trivial change, but if the virus author had decided, it could have been looking for anything he fancied, and changed it to anything else.

Every few minutes Solano looks at a random place on the screen to see if there is a digit there. If there is, and there is also one on the right of it, it transposes the two. Fumble does nothing, unless you type at least two keys in succession at a rate of five characters per second. In that case, the second character is replaced by the one immediately to the right on the keyboard.

So that is the kind of deliberate direct damage that viruses can do. Next, the accidental direct damage. Most viruses either have bugs, or were not tested in a wide variety of environments. A virus author can get away with programming techniques that a normal software house must avoid, since he won't be getting support calls. For example, Jerusalem virus uses interrupt 21h, function ddh, deh and e0h as part of its internal workings: unfortunately, so does the Novell shell, and that leads to the workstation finding itself cut off from the network if Jerusalem virus is run. Stoned virus was not designed with 1.2 Mb diskettes in mind, but unfortunately, it still infects them, which overwrites the third directory sector. Some of the self-hiding viruses trap many DOS functions, and some even put the processor into single step mode, which can lead to a considerable slowing down of the computer. In my experience, a virus is noticed quite often because of an unintended side effect.

The next category of damage comes about as a consequence of the first two. If a virus is discovered in a company, it is my experience that the decision to eradicate it is always made, sometimes without even considering the possibility of not doing so. The eradication of the virus is an operation that is going to consume time and resources, and lead to a certain amount of disruption to the business (hopefully, this will be minimised). My estimate of the time needed to eradicate a virus is based on the assumption that it is intended to become as close to 100 per cent clean as possible, and if done over a weekend, will require a number of people that is between 5 and 10 per cent of the number of computers. This is not such a big operation as to be a major catastrophe, by any means, but neither is it something that you want to do every weekend.

The fourth category of damage is becoming the most pervasive. Because of the existence of viruses, we are forced to modify the way we use computers. Some people run memory-resident software that permanently occupies a slice of precious memory, and also affects processing time. Other people prefer to do a virus check once per day, but that also is a use of resources that would not be necessary in a perfect world. Time must be wasted on sheep-dipping incoming diskettes. This category of damage, which perhaps should be called something other than damage, is perhaps the most costly of them all, as it is a continuous, ongoing process, consuming resources on many machines in many places, even though there is no virus there. If there are 50 000 000 computers in the world, and each of them wastes a minute per day on anti-virus precautions, what is the overall value of this wasted computer time?

1.2.2 Viruses on the LAN

The usual picture that is painted is completely wrong. The myth is that once a virus is on a LAN, it flashes across the LAN infecting everything. The truth is that although a LAN can help a virus to spread, a properly set up and managed LAN can be a considerable hindrance to viruses.

The key is to use the network security facilities, and to make as many executables as possible read-only. If the user does not have the privilege to write to the file, neither does the virus. Unfortunately, it is not always possible to make the executables read-only, and it isn't always possible to devote the necessary manpower to ensuring that this is done.

The full answer on a network is to run a cryptographic checksummer, which works by detecting changes to executables. In order for a virus to be a virus, it must replicate. In order to replicate, it must make a change to another executable. If we detect a change to an executable, we can take immediate action.

If a network has never had a virus, or has only had one that is a slow spreader, then it is sufficient to run the cryptographic checksummer once per day, perhaps in the same batch file that does the backup. But if a network has recently had a fast-spreading virus, you should consider attaching a workstation to the network that does nothing but continuously checksum in a looping batch file, so you get an even earlier warning of an executable changing. For example, I would recommend this in the case of Frodo or Dark Avenger. In one case of Frodo, the checks were being done every minute, and a message was sent to the network administrator via email if anything changed, as well as a loud flashing alarm being triggered. The reason for wanting this is that Frodo spreads so quickly that it was important to take immediate action if a user logged on while infected.

If a network becomes infected, it is generally easy to clear it up, because a network is (at least logically) all in one place. The clear-up can be done in three stages. First you boot from a clean diskette, and run only known clean software as you log in. Once logged in, you should check that you do not have the virus memory resident, in case logging in runs something that you didn't know is run, and which is infected. Next, you can run a virus finder program, to discover which files are infected, and perhaps log that to disk or printer. You can also use a program to either clean, rename (from COM to VOM, EXE to VXE and so on) or delete infected files.

The ideal clean-up consists of deleting infected files, and re-installing clean copies of the software. But that might be time consuming, and as a temporary measure, you can use a virus-cleaner to remove the virus from all infected files. Terms used by anti-virus software for this procedure include "heal", "repair" and "remove". But I would still recommend replacing these executables in the longer run, as sometimes a virus overwrites part of a file while infecting it, and then the damage cannot be reversed. It isn't usually possible to detect that this has happened; the result is that the software might not work properly. The most likely effect would be that it would not load at all; the next most likely effect is the computer hanging. The advantage of using this technique is that it is a very rapid way to make sure that the virus is eliminated, and yet the user is able to carry on doing his job; the re-installation of clean software can be done as a second stage.

At the same time as dealing with the network, you have to clean the local hard disks. This is slightly more tedious, as there will be a number of offices to visit, and the site must be systematically toured. One useful tip is not to work from an asset register, as there are usually computers around that are not listed. Instead, tour the offices.

The final, and worst, problem is the floppy diskettes. Each floppy disk will take just a few seconds, but there are likely to be a large number of them. In my experience, you should expect between 50 and 100 floppy disks for each computer, and you will have logistical trouble dealing with them. Most of the organisation of a virus-hunt is associated with the floppy disks; see the chapter on how this is done. Most companies these days buy or rent an autoloader – a hopper-fed machine that can process hundreds of diskettes per hour.

The clean-up operation is not the end of it, though. There will usually be a re-infestation if it is left at that, as there might be an overlooked infected floppy, or else the infection might come back in the same way it did the first time. It is necessary to install an early warning system on each computer to avoid having to do the job all over again. There are three possibilities for this early warning system.

The first possibility that springs to mind is a memory-resident virus detector that constantly monitors and reports on any virus that arrives. There are a number of problems with this method, though. First, the software will consume a quantity of memory – how much will depend on how well it was written. Second, problems of clashes between memory-resident utilities and network shells are too well known to need covering in detail – again, much will depend on how well written the program is, and which networks it is known to be compatible with.

Another problem with this method is that the memory resident program is either virus-specific, or else it isn't. If it is virus-specific, then it will need upgrading frequently, and you should never go for a virus-specific solution unless you can solve the logistic and support problem of frequent upgrades. Alternatively, it is non-virus specific, in which case there are almost certainly viruses around which have been written specifically to counter the methods it uses; the virus writers are taking such software as being a challenge. In particular, for any given non-virus-specific program, it would be extremely easy to write a virus that simply patched it in memory and disabled it, as there is no way that any process can be prevented from addressing any part of the memory in a computer running under DOS.

The next possible solution is one that is used quite commonly. This is to use a virus finder or scanner program. This works by identifying known viruses in files, using either a series of bytes from the virus as a signature, or else by some other method. This works, but again, you must solve the logistic problem of upgrades before you adopt it. Also, you should ensure that the scanner that you choose has sufficient speed to be able to scan for not merely the hundreds of viruses that are around today, but for the possibility that there may be thousands in the future. Some scanners do have adequate speed to make this possible; some do not. If you choose a scanner that can cope when the count of viruses is 100, but is unusably slow at 5000, you should not pretend to be surprised when there are 5000 viruses.

The third possible solution is to use a cryptographic checksummer, as described above. The advantages of this are quite large: because it is non-virus-specific, there is no logistical upgrade problem, nor will the runtime grow with the number of viruses. The main downside is that each time the software is changed, the checksums must be recalculated, but that is not an arduous task.

Once the early warning system has been installed, there must be a support infrastructure – if the alarm is raised, it must be responded to rapidly. There should be resources available at each site to deal with a virus on a computer, so that the outbreak can be dealt with quickly and efficiently, before it has a chance to spread.

1.2.3 Network Specifics

With Novell Netwire, there is a bonus, and an unfortunate happenstance. It is unfortunate that Novell Netwire uses some of the interrupts that Jerusalem (and several other) viruses use, and so if a workstation on a Novell network gets this virus, it takes that workstation off the network. Jerusalem uses interrupt 21h function 0ddh, 0deh and 0e0h, and so does Novell. On the other hand, it means that the virus is very quickly detected, and can then be eradicated. The bonus is that Novell lets you apply a strong security system; if you make executables read-only, then if a user only has that privilege, then so does any virus that he may be running. It is good network management to make all executable files read-only, using the network operating system security. A virus will not be able to get through this security, except by continually retrying, until one day the privileges are temporarily changed by the system supervisor (perhaps to do an upgrade).

There has been a rumour of a version of Jerusalem that can penetrate Novell Netware security. This rumour is wholly false, and was caused by the virus getting on to the network via a file that had not been secured. It is easy for a fallible human to forget to make a file read-only.

With Banyan Vines, the security system is less flexible, and it might not be possible to make all executables read-only. In this case, you should make as many as possible read-only, and rely on the cryptographic checksummer to do the rest.

PC Lan has a very inadequate security system, and the checksummer will have to do the whole job.

1.2.4 PC Viruses on Mainframes

PC viruses cannot infect mainframes. If the mainframe stores a PC file, and that file is an infected executable, then the mainframe is not infected. It is analogous to the situation of a person holding a cat with cat flu. Cats get cat flu; people, with a different internal architecture, cannot get cat flu. If a person holds a cat with cat flu, then that person has not got cat flu, he has a cat with cat flu. If another person has a cat, and holds it near to the cat with cat flu, then the cat flu can be transmitted from cat to cat, but neither of the people holding the cats have cat flu. Mainframes cannot get PC viruses.

It is theoretically possible to write a mainframe virus, but none has been written so far. What has appeared on mainframes is worms. A worm is the electronic equivalent of a chain letter; a message is sent to a user, and that message triggers other messages to be sent to other users, and so on. The worm can be human-assisted, as in the case of the IBM Christma Exec, or it can be autonomous, as in the case of the Usenet worm.

1.2.5 Trojans in the Corporate Environment

The most famous trojan in recent times was the AIDS Information Introductory Diskette. This was mailed to 20 000 users in December 1989. It came with a licence agreement stating that if you ran the program, you would owe PC Cyborg Corporation $189, and that there were certain program mechanisms to ensure payment, and that these mechanisms could interfere with the operation of the PC. If you installed it (as several hundred people did), it created hidden files and subdirectories on the hard disk, and changed the AUTOEXEC.BAT. The new AUTOEXEC ran a hidden program each time you started up the computer, and after 90 boots, the trojan triggered. The trojan would encrypt all the filenames on the hard disk, leaving one file, which was a request for payment. It is alleged that this act was criminal (blackmail), and that the perpetrator was Dr Popp.

The simplest way of dealing with the trojan was to simply not run it, but once run, it could be cleared out fairly easily – the magazine whose mailing list was used commissioned a program to do this. After the trojan triggered, the damage could still be undone quite easily, as the encryption scheme was so simple as to scarcely be worth calling encryption; again, the magazine provide a program to do this.

It could easily have been worse. The encryption could have been a real encryption system; in that case, some users might have been willing to pay to get their data back. It might have been more damaging than encryption; perhaps an erasure, or even a corruption of the data. Companies should be aware of the possibility of such a threat, and the trust shown by so many users in an unknown program.

The AIDS trojan has resulted in a large number of companies introducing rules about the sources of software – hopefully, such a thing could not happen again. However, the ease with which the AIDS trojan happened probably means that there are several other ways that such a thing could happen. Magazines still offer their mailing lists to all and sundry, and if users received an attractive-sounding diskette from a company that they had heard of and trusted (it is very easy to pretend to be another company), then the incident could be repeated. How can this be prevented? It is very difficult to get people to abandon their naturally trusting nature. Perhaps it is necessary to use technical means, to ensure that each computer is only able to run software that has specifically authorised. This would mean that an incident similar to the AIDS diskette would require the PC Support staff to be taken in as well, and they are more likely to be suspicious of, for example, a diskette that comes from a company with a return address that is PO Box 7, Panama.

1.3 Viruses in the Academic Environment

The academic world has a particular problem with viruses, for two reasons: (i) under-resourcing, and (ii) public access computers. The ratio of PC support staff to users is particularly low in the academic world, because it is more difficult to finance than in the commercial world. As a result, once a virus does come in to the organisation, it can be hard to find the manpower resources to eradicate it. Also, the importance of the data on academic machines is often perceived to be less than in the business world.

The second factor that leads to more viruses is the existence of public access computers. These are computers that anyone can use, and which therefore belong to no one. This is an excellent system for the users, but an ideal breeding-ground for viruses to spread.

So what can be done? Prevention is the first measure, but in most academic sites, this is not going to be the whole answer. There should be a sheep-dip computer in each public access area, with firm, clear instructions about using it. Ideally, the sheep-dip machine should be capable of repairing infected files as well as detecting them, since the population that will be using them is likely to be impatient about re-installing clean software. The public access computers should also have a cryptographic checksummer installed, which can be run perhaps weekly (more often if resources permit) by the PC Support staff. If the software on the public access computers is changing very rapidly, then a virus finder should be run instead, but it is important to run some kind of detector on a routine basis.

It might also be a good idea to run a memory resident virus finder, that checks each file as it is copied or run, and each floppy diskette that is accessed.

At some sites, the public access machines might not have hard disks. This is also useful as an economy measure, as a network card is cheaper than a hard disk, and the students can keep their work on floppy diskettes. If this is done, and a network operating system with flexible security is used (such as Novell) then all executables on the network can be made read-only, which will reduce the virus problem to manageable proportions. If the local hard disks are kept, they can be checked whenever a user logs in to the network as part of the login script.

Users should be educated about viruses; there should be talks about what a virus is and how it works, and the downsides of having a virus should be clearly explained. In particular, it should be pointed out that there is a possibility that the users could lose some or all of their hard work. The use of the sheep-dip should be explained, and the use of the write-protect tab. Do not even try to ban the playing of games, but insist that all software, from whatever source, is sheep-dipped before it is used. Also, all diskettes that contain software and which will not be written to, must be write-protected.

When students are sent out on work experience, or summer jobs, they should be strongly encouraged to sheep-dip all their diskettes first; if a virus is passed on to a friendly local business, it might affect the future prospects of co-operation.

If there is an outbreak of a virus, the traditional virus-hunt that is used in the commercial world might not be possible, because of lack of resources. Instead, a gradual strategy of attrition can be pursued. For some viruses, it is possible to inoculate the disks or files so that the virus thinks that they are already infected, and doesn't infect a second time. For example, this technique can be used to contain and gradually eliminate outbreaks of Stoned, Italian and Jerusalem. If diskettes are inoculated in quantity, the virus finds that it cannot spread as freely as it could; if this is combined with an eradication campaign, it is possible to eliminate the virus without a major effort.

As well as the public machines at academic sites, there are also the computers used for administration. Here, there can be much tighter controls, as the situation is more like that in the commercial world. The main difference is that because of the location of the computers, there must be a greater risk of viruses. A cryptographic checksummer should be run every day, and sheep-dipping should be done for all incoming diskettes, even if they have just come from another part of the academic site.

Possibly the enthusiasm of the students can be harnessed; each public access site could have a student virus-hunter appointed. They can be armed with suitable anti-virus software, and educated in the technical aspects of computer viruses, and then they will be a powerful force against viruses. It can be part of their duty to virus-check the computers each day, and perhaps even to do a clean-up, where the outbreak is small and easily dealt with. If a virus outbreak is detected early, then the clean-up can be quick and not too difficult.

1.4 The Future

The first PC virus, Brain, appears to have been written in 1986. However, Ashar, which appeared in 1989, looks very like an antecedent to Brain, and possibly predates it. In 1987, Lehigh, Vienna and Jerusalem appeared. The three Suriv viruses appear to precede Jerusalem, as Jerusalem seems to be the final version that these were leading up to. By the end of 1988, Stoned and Italian virus came out, and Yale and Cascade had probably been written by then. I call these the "classic" viruses; Lehigh and Yale are not very infectious, but the other six account for the majority of outbreaks.

In addition, they inspired imitators. Jerusalem has many viruses based on its code, from minor variants such as Jerspain, Payday, Mendoza, Anarkia and Sunday to viruses that are considerably different such as PSQR, Fu Manchu and Zerotime. Other viruses, such as Anticad, clearly owe part of their code to Jerusalem.

There are a number of minor variants on Cascade, such as 17Y4 (with just one byte different), 1701FRMT (which replaces the falling letters display with a hard disk format) and Jojo, which omits the encryption of the code.

The virus that inspired the greatest number of imitators is Vienna, and that is probably because a disassembly of it was published in a book, making it easily accessible. There are several rewrites of it, in a steadily decreasing number of bytes, that come from Bulgaria. W13, Ghostballs and Lisbon clearly show their descent from Vienna, and although the Chameleon is a substantially different virus, Vienna still shows through.

By the end of 1989 it became difficult to count the number of viruses; one could argue figures between 30 and 50, depending on how you count different viruses. By the end of 1990, one could easily justify counting up to 350.

Any forecast for the number of viruses would fall between two stools; a small increase would almost certainly be optimistic, whereas a large forecast increase could be regarded as alarmist. When asked to forecast the future number of viruses, I normally take refuge by quoting the past figures, which certainly show a marked upward trend which I have no reason to suppose will diminish.

There are grounds for optimism for the future, but also pessimism. On the bright side, people are now beginning to recognise the possibility of viruses, and to take steps to prevent them – my simulation model of virus propagation shows that if the probability of detection is raised, this has the effect of dramatically curtailing the spread of a virus.

Another hopeful note is that people are beginning to stop regarding a PC virus as some kind of special problem, and are starting to treat it as just another PC problem, to be put alongside all the hundred and one other problems of using a computer. In particular, the notion that a PC virus is in some sense shameful is dying out, and it is becoming possible for companies to share their experiences in this area. There was a time when the existence of a virus outbreak was concealed even from other parts of the company, which meant that the company could not learn from its own experience. Now, such outbreaks are reported up through the appropriate channels, and PC Support staff talk to their counterparts in other companies.

On the down side, the viruses are getting more common, more diverse, and more sophisticated. The replication routines are improving, the newer viruses are better able to hide themselves, and the damage routines are getting more subtle.

There are no hard statistics on the number of virus outbreaks, and reports in the press are a poor guide. Many outbreaks are not reported (even though it is just a small problem, why should a company shout about it?) and those that are, are either treated in a sensationalist way (if the company is an interesting one) or else ignored, since yet another virus outbreak is not newsworthy.

As a result, it is not possible to make any estimate of the number of outbreaks per month. The increased popularity of the various virus newsletters and the increasing number of vendors of anti-virus products cannot be taken as evidence that the number of outbreaks is increasing; these are only an indication that there is an increased interest in the subject. The increased interest could be caused by the viruses being more widespread, or it could have other causes, such as the marketing efforts of the vendor companies.

My opinion, which is based on the number of virus outbreaks that are reported to me, is that the classic viruses (Stoned, Jerusalem, Cascade) are still on the increase, while Brain and Italian are declining – Brain is almost becoming an endangered species. In particular, I am finding that if a virus has very noticeable effects, its population is tending to decline, as I would expect from my model.

The number of different viruses is difficult to count, as different researchers use different counting methods. For example, if a virus is the same as an old one, but with a difference in one of the text strings, is it a new virus, a new strain or a variant? Different researchers use different names for the same virus, and sometimes the same name is used for different viruses. In spite of all this confusion, it is clear that the number of viruses has increased substantially, and there is no reason to suppose that this trend will stop. Words like "strain", "variant", "version" and "mutation" have no commonly agreed meaning.

The fact of an increasing number of viruses is going to pose a new problem. If a company wishes to stop viruses from coming in, it has to sheep-dip all incoming disks and files. But as the number of viruses grows, so does the task of doing this. Scanners tend to run more slowly as the number of viruses scanned for increases, and memory-resident virus-specific software will slow down and require more space. This means that it will become increasingly important to use software that is efficient in resource consumption, and that virus-scanning will consume an increasing amount of resource.

The replication mechanisms of viruses are improving. For example, mid-1990 saw the first virus which was both a file virus and a boot sector virus. Using two replication strategies means that it will spread more widely, and also increases its chances of surviving a clean-up operation.

Viruses are also getting better at hiding themselves. There are now several viruses which, if in memory, hide the increase in file size from sight. Frodo and 666 (Number of the Beast) both hide from sight the entire virus in the file, if in memory. The sector redirection trick that was first used by Brain, is now used by other boot sector viruses (such as EDV), in order to hide the altered boot sector from inspection, and from anti-virus programs.

Another trend is viruses that make it more difficult to write anti-virus programs. For example, Chameleon includes code to prevent single-stepping through the virus, and it has an additional layer of encryption that is only removed at runtime. The encryption key is changed with each instance of the virus, and the decryptor-loader is shuffled around for each instance. As a result, it is not possible to write a simple string-search that can detect it, and a more sophisticated algorithm must be used. This more sophisticated algorithm requires time to develop, and some anti-virus software vendors might decide that this virus isn't worth scanning for. Other viruses use similar techniques to make scanning for them more difficult.

Another trend towards countering anti-virus software is the virus's movement towards using the firmware directly, instead of via the PC interrupt system. A number of viruses are using undocumented DOS functions to discover where the firmware for the disk is in the memory map, and then doing far calls to the firmware, which evades memory resident generic anti-virus traps.

The damage routines are getting more subtle. The earlier viruses included routines that could be regarded as a joke; the bouncing ball of Italian, for example, or the letter-fall of Cascade. Even the deletion of executable files on Friday 13th that Jerusalem does is not too damaging, as executables are easily replaced.

Most of the viruses I see are still in this class. A few, however, are aiming to do more damage. Datacrime, for example does a low level format of cylinder zero of your hard disk, and Ogre encrypts the FAT and directory, and works its way down the data area. An increasing number of viruses are designed to do something quite nasty when triggered.

More recently, I have seen viruses that work in a more subtle way. Dark Avenger gradually corrupts the data on the disk, which will be copied onto backups until the virus is discovered. Syslock works its way progressively down the disk, changing each instance of "Microsoft" to "Macrosoft".

I would expect an increase in the trend to more sophistication in the viruses. Some of the virus authors are creating a series of increasingly sophisticated viruses, and as new authors start writing viruses, some of them will learn from the older ones; there are quite a lot of disassemblies, and original source code, in circulation. Some commentators have expressed the hope that the virus authors will get tired of the game and go and do something else, but this assumes that there is a fixed supply of virus authors.

I think that viruses will become an increasing nuisance, although never much more than a nuisance. Rather like garden pests, they will detract slightly from the value of the computers that we use. They will always remain under control, but never be eradicated completely.

In the very long term, I would expect the hardware to change; there is a change in computer architecture every few years anyway, and I think that some future change will incorporate intrinsic security features. For example, I think that cryptographic checksumming might be incorporated in the hardware or firmware.

Those two brothers in Lahore certainly started something.

Chapter 2
What is a Virus?

2.1 Bugs, Clashes, Trojans and Viruses

There is still a certain amount of confusion about what a virus is. I shall start with some definitions.

First, let's define "bug", a word that is sometimes used by the media as a synonym for virus. A bug is not a virus, it is a mistake in the program. People make mistakes, and programmers, being human, also make mistakes. Like other humans, they don't really like admitting their fallibility, so these mistakes are called bugs, with some kind of implication that they come from an outside agency. This is perhaps what has caused the confusion.

All sufficiently complex programs have bugs, and sometimes the bug can be quite damaging to data. I usually cite as a good instance of a damaging bug the DOS critical error bug, which has been responsible for a lot of people losing a lot of data. Here's how it works.

Take one write-protected floppy diskette, with a few files on it. Take another floppy diskette, with some different files on it. Now try to copy a file onto the write-protected diskette. DOS will say, "Write protect error, Abort, Retry, Ignore", or a similar message for other versions of DOS. So, you take out the write-protected diskette, and put in the write enabled one, that you had meant to use, and press R for Retry. When you look at that diskette, you'll find the directory (and FAT) of the first diskette all over the second.

That bug has been in DOS for a great many years – it is only in DOS 4 that Microsoft dealt with it. If there are bugs like that in DOS, which is a small (less than 60 k) program, and has been in use for several years, what do you suppose it is like for multi-megabyte applications that have been around for a couple of months?

Another thing that is not a virus is a hardware failure. I get a number of people trying to report Cascade (1701) virus; some of these are genuine, of course, but many of them are one of two things. The first is the "1701" diagnostic message that the PC BIOS gives when the disk fails. This is analogous to the 301 message for the keyboard, and the 601 for the floppy drive. It means hardware failure. Another thing that I occasionally get reported is that there is Cascade virus in the interrupts. This misapprehension comes from the fact that the hardware architecture of the AT doubled the number of hardware interrupts by cascading the controller chips (so that an interrupt on the lower one triggers an interrupt on the upper one. Some diagnostic programs report these cascaded interrupts very briefly, as "Cascade".

Quite often, a hard disk will develop bad sectors, especially if it has been used for a long time, and is a stepper-motor drive. Floppy disks develop bad sectors even more often, as the recording surface is open to the air and dust. 5¼-inch floppies are especially vulnerable, as the recording surface can be touched quite easily. If a sector of the disk cannot be read, DOS will report "Sector not found", or "Data error" or some similar message.

All hardware fails – it is simply a matter of time. In particular, anything that is mechanical will wear. Manufacturers quote a mean time between failure (MTBF) for hard disks which is from 12 000 hours upwards to 100 000. The cheap-and-cheerful drives tend to be the ones with the low MTBF; 12 000 hours is a year and a half. Switching the computer off when not in use might not extend the life of the drive, as the surge of current needed to start up the drive is one of the most stressful experiences that the drive gets. Some people suggest that not switching the computer off would extend its life.

So how do you insure against the inevitable failure of the hard disk? By taking backups. Ideally, on the day that the drive fails, there is a full backup from the previous day. Unfortunately, although the drive failure can be predicted reliably, the date of the failure is completely uncertain. So you have to behave as if any day might be the last day, and take backups accordingly.

Unfortunately, programmer's errors and fallible hardware are not the only hazards to computing today. There are also people that deliberately aim to reduce the usefulness of the computer.

A trojan is a program that does something nice, or useful. But it also does something that you aren't told about, and which you would rather it didn't – this is called the "hidden agenda". The difference between a trojan and a bug is that with a trojan the programmer has done it deliberately.

The best-known trojan for the PC was the Aids Information diskette. This was a 5¼-inch floppy diskette that was mailed to several thousand PC users in the middle of December 1989. It is generally called a trojan, but it is arguable about whether this is the case.

The diskette came with a licence agreement, which said that if you installed the software, you owed $189 to PC Cyborg Corporation, and that the software contained certain mechanisms to ensure payment. It said that these mechanisms could interfere with the proper operation of the PC, and that other programs could be affected also. In other words, if you read the accompanying licence, you were told fairly clearly that there is a hidden agenda, and that it will cause problems. I do not want to cover the legal aspects of the case, as the law varies from country to country, but it is this warning of the damage that blurs the question of whether this was a trojan or not.

In practice, of course, very few people would have read the small print on the licence carefully enough, or tried to understand its meaning. Those people who did install it (and there were hundreds) had the following happen.

On installation, the program creates hidden subdirectories with invisible-character names, and hidden files. It hides the AUTOEXEC.BAT, but the AUTOEXEC calls another batch file, AUTO.BAT, which the user is supposed to use instead. Each time the computer is started up, there is a harmless-looking REM statement in the AUTOEXEC which is executed, but the REM has an invisible character 255 after it, so it actually runs a program called REM# (for clarity, I will use the # to represent character 255, which is invisible). The REM# program counts to 90, so that after executing the AUTOEXEC 90 times (which would normally mean 90 boot-ups) the trojan triggers.

The trojan consists of encrypting all the file names on the disk (using a very simple, and reversible scheme), and making all the files hidden. When you boot up, a DOS emulator is run, which refuses to do very much. If you boot from a floppy, it seems that there is almost nothing left on the disk, apart from a file that contains a request for payment to PC Cyborg.

The trojan has triggered in at least a few cases, but even where it hadn't, the user was put to the trouble of removing the files from the diskette.

The diskettes were mailed to several thousand people on the distribution list of *PC Business World*, as well as names gathered from other sources. It was really quite hard for any major company to avoid receiving at least one of the diskettes; the differences arose from how the incoming diskettes were treated. In one company, the PC Support staff handed out leaflets to users as they came in. In others, there are firm rules about what software can be run on the computers. But in many companies, there were no rules about incoming diskettes, and people can be very trusting.

Another type of trojan is something that is added to a program that is intended to be passed around. The most interesting of these is Twelve Tricks. I have found this in three programs now, all shareware, and it may be in others. Twelve Tricks only activates if you have one of five hard disk controllers; one of these is the standard IBM XT controller. When you run a program containing Twelve Tricks, it installs itself on the partition record, using a far call to the firmware to do so; this ensures that it will not be detected by programs that intercept and filter interrupt calls. Once it is on the partition record, it is run every time the computer is started up. It chooses one of twelve tricks to play, at random; these are described in detail elsewhere in this book. The overall effect is that of an unreliable computer.

If a trojan causes sudden and obvious damage, it is unlikely to survive. Such a trojan must be delivered in large quantities (such as by mail-out) if it is to hit a substantial number of machines. If a trojan is intended to be passed around, the damage must be very occasional, or else minor (possibly cumulative), otherwise it will not be passed from computer to computer.

The main defence against trojans is to get all your software from a reputable source. This does not rule out public domain software, or bulletin boards, however. For example, the Novell Netwire service is an excellent source of information and updated drivers; if a company were to stop using that, and services like it, it would be a considerable loss. At the other end of the scale, a BBS with a name like "Nasty Banana" (with apologies if there is a BBS with this name) run by heaven-knows-who could contain anything.

Likewise shareware. The place to get shareware from is a reputable shareware vendor, or a User Group, which is taking care over its collection. Another good source is if the PC Support centre maintains a collection of shareware for users in the company. A disreputable source of shareware is some guy you met in a bar, or your next door neighbour.

The next category to look at is the worm. Consider how a chain letter works; you receive the letter, and mail off four (or ten, or whatever) copies to friends. You do this because you hope to benefit in cash, or because it is unlucky not to, or because someone wants a lot of get-well cards.

Suppose the scheme works as designed, and everyone co-operates, and mails out ten letters within a week. After two weeks, this is 100, after 6 weeks it is a million, and after three months 10 million million letters are posted. At some point, the postal system is so overloaded that normal mail is not received. Of course, the chain breaks long before that point, and most people are properly sceptical of such schemes. More recently, I have seen the chain fax; you are supposed to on-fax a copy of the fax to ten other people. A chain fax is easier to do, as sending a fax is so simple, and many people will have plenty of numbers pre-programmed in their fax machines. Again, after a short period of time, the entire world fax system would be sending nothing but this fax; nothing else could get through. Thank goodness most people are not that gullible.

Now let us bring computers in to this idea. Suppose it is almost Christmas, and you receive electronic mail from a friend who you know and trust. The email tells you not to just browse the mail; you should type "CHRISTMA". So, because it comes from a friend, you do just that, and you see a Christmas tree on your screen.

What you don't know, is that you've just run a Rexx file, which has read your list of email addresses, and emailed itself to each of them. So each of them receives a message from someone that they know and trust, suggesting that they type "CHRISTMA", and so on and so on.

This happened in December 1987, on the IBM internal network. Lots of people typed CHRISTMA, and pretty soon, there were so many copies of the file flying around that it took up a noticeable proportion of the network bandwidth. Of course, it was very easily fixed, by persuading people not to type CHRISTMA. Although, if you were to get an email message telling you "Don't type CHRISTMA", what's the next thing you do?

It's an interesting question whether you can call this a worm, since it needed human intervention to propagate. The effect on each user, is optional – you don't have to type CHRISTMA. But the effect on the network was pretty inevitable, people being the way they are.

The Internet worm was less ambiguously a worm, as it operated without any human help. It was launched by Robert Morris, and it spread very rapidly, reaching a large number of computers (estimates vary from hundreds to thousands) in a very short time.

It worked on Unix systems, spreading itself via the connections between Unix machines called the Internet. Most academic sites are on Internet, and many commercial sites, plus some non-sensitive US military computers. Internet is connected to, and includes, several other networks, such as Arpanet, Janet and Bitnet. First, it would log into a remote computer, and then send a small process down to it to run. This would then create a process that brought the full worm to the remote site, where it would run. It looked for user names and passwords, using some automatic password breaking routines, and would successfully crack a surprising proportion of them. It would then log into remote computers under these names, and the process would continue.

The Internet worm used a number of security holes in Unix; these holes turned out to have been known by many Unix experts, but no one had done enough to close them. For example, at one point, the worm used a bug in a commonly accessible program to patch the system in a way that should not have been available to that process. A number of detailed reports on the Internet worm have been prepared, and are available via Internet.

It is not clear how much damage was done. Certainly, a number of people had to do work to remove the worm from their systems, and some systems were taken off the network for a while. Estimates of the dollar value of this work vary widely, from tens of thousands, to tens of millions. These estimates depend on many guesses, such as the number of computers affected, the dollar value of computer time wasted, and the dollar value of the human time wasted. Robert Morris was tried, convicted, and sentenced.

Worms tend to be occasional, one-off jobs. They are launched, move rapidly, are noticed because of the resources that they consume, and are killed. They must either persuade humans to help them (like CHRISTMA) or else exploit holes in system security; this makes them difficult to create. I do not expect there to be very many worms each year, and once a worm has been dealt with, that's the end of it.

A computer virus is different. First the definition – a virus is a program that copies itself. To this definition, I should add the proviso that the different instances of the virus don't have to be identical; for example, each instance could be encrypted using a different key (as in Cascade and several others).

A virus might or might not contain a trojan. Many viruses have no payload at all – for example, the Tiny series of viruses. But a virus can contain a payload, and many do, and this can be anything that the virus author can program.

There are two kinds of virus; boot sector and file viruses. Boot sector viruses replace or modify the boot sectors of floppy disks, and the boot sector or partition sectors of hard disks. File viruses attach themselves to files, and this usually makes the file longer (but some viruses infect inside the file). The virus can go to the beginning, the middle or the end of the file.

File viruses can be memory resident (indirect action) or not (direct action). If the virus is direct action, then running an infected program infects one or more other programs. If the virus is indirect action, then running the virus installs part of it in memory, and from there it infects files. I use the term "indirect action" rather than "memory resident", because a direct action virus can also make part of itself memory resident, perhaps to implement a trojan.

Indirect action viruses are more infectious than direct, because it is more likely that a file on a floppy disk gets infected using this mechanism, and so the virus moves from machine to machine. Jerusalem virus (indirect action) is one of the oldest, and most widespread viruses; Vienna (direct action) is slightly older, but not nearly as common, in spite of getting a boost by being published in a book, and then being typed in by people.

Some virus are both boot and file viruses. This is a particularly good replication mechanism, because it means that the virus makes lots of copies of itself on the hard disk, as well as on to lots of floppies. It makes it more likely that an instance of the virus will be overlooked in the clean-up operation, and gives it two ways to pass from computer to computer.

The virus authors are now starting to build into their viruses various forms of protection from anti-virus software, so there is a constant state of struggle between them and the virus detectors. For example, Brain (one of the first viruses on the PC) uses sector redirection to hide the infected boot sector. If Brain is in memory, any program that uses the normal interrupt 13h to read the boot sector gets shown the original boot sector before Brain replaced it with its own. This effectively hides the virus from scanners and cryptographic checksummers.

For a while, Brain was the only virus that attempted to conceal itself, but a similar approach has been taken by other viruses since 1990. EDV is another boot sector virus that uses the same redirection trick, with the additional feature that if you look at the sector where the original boot sector is stored, the BIOS returns a "Can't read" error.

Frodo uses some cunning tricks to conceal itself. First of all, if Frodo is in memory, any attempt to read infected files from the disk is filtered by the virus, and only the bytes from the original file are presented to DOS. Secondly, Frodo doesn't change the interrupt vector table when it captures interrupt 21h; again, to elude detection. Several viruses use their capture of interrupt 21h to conceal the increase in file size, which is one of the most obvious give-aways of their presence.

Another way that viruses seek to evade detection is by tunnelling under the interrupts. When a program reads or writes a file, it is supposed to use interrupt 21h; when it reads or writes a sector of disk, interrupt 13h. There are various programs (called active monitors) that aim to prevent a virus from doing this. Some of the viruses evade such programs, by writing to disk without using the normal interrupt system.

They can do this using several methods. They might search in memory for the firmware that controls the disk, and call this without going via the interrupts, or they might use an undocumented DOS function that will give the address of the firmware to any program that calls it. This might be an unreliable way to go, because only some DOS versions might support this undocumented function, but a virus doesn't need to be reliable. Similarly, a virus can search memory for the bytes of interrupt 21h, and do a far call to the DOS kernel instead of executing the interrupt; one of the Icelandics does this.

Another way that virus authors have make the anti-virus job more difficult, is by writing viruses that change themselves. The simplest form of this is a virus that is encrypted, and the encryption key is chosen randomly for each instance of the virus. But then the decryptor/loader is a constant that can be scanned for. So the next step is to ensure that the decryptor/loader changes with each instance, by juggling the bytes around while retaining the same function, by adding random bytes that do nothing, or by using instructions that are different, but functionally equivalent. Examples of this are Virus-101, the Life-after-Death series, and Chameleon (1260).

It would, therefore, seem that there is a constant struggle between the virus authors and the anti-virus programs, with the viruses always being one step ahead. But there is a way that this can be avoided – it is possible to run a cryptographic checksummer, which detects changes in software, and which therefore is not virus-specific. Of course, to do that, you have to put a stop to the self-hiding tricks, which you can do by cold-booting from a clean DOS diskette, thus ensuring that the cunning of the virus author is nullified by the fact that his software isn't running.

What can a virus do? The answer is, anything that is possible in software. Deleting files and formatting disks is not actually something that most people should worry about – the damage is so obvious and immediate that you can see the problem, and then restore a backup. People are much more concerned about the possibility of gradual and progressive data corruption, such as happens with Dark Avenger, or even changes to data, such as happens with Syslock (each instance of the word Microsoft is changed to Macrosoft). The Anticad series of viruses react damagingly to any attempt to run any program with the name ACAD.EXE; the Anti-Pascal viruses aim to wipe out Pascal source code. Solano swaps a pair of digits on the screen, and the Dbase virus swaps all pairs of bytes in the file while making the file appear normal.

The main threat of the virus is in the fact that it replicates itself, and in addition can do whatever the author designs. Unlike a trojan, a virus will continue to spread around the world almost indefinitely; the commonest viruses were written years ago.

How much damage do viruses do? The worst damage is done to confidence; a few years ago, you could run any program from any source, and the worst that would happen was a bug. Today, you have to exercise a degree of caution.

It is difficult to put a value on the damage done by PC viruses; the most difficult problem is that any estimate is likely to be either an underestimate, or else it will be branded as scaremongering, or possibly even both. In my view, the virus threat is no more than a nuisance, albeit an increasing one – even so, a nuisance costs time and therefore money to deal with. In a site that has been hit, it is common practice to do a full clean-up operation, checking all the clean computers as well as the infected ones, as you don't know which are clean until you have checked. A clean-up such as this takes something like five or ten man-days per 100 computers, including the checking of floppy disks. In addition, anti-virus software will probably be installed on all the computers.

This gives us a rough idea of the cost of this nuisance. If we estimate £25 per hour for the cost of people's time, and £5 for the cost of purchasing and installing the software, we come to a figure of $5 \times 25 \times 8 = £1000$ for the time, and £500 for the software. So the virus threat costs perhaps £15 per computer; not much more than a nuisance. But there are perhaps 50 million PCs in the world, and the percentage that have been hit by a virus, or were on a site that was hit must be at least 1 per cent, and may be rather more.

You can plug your own figures into this calculation; your staff might be more or less expensive, and you might be paying more or less for software. You can arrive at your own estimates – the situation is not static, and in a few years could be completely different.

It is worth remembering, though, that the most common disaster that happens to computers is still operator error, followed by hardware failure. The best insurance against data loss is a good, recent, restorable backup. I would strongly recommend that a good backup strategy is still more important than an anti-virus strategy.

2.2 How to Identify a Virus

A virus is a program that copies itself, without the user being aware that it is happening. So the most important symptom of a virus is that it alters executable code. This might be COM or EXE files, or SYS, OVL, OVR files, or the boot sector or partition record. You can use Peeka to check your partition record and boot sector, and you can use COMP (on your DOS diskette) to check that your executable files are unchanged.

This could mean a lot of work. So you can use a cryptographic checksummer to lock up your hard disk, and see if anything changes that shouldn't. If any executables are changed you quite possibly have a virus, unless, of course, you can find another explanation for an executable changing. That isn't unlikely, actually. Some programs patch themselves if you re-install them, and of course any version upgrade will appear to be a changed executable.

So how do you know if you've got a virus? Good question. Very often, you only find out by accident. One company discovered that they had Cascade virus purely because they had Vienna virus, and acquired a copy of the Toolkit to clean that out. Imagine their surprise when, in the middle of the operation, FindVirus informed them that they had Cascade as well. Another company found out they had Italian virus when a backup utility was refusing to back up onto diskettes, on the grounds that those diskettes were not 100 per cent perfect, because they had 1 k in bad sectors. Another company found that they had Stoned when someone used an Unerase utility to unerase some files, and then, for no particular reason, had a look at various sectors on the disk, including the boot sector, whereupon he saw "Your PC is now Stoned".

A lot of people seem to find out that they've got a virus by accident, which probably means that a lot of people probably don't. Back to the outbreak of Stoned – they would have found out that they had some problem eventually, because Stoned infected one hard disk that was set up with the boot sector immediately after the partition record, which Stoned does not expect, so it overwrote one of the FAT sectors, and any files that used parts of the disk that were referred to by that sector would have been trashed. They hadn't yet used any of those files.

Because so many viruses are not obvious, it is impossible to say how many computers are infected. I do know that I get several reports each day of one or another of the existing viruses, plus a very occasional report of a new one.

Which brings me back to the original problem – how do you know if you've got a virus? The classic virus symptom is when you have the same problem on several computers. Several problems on one computer could be hardware, or software, or both, but the same problem on several computers means the same software bug in the application program, the same network problem, the same dirty electricity problem, or possibly a virus.

So how do you tell the difference? There are now hundreds of PC viruses, all with their own set of symptoms. It would not be practical to try to diagnose a virus by looking at the symptoms that are noticeable, and then matching this against the possible viruses. And anyway, there is a much easier way to do it – you run a program that looks at your files, and decides whether one of the known viruses is in each file.

A virus is just a program, and therefore has program code. The program code is a set of bytes, in sequence. So if you take a group of these bytes (called a "search signature") and search the target files for that signature, you can detect each virus. All you need is an appropriate signature for each virus. Programs that work this way are called "signature scanners", and they are very easy to write. You just have to write a program that reads each file on the disk, and searches that file for one of a database of signatures.

Where do you get the database of signatures? There are three ways. You can look at each virus, pick a sequence of bytes that you think will be appropriate for the purpose, and do that for each virus. To do that, you have to have a copy of the virus, and you have to understand it well enough to be sure that you don't pick a part of the file that is different in different instances of the virus, such as a data storage area.

The second way is to use a published signature – a number of magazines publish virus signatures. Unfortunately, these lists are rarely complete, and may contain the usual typographical errors. The third way is to look at someone else's program, and reverse engineer it sufficiently to extract the signatures that it uses. This third method may or may not be in breach of copyright, depending on the laws of the country where it is done. But it certainly is one of the most widely used methods.

It is a pity that this is true, because many companies report that they are using more than one scanner, on the assumption that perhaps the second scanner will pick up anything that the first misses. If the two scanners are using the same database, then they are really using one scanner. Unfortunately, scanners tend not to admit that they are using signatures culled from another source.

There are some viruses that cannot be identified this way. For example, the 1260 virus encrypts itself, and only decrypts itself in memory at runtime. The decryptor/loader is, of course, not encrypted. But the order of the instructions in the loader is varied from instance to instance of the virus, and also some do-nothing bytes are interspersed between the significant ones. The upshot is that you cannot rely on any constant sequence of bytes in that virus;

there are other viruses that achieve the same end, by the same, or other, means.

So a signature scanner cannot be used for such viruses. It is necessary to generalise the technique, and create a program of the type called a "virus finder". A virus finder might use signature scanning for those viruses for which this will work, but it uses whatever other methods must be used for other viruses. A virus finder is harder to write than a simple scanner, and it cannot be done from the descriptions of the viruses that are published – they simply are not detailed enough. Also, it is very much harder to extract a finding method from another program, than it is to extract signatures.

The other classification of virus finder programs is based on where they look for the virus. The "brute force" scanner searches the entire file for the virus, whereas the more sophisticated "targeted" scanner looks in the file for where the virus has to be. Once a virus has been analysed, the place where it must be in a file is entirely predictable. So there is no point in searching those places in the file where the virus cannot possibly be, and to do so is time-wasting. The speed at which a scanner operates is becoming more and more important as the number of viruses grows; a targeted scanner can be orders of magnitude faster than a brute force scanner. If it takes some hours to scan a disk, it is unlikely that it will be done very often, and I am beginning to hear that some scanners will be offering the option of scanning for only some of the known viruses, in order to work more quickly.

Again, it is much easier to write a brute force scanner than a targeted scanner, and the programs that rely on indirect sources of information about the viruses, are constrained to the brute force approach.

My approach has been to write a virus finder rather than a scanner, on the assumption that some people will not want to omit the viruses that cannot be found with a simple scanner. Likewise, I have adopted the targeted approach rather than the brute force way, because I believe that people will want to search for all the viruses, even when the total number is considerably greater than currently.

2.3 False Alarms

A false alarm is a symptom on your computer which leads you to believe that you have a virus when you haven't.

One common false alarm is Chkdsk reporting a hidden file zero bytes long which is actually a volume label. This can only be regarded as a minor bug in Chkdsk. Other programs, such as PC Tools, correctly report it as a volume label.

There are many programs that report the space used and available on disks and diskettes. This calculation can be done in many ways, so the different programs don't always agree with each other. For example, one might add up the number of bytes used by each file, whereas another might add up the space allocated by DOS to each file. On most hard disks, space is allocated in units of 2048 bytes, so that even a 1-byte file uses up 2 k.

I have heard rumours of viruses on various demo diskettes – so far, most of these rumours have had no good foundation. The usual course of events is that a PC Support group sends round a note advising users not to run a demo, one of the users phones up a colleague in another company and tells him that the diskette has had this note round saying not to run it, he tells a friend that the diskette is suspected of having a virus, and via the normal system of Chinese Whispers, the rumour takes hold that there is a virus on the diskette.

If you take a 360 k diskette (double sided, double density) and format it as if it were a 1.2 Mb diskette (double sided, high capacity) then it will format and give you several hundred kilobytes of space, and a few hundred kilobytes of bad sectors. As the diskette is used, some of the space marked as usable will deteriorate, and you'll begin to get read or write errors. I've had this effect reported as a virus a few times.

If your PC fails to boot and the message "1701" comes up on your screen, this is not a symptom of 1701 (Cascade) virus. 1701 is a standard PC error message meaning hardware failure on the hard disk, and could be caused by worn bearings, loose cables or several other things. Call a hardware engineer.

I've had some calls from people who have had "Sector error reading drive C", and are worried that it might be a virus. None of the existing viruses do that: it is a symptom of a deteriorating drive. Don't panic, but do an immediate and full backup, and then call a hardware engineer. A low level format will fix this problem temporarily, but in my experience the disk will fail even if you do this. If you do decide to continue using the disk, then take a backup every day.

Many partition sectors are signed by the author – programmers have a habit of signing their work. The partition sector program is very much smaller than the size available in the partition, so there is plenty of room there. The most common signature is David Litton – he wrote the one in PC DOS. Some people, seeing this signature, have been concerned, but there is absolutely no cause for alarm.

Sometimes, when a program crashes, the screen fills with garbage. This is because the errant program has written to memory in an uncontrolled way, and written into the screen buffer. Certainly this is a problem, as the program needs sorting out, but it isn't necessarily a symptom of a virus.

Friday 13th, April 1st and other interesting dates in the calendar always cause a stir in the media. There are viruses that have a special relationship with certain dates, and these are documented in this book. Jerusalem is tied to Friday 13th, Datacrime is tied to October 13th, the Surivs are tied to April 1st. But most viruses are not tied to any date in particular, and the media always overdoes it. My advice, as one of these dates approaches, is to work normally. Working normally, of course, includes taking backups as often as your procedures specify.

Finally, now that there are a number of anti-virus products on the market, many companies are running more than one virus scanning program, and occasionally one will report a virus whilst the other doesn't. This might, or might not, be a false alarm. Read the chapter in this manual about that virus, and you can then do further tests based on that information. For example, some products do not encrypt their virus signatures, and then another product might look at the first product, identify the signature, and give a false alarm.

Another problem is that some products are written using published search strings, and if the context of the publication is not read carefully, the search string may be used inappropriately. For example, I published a search string so that people could check for Twelve Tricks in their partition record. Some products have taken this string, and applied it to searching in files, and incorrectly report Twelve Tricks in the file.

A third problem is that a set of viruses circulates round the virus research community; these are carefully controlled, and are used for writing anti-virus products. Sometimes, a researcher will include something of interest on the diskette, which is not a virus – often the researcher will include an uninfected copy of the test file that he uses for infecting, for comparison. There has been an instance of a product that reported one of these test files as a virus, and there have been instances of other perfectly harmless programs being identified by a scanner as a virus, simply because the program had found its way onto one of the disks sent between researchers.

There are programs that simulate the appearance or effects of viruses; if one of these is used as a practical joke, this could cause an unnecessary false alarm.

Chapter 3
The Types of Viruses and How They Operate

3.1 Boot Sector Viruses

The boot sector is the very first sector on the diskette. On a hard disk, it is the first sector of the DOS partition. It contains information about that disk or diskette (such as the number of sectors in the logical volume), plus a little program. When a PC starts up, it reads the boot sector of the diskette in drive A, if it can, and then loads what it finds into memory and runs it. A boot sector virus (BSV) replaces the diskette boot sector with its own code, and moves the original boot sector to somewhere else on the diskette, so that it can be loaded after the virus has finished, and the original boot process can continue.

A BSV gets into the computer at boot time, before any software can be run. So prevention programs are defenceless against it. There are only two ways to prevent a BSV getting in. The first is to make the BSV think that it is already in, and so it won't try again. That is what inoculation programs do. But tinkering around with the highly vulnerable areas on someone else's hard disk can be dangerous. Inoculating diskettes is usually safe, but if you inoculate a hard disk, you could find that it no longer boots up (or is even completely inaccessible).

The second way to prevent a BSV getting in is with hardware, and there are a few products around for doing this, but they are mainly of interest to virus researchers.

Once a BSV is on your boot sector, it runs every time you boot up. So that every time you start the computer, the BSV loads itself into memory and protects itself by flagging that memory as in use. The BSV hooks some of the PCs interrupts – typically interrupt 13h, the disk read/write interrupt. So that whenever you read or write to a disk or diskette, the virus runs first.

Whenever you access the disk, the virus checks to see if it is already installed on that disk, and if not, it installs itself. Some BSVs only infect diskettes, others infect hard disks as well. If a BSV has infected a hard disk, or a bootable DOS diskette, then there will be an immense number of infected floppies around.

Brain and Italian are the commonest examples of BSVs.

3.2 Partition Sector Viruses

The partition sector is the very first sector on the hard disk. It contains information about that disk (such as the number of sectors in each partition, and where the DOS partition starts), plus a little program. When a PC starts up, it reads the partition sector on the disk, and executes the code.

A partition sector virus (PSV) is just like a BSV, except that it is harder to find, since many disk snooping tools (such as Debug) don't let you see the partition sector. Floppy disks don't have a partition sector, so on a floppy, a PSV is the same as a BSV. The code on the partition sector is run before the boot sector, so again, software that is run under DOS is running under control of the virus, and so cannot be relied on. Stoned is the commonest PSV.

3.3 File Viruses: Direct Action

A direct action file virus (DAFV) appends (or inserts or prepends) itself to an executable file. This could be a COM file or an EXE file, but could also be a SYS file, or an overlay file, which could have any extension.

Most COM files have three bytes at the beginning, which are a jump to the start of the actual program. The virus might append itself to the end of the file, patch the jump so that it jumps to the virus code, and the last instruction of the virus code is a jump to the original program, so that it runs in an apparently normal way, and the user's suspicions are not aroused. The virus could alternatively prepend itself, or even locate itself in a sufficiently large block of zeros in the code.

COM file viruses are easier to write than EXE file viruses, as the COM file has a very simple structure that lends itself to being infected quite easily. EXE file viruses are therefore less common, but should not be ignored. It is possible to write a virus that infects both COM and EXE files, but the virus then has to detect which kind of file it is infecting, and take different action accordingly. Syslock is one of these.

It is sometimes thought that a file infected with a file virus would have a changed date and time. It is very easy to read the date/time of a file, and equally easy to set the date/time after changing it. In fact, this is done by almost every file virus that I've met so far.

Nor, of course, does it make the slightest difference if a file is read-only. It is very easy to discover the attribute of a file, set it to read/write, do whatever you like to it, and then reset the attribute back the way you found it.

On a network, however, things are different. Network security can be effective against viruses, as the virus has the same privileges as the logged-in user. For example, if you have a Novell network and you make a file read-only then a virus would not be able to make it read/write, unless the logged-on user has that privilege.

A DAFV operates each time you run an infected file. The virus code searches for an uninfected file, and infects it; after doing so, the original program runs.

3.4 File Viruses: Indirect Action

An indirect action file virus (IAFV) also infects COM and EXE files. The difference between an IAFV and a DAFV is that an IAFV installs itself into memory, usually by replacing interrupt 21h, the DOS function interrupt. But it could replace any other interrupt that is called regularly. A good one to intercept is interrupt 21h, function 4bh (Load and Execute a program) as this is only called when DOS tries to load an EXE or COM file, which are exactly the files that the virus wants to infect. Other viruses use other functions to trigger the infection routine, such as open file, close file, or even the function to look at the file's directory entry.

This means that once the virus is installed in memory, every time DOS does anything the virus has control. The virus will do whatever it wants to first, and will then pass the original request on to DOS, either intact, or in a modified form.

This means that you only need to run an IAFV once, in order to infect lots of other files. It also means that a machine running under control of the virus is unpredictable.

3.5 How do Viruses Spread?

The most frequent spreader of viruses is, surprisingly enough, the PC Support group, although of course this in completely unintentional. The usual way this happens is that a user gets a virus, and at some stage, PC Support is called out to give some help with some minor problem. In giving this help, the PC Support staff member infects one of his diskettes, and thereafter, that diskette infects many other computers. I advise all PC Support staff to write-protect all their tool diskettes, so that this cannot happen.

So how does the virus get into the company in the first place? It is commonly believed that the virus gets in on a game, or on pirated software. This is not my experience. When you read about the infective mechanisms of the viruses, you'll see that many other routes are possible. BSVs tend to come in on data diskettes, and file viruses can come in when a salesman runs a demo program that he has run on many other computers before, one of which, unknown to him, had a virus.

An additional vector for viruses is the hardware engineer. These are like busy little bees, flitting from PC to PC, carrying their diagnostic disks with them. If those diskettes are not write-protected, then an infection picked up from one customer can be passed on unwittingly to the next. Please ensure that any hardware engineer write-protects his diskettes before putting them in your drive, and explain to him why. It costs nothing, and closes down one more route for viruses to spread on. This is too late to protect your disk, of course, but at least from now on his disks will remain virus-proof. PC Support staff should also write-protect their diskettes, for the same reason.

Whenever you get new software, write-protect the diskette it came on before even putting it into your diskette drive. This will mean that you will never accidentally infect the distribution diskette.

3.6 Viruses on Networks

Networks are different to stand-alone PCs in one major and obvious way – it is much easier to share things across computers. With stand-alone machines, a virus can only spread via a floppy disk, whereas on a network, some viruses can also spread that way. On the other hand, there are usually ways in which good network management can offer a substantial barrier to the spread of viruses.

Here is how a file virus can spread over a network; to be specific, let's take Jerusalem as an example. The virus would come in somehow (perhaps on an engineer's diagnostic disk or a salesman's demo) and remain installed in memory after the visit. The first program run by the user becomes infected, and thereafter each program run is likewise infected. When the user reboots, the virus is cleared from memory, but the first infected program run re-installs it, and thereafter, once again, each uninfected program run becomes infected.

Eventually, the user runs a program that is stored on the file server, and so that program is infected. Suppose another user runs that program; the virus installs into the memory of his machine, and from there infects any program that he runs thereafter, from whatever device the program is on. Likewise, other users on the network can become infected, and so the infection becomes widespread rather more quickly than if the PCs were stand-alone.

The first line of defence should be ordinary good network management. Most good network operating systems have a way of allowing or denying various classes of access to files. A good start is to make all COM and EXE files read-only using this. Although nearly every virus uses DOS calls to make a target file read/write before attempting the infection, this will fail if the network software refuses permission. For example, you can use Novell in this way. It would also be useful if you could arrange for any attempt to write to a read-only file to trigger an alarm.

The second line of defence should be a cryptographic checksummer. Running this on a network is obviously harder than running it on a stand-alone PC. First you will have to ensure that the diskette you boot from is truly clean, and then you should log on as a special user, in order to get access to all the necessary files. Ideally, you should do this at a time when the network is used lightly or not at all, as the checksummer will try to read and verify every file on its list.

Perhaps insufficient precautions have been taken, and you have a virus on the network. The most important rule is not to panic, and not to take precipitate action that could actually cause damage. Removing a virus from a network is exactly the same as removing it from a stand-alone, except that you will have to take everybody off the network while it is being done, and you should ensure that the workstations are clean as well, before allowing users to log on again.

If you need to reformat the server, do not rely on a single tape backup, as these sometimes fail to restore. You should take at least two backups, using as completely different methods as you can, and you should verify that at least one of them will restore, if you can, by restoring it on another computer.

There is a particular problem with Novell networks and Jerusalem virus, as the virus tries to use interrupts that Novell uses. As a result, this virus causes particular problems on Novell systems.

Network drives are checked in exactly the same way as local hard disks, except that you should tell FindVirus not to check for BSVs, as these cannot be checked over a network. To check the network for BSVs:

- If the server is Novell, there won't be any BSVs – if there are, the server won't boot at all
- If the server is running under DOS (PC Lan, 3COM and others) then run FindVirus on the server itself
- If the server is running under OS/2 (3 Plus Open, others), then boot under DOS from a DOS diskette, and run FindVirus on the server itself

Chapter 4
The Known PC Viruses: Recognition, Analysis and Cure

The study of viruses is a very new field, and the terminology has not settled down yet. File viruses are also called "link" viruses and "parasitic" viruses, for example. But the worst confusion is in naming the viruses. The same virus is rediscovered several times, and given a name by each discoverer. In this chapter, I try to give all the common names for each virus, but the confusion will always persist.

In this chapter, I cover the PC viruses one at a time. Under the heading for each virus I cover recognition and detection, so that you can tell whether you have that virus. I explain how the virus copies itself, so that you can understand how it got into your organisation, and where it might have spread to. I cover what the virus does, which can be anything from nothing at all (as in Yale virus) up to making your hard disk inaccessible (Datacrime) by doing a low level format. Some viruses have a lot of different effects (such as Jerusalem).

Next, I explain how to get rid of it. Here, I explain the procedures that you have to go through to eradicate the virus. These will depend on the virus and how it works. Every organisation that I have ever worked with has decided to eradicate the virus from all their computers.

Where I suggest using FindVirus to check for the existence of the virus, any virus finding program that can reliably detect the virus in question will do; likewise where I suggest using an inoculator. UnVirus can be replaced by any virus removal program.

Some packages come with programs that remove the virus from infected files (this is also called "repair" or "healing"). In general, I would not suggest using such a facility, unless it is really necessary. Instead, I would recommend deleting the infected file, and replacing it with a clean copy by re-installing the software. But this is not always practical – consider a file server with thousands of infected files, or a site with hundreds of infected computers, or a situation where it will not be possible to get clean replacement software for several weeks. In such a situation, it is a good idea to use a virus removal system, and so there is such a facility built into FindVirus. In general, though, I do not mention this possibility in the chapter on virus eradication, as it is preferable to replace the infected file.

After eradicating the virus, you should expect that it will return, as you might have overlooked an infected diskette, or failed to find the source of the virus. To guard against this possibility, you should install some anti-virus software on each potentially infectable machine, and I would normally suggest a cryptographic checksummer for this. ChkVirus is one such, but there are several others available, so where I recommend installing ChkVirus, you can install any similar system.

Next, I present other information about the virus – this might be interesting information about its origin, or where it has been seen. Finally, I give technical information, which might be of interest to technical support staff, about the mechanisms used by the virus.

4.1 Brain

Other names: Pakistani, Lahore. Major variant: Ashar. Minor variants: the message in the boot sector can differ slightly, or (in the "telephone numbers" variant) considerably
Infects: any 5¼-inch 360 k diskette, any computer
Classification: boot sector virus

4.1.1 Recognition and Detection

You see "(c) Brain" as a volume label on diskettes, and diskettes have 3 k of bad sectors. Brain only affects 5¼-inch diskettes in all the versions that I've seen. I've heard reports of hard disk versions, but never seen one.

You can detect infected diskettes by running Chkdsk (which comes with DOS). If you get 3 k of bad sectors, that's an almost sure sign of Brain or Ashar, as FORMAT marks an entire track (5 k on a 360 k diskette) as bad if it finds a defect. You can also use FindVirus to detect Brain, and a disk sector editor will confirm it, since the boot sector is so distinctive. You must, of course, boot from a clean DOS diskette before running any anti-virus software.

4.1.2 How the Virus Copies Itself

When you boot from an infected diskette, the virus goes memory-resident; this is true whether the diskette is a boot disk or not. So the usual thing is for someone to have an infected data diskette, which they leave in drive A when they shut down. Next day when they start up the computer, it attempts to boot from that diskette: if it isn't a system diskette, you see the message "Not a system disk. Please insert a system disk and retry". If that diskette was Brain- infected, Brain is now in memory, and when you continue the boot it remains there.

While it is in memory, any diskette that you put into any floppy drive is liable to be infected. If you access the diskette (whether read or write) and the diskette is write-enabled, and there is space on it for Brain, then Brain will replace the boot sector with its own code, move the boot sector further up the disk, add the rest of the Brain code, and mark these sectors as bad in the FAT.

4.1.3 What the Virus Does

The virus has no ill-effects, apart from slowing down the floppy drive because of the infection attempts, and making 3 k of the diskette and 7 k of memory unavailable to DOS.

4.1.4 How To Get Rid of It

Boot from a clean DOS disk; this is a DOS diskette that has come from the manufacturer, and has never been write-enabled. This ensures that there is nothing unwanted installed in memory. Use FindVirus to determine which diskettes are infected.

Treatment consists of simply copying all the files off an infected diskette (using "COPY *.*"; do not use Diskcopy or any image copier), and reformatting the diskette (see below for details). Alternatively, you can use UnVirus to remove the infection from a diskette; UnVirus or any virus removal program is a lot faster.

If a large number of diskettes are potentially infected, then you should consider borrowing a hopper-fed diskette cleaning machine, which can handle up to 700 diskettes per hour, sorting them into clean and contaminated bins.

If you have an outbreak of Brain, then after it is cleared up you should use Inoculate or any other inoculator on all diskettes. This works by putting the Brain signature (just two harmless bytes) on the boot sector of the diskette. If Brain sees that signature, it thinks that the diskette is already infected, so doesn't attack it.

4.1.5 Other Information

The story says that this virus was written by two brothers, Basit and Amjads, from Lahore, Pakistan. The story says that whenever a foreigner came to their shop to buy pirated software they gave him an infected disk, but locals got uninfected disks. In my opinion, this practice would have soon led to confusion, and infection of their own diskettes.

Another version of the story says that they wrote it to track down pirate copies of their own software. Since Brain travels equally well on data diskettes with no COM or EXE files as it does on diskettes with programs on, this is hard to believe.

Another part of the story says that there is a phone number on the boot sector, and if you phone that number you get through to the brothers, who cheerfully admit to having written the virus, and express surprise that it has travelled so far. I have only ever seen a few Brain-infected disks that had phone numbers on – most Brain disks have nothing except the "Welcome to the Dungeon" message.

This is the text that you find on the boot sector. I've left in the spelling and grammatical mistakes. There is a minor variant of this in which "pvt" is replaced by DLC, and the major variant in which the message is completely different.

Welcome to the Dungeon
(c) 1986 Brain & Amjads (pvt) Ltd
VIRUS _SHOE RECORD v9.0
Dedicated to the dynamic memories
of millions of virus who are no longer with us
today - Thanks GOODNESS!!
BEWARE OF THE er..VIRUS : this program is catching
program follows after these messeges….. $#@%$@!!

None of the known versions of Brain infect hard disks, although this isn't a safe assumption to make about future versions, as I have heard rumours about versions that will infect hard disks. It is widespread in the Philippines (Manila), in Indonesia (Jakarta), and in Pakistan. It has spread through a number of US colleges, and is fairly widespread in UK technical colleges and a few universities. It has infected a UK software house, and (perhaps through them) Saudi, Qatar and Abu Dhabi, including a hospital there.

4.1.6 Technical Details

When a diskette is infected, the virus puts a pseudo-volume label onto it. If there are no files on the diskette, then it puts it as entry number three, which means that the label won't be seen until after two files have been added to the diskette, at which point you see the "(c) Brain". The fake bad sectors are some way down the diskette, at cluster number 55 if the diskette was empty, or after that if necessary, wherever Brain can find three contiguous unused clusters.

Probably, the intention was to make it possible to put the DOS system files on an infected diskette; the DOS system files want to be the first directory entries, and must be contiguous files, so a bad sector in the middle would stop that happening. So the purpose of this ploy is to avoid detection when bootable diskettes are made. This, plus the fact that Brain doesn't infect hard disks, means that it was probably written by someone who didn't use a hard disk.

Brain has a very interesting trick. Whilst the virus is active, if you look at the boot sector it looks completely normal. This is because the virus redirects any attempt to look at the boot sector and shows you the original boot sector. This may be an attempt to make programs that read the boot sector run normally, but it is more likely to be camouflage, so that you won't detect the virus. Ashar is a related virus.

4.2 Ashar

Other names: Pakistani, Lahore. It is a variant of Brain
Infects: any 5¼-inch 360 k diskette, any computer
Classification: boot sector virus

4.2.1 Recognition and Detection

You see "(c) Ashar" as a volume label on diskettes, and diskettes have 3 k of bad sectors. Ashar only affects 5¼-inch 360 k diskettes. You can detect infected diskettes by running Chkdsk (which comes with DOS). If you get 3 k of bad sectors, that's an almost sure sign of Brain or Ashar, as FORMAT marks an entire track (5 k on a 360 k diskette) as bad if it finds a defect. You can also use FindVirus to detect Ashar, and a disk sector editor will confirm it since the boot sector is so distinctive. You must, of course, boot from a clean DOS diskette before running any anti-virus software.

4.2.2 How the Virus Copies Itself

When you boot from an infected diskette, the virus goes memory-resident; this is true whether the diskette is a boot disk or not. So the usual thing is for someone to have an infected data diskette, which they leave in drive A when they shut down. Next day when they start up the computer, it attempts to boot from that diskette; if it isn't a system diskette, you see the message "Not a system disk. Please insert a system disk and retry". If that diskette was Ashar- infected, Ashar is now in memory, and when you continue the boot it remains there.

While it is in memory, any diskette that you put into any floppy drive is liable to be infected. If you access the diskette (whether read or write) and the diskette is write-enabled, and there is space on it for Ashar, then Ashar will replace the boot sector with its own code, move the boot sector further up the disk, add the rest of the Ashar code, and mark these sectors as bad in the FAT.

4.2.3 What the Virus Does

The virus has no ill-effects, apart from slowing down the floppy drive because of the infection attempts, and making 3 k of the diskette and 7 k of memory unavailable to DOS.

4.2.4 How To Get Rid of It

Boot from a clean DOS disk; this is a DOS diskette that has come from the manufacturer, and has never been write-enabled. This ensures that there is nothing unwanted installed in memory. Use FindVirus to determine which diskettes are infected.

Treatment consists of simply copying all the files off an infected diskette (using "COPY *.*"; do not use Diskcopy or any image copier), and reformatting the diskette (see below for details). Alternatively, you can use UnVirus or any virus removal program to remove the infection from a diskette; UnVirus is a lot faster.

If a large number of diskettes are potentially infected, then you should consider borrowing a hopper-fed diskette cleaning machine, which can handle up to 700 diskettes per hour, sorting them into clean and contaminated bins.

If you have an outbreak of Ashar, then after it is cleared up, you could use Inoculate or any other inoculator on all diskettes. This works by putting the Ashar signature (just two harmless bytes) on the boot sector of the diskette. If Ashar sees that signature, it thinks that the diskette is already infected, so doesn't attack it.

4.2.5 Other Information

Ashar is very similar to Brain, which has been described above, but there are some interesting differences, which are worth documenting.

Difference 1 The volume label that is put on the diskette is "(c) ashar" instead of "(c) Brain". The text in the boot sector contains "(c) 1986 ashar & ashars (pvt) Ltd VIRUS_ _SHOE RECORD" and the "v9.0" is absent. The rest of the text "Dedicated to the dynamic memories" etc. is exactly the same, including the misspelling of "messeges" and the grammatical errors.

Difference 2 In Ashar, the volume label is put into the first available directory entry, whereas with Brain, it cannot be put into the first or second entry. If there is a volume label on one of the first two entries, an attempt to install the system will fail, making the virus more noticeable and more of a nuisance.

Difference 3 The body of the virus, and the stored (original) boot sector, is placed in three fake bad clusters. In Brain, this must be on or after cluster 55; the purpose of this is probably to allow space for the DOS system files. Ashar allows the body of the virus to be on any free cluster on the diskette.

Difference 4 Brain uses quite a complicated encryption scheme to encode the volume label that it places on diskettes, presumably to make it harder for someone to change it. Ashar uses a much simpler scheme. It stores the volume label as a character string, in negated form, so that all you have to do to decode it is a NEG instruction. There are 11 bytes in Brain which were previously thought to contain rubbish. These 11 bytes are the negated "(c) ashar". Immediately after these, there is "(c) ashar $" in clear. These 11 bytes and the clear text are unused by Brain.

Difference 5 Ashar resets the floppy disk controller before reading or writing to the device in a number of places that Brain doesn't.

Difference 6 When Brain is installed in memory, and you try to look at the boot sector of a diskette, Brain reads the original boot sector that has been stored further down the diskette, and shows you that normal boot sector instead. This applies to programs that use the data in the boot sector, but also to Debug, Norton, Mace, PC-Tools and other disk sector editors. One of the effects of this is to mislead you into thinking that the diskette is normal.

Ashar stores the original boot sector of the diskette, and uses it to continue the boot process after an attempt has been made to boot from an infected floppy, but it does not redirect subsequent attempts to read the boot sector. When you look at the boot sector, you see an infected boot sector.

Conclusion on Ashar/Brain Ashar and Brain are definitely two versions of the same virus; the code is nearly the same, apart from the differences documented above. But Brain has sophistications that Ashar doesn't have, such as the boot-read redirection, the space left in the FAT and directory for the installation of the system, and the greatly improved encryption system.

Brain contains, as an unused remnant, the NEG-encrypted Ashar volume label. That would tend to imply that Ashar predates Brain, and the greater sophistications in Brain tend to confirm this. This would imply that Ashar was the precursor to Brain.

If this is true, then the version of Brain which has not got the telephone numbers on the boot sector (but has "Dedicated to the dynamic memories") is previous to the version with the telephone numbers, which would imply that the telephone numbers version is a hack of the real Brain. It is very easy to change the boot sector – any disk sector editor would allow that.

4.2.6 Technical Details

When a diskette is infected, the virus puts a pseudo-volume label onto the diskette. The fake bad sectors are wherever Ashar can find three contiguous unused clusters.

4.3 Italian

Other names: Ping Pong, Bouncing Ball
Infects: the boot sector of any writable diskette or hard disk on 8088 or 8086 computers
Classification: boot sector virus

4.3.1 Recognition and Detection

Once every half hour, if you are accessing the disk, the bouncing dot is triggered. The dot bounces off the edges of the screen, and passes through any text, with replacement after it. Sometimes this doesn't work properly, and screen displays are slightly messed up. If you look at the boot sector using Peeka or Norton, it will be full of program code, without the usual messages like "Not a system disk".

You can detect infected diskettes by running Chkdsk (which comes with DOS). If you get 1 k of bad sectors, that's an almost sure sign of Italian, as FORMAT marks an entire track (5 k on a 360 k diskette) as bad if it finds a defect. You can also use FindVirus to detect Italian.

4.3.2 How the Virus Copies Itself

When you boot from an infected diskette, the virus goes memory-resident; this is true whether the diskette is a boot disk or not. So the usual thing is for someone to have an infected data diskette which they leave in drive A when they shut down. Next day when they start up the computer it attempts to boot from that diskette; if it isn't a system diskette, you see the message "Not a system disk. Please insert a system disk and retry" or a similar message. If that diskette was infected, the virus is now in memory, and when you continue the boot, it remains there.

While it is in memory, any disk that you access is liable to be infected. If you access the diskette (whether read or write) and the diskette is write-enabled then Italian will replace the boot sector with its own code, move the boot sector further up the disk, add the rest of the Italian code, and mark these sectors as bad in the FAT. Italian also infects hard disks.

4.3.3 What the Virus Does

The bouncing ball display is the main outcome of the virus. In addition, infected diskettes lose 1 k of space to the fake bad sectors that Italian creates (hard disks lose one cluster, which usually means 2 k). Attempts to infect slow the computer down, although not noticeably.

4.3.4 How To Get Rid of It

Boot from a clean DOS disk; this is a DOS diskette that has come from the manufacturer, and has never been write-enabled. This ensures that there is nothing unwanted installed in memory. Use FindVirus to determine which diskettes are infected. Treatment consists of simply copying all the files off an infected diskette (using "COPY *.*"; do not use Diskcopy or any image copier), and reformatting the diskette (see below for details). Alternatively, you can use UnVirus or any virus removal program to remove the infection from a diskette; UnVirus is a lot faster.

If a large number of diskettes are potentially infected, then you should consider borrowing a hopper-fed diskette cleaning machine, which can handle up to 700 diskettes per hour, sorting them into clean and contaminated bins.

If you have an outbreak of Italian, after it is cleared up you should use Inoculate or any other inoculator on all diskettes. This works by putting the Italian signature (just two harmless bytes) on the boot sector of the diskette. If Italian sees that signature, it thinks that the diskette is already infected, so doesn't attack it.

In the case of a hard disk, you could use a disk sector editor. Find the original boot sector (it will be in the bad sectors) and copy it back to the place where it should be, at Logical Sector Number zero. I would recommend that you take a full backup before doing this, as if you get it wrong, you could make your disk inaccessible. You could then patch the FAT to mark the bad sectors as usable. I have not provided a utility to do this, as there are so many different layouts of hard disk to cope with.

An alternative, and much easier method, is as follows. First boot from a clean DOS disk. Then make two backups of the hard disk (the second backup is in case you find that you have a problem restoring the first backup). With most versions of DOS, SYS will replace the boot sector, and you can use FindVirus to check that this has worked, but this still leaves you with the 2 k in bad sectors; this is now quite harmless and can be ignored. Alternatively, you can format the hard disk, using "FORMAT /S/V" and restore the backup; this has the advantage of reclaiming the fake bad sectors.

4.3.5 Other Information

It was first sighted in Turin, Italy, and is to be found on the south coast of England where it came in via a technical college, and in the City, as a dealer there had an infection for some time. It has also been found at other sites, scattered around the country.

4.3.6 Technical Details

Italian fails to infect 80286 and 80386 machines, because of a bug in the virus. Another interesting detail about this virus is when it writes to the FAT, it only writes to the first copy, relying on DOS to copy that to the second FAT copy.

4.4 Stoned

Other names: New Zealand, Marijuana, Australian
Infects: the partition sector of hard disks, the boot sector of
floppies in drive A
Classification: partition sector virus

4.4.1 Recognition and Detection

Every eighth infective boot-up, you see "Your PC is now Stoned".
The boot sectors of infected diskettes are obviously abnormal, and
include that message. FindVirus will detect Stoned, or you can look
at the partition sector with Peeka or another low level disk sector
editor. If you do, you will see the "Stoned" message, as well as
another text string "Legalise Marijuana". There is a variant where
the "Legalise Marijuana" string has been replaced with random
bytes. Another variant replaces the word Stoned with Sanded.

4.4.2 How the Virus Copies Itself

When you boot from an infected diskette, the virus goes memory-
resident; this is true whether the diskette is a boot disk or not. So the
usual thing is for someone to have an infected data diskette, which
they leave in drive A when they shut down. Next day when they
start up the computer, it attempts to boot from that diskette; if it isn't
a system diskette, you see the message "Not a system disk. Please
insert a system disk and retry" or a similar message. If that diskette
was infected, the virus is now in memory, and when you continue
the boot, it remains there.

It is also written immediately to the partition sector of the hard disk,
if one is present. While the virus is in memory, any disk in drive A
that you access is liable to be infected. If you access the diskette
(whether read or write) and the diskette is write-enabled then Stoned
will replace the boot sector with its own code, move the boot sector
further up the disk and add the rest of the Stoned code.

4.4.3 What the Virus Does

No intentional damage is done. However, because the place that
Stoned stores the original boot sector does not change according to
the kind of diskette it infects, it causes problems on 1.2 floppies if

they have more than 32 files, by overwriting the directory entries for files 33 to 48, and would also cause problems on 3½-inch diskettes. On a small percentage of hard disks, it overwrites part of the FAT, because it assumes that cylinder zero, head zero has nothing on it after the partition sector, whereas there are some disks that begin the DOS partition immediately after the partition sector.

4.4.4 How To Get Rid of It

You can use FindVirus to detect Stoned, and a disk sector editor will confirm it, since the partition sector (boot sector on diskettes) has the distinctive message.

Boot from a clean DOS disk; this is a DOS diskette that has come from the manufacturer, and has never been write-enabled. This ensures that there is nothing unwanted installed in memory. Use FindVirus to determine which diskettes are infected.

Treatment consists of simply copying all the files off an infected diskette (using "COPY *.*"; do not use Diskcopy or any image copier), and reformatting the diskette (see below for details). Alternatively, you can use UnVirus or any virus removal program to remove the infection from a diskette; UnVirus is a lot faster. You can also use UnStone or any similar remover for Stoned virus to remove it from a hard disk; this is the simplest method.

In the case of a hard disk, you could use a disk sector editor. Find the original partition sector (it will be at cylinder 0, head 0, sector 7, although there is supposedly another version which puts it at 0, 0, 2) and copy it back to the place where it should be, at Physical Sector Number zero. I would recommend that you take a full backup before doing this, as if you get it wrong, you could make your disk inaccessible.

If the hard disk is the kind that has the boot sector immediately after the partition sector, Stoned will have overwritten one sector of the first copy of the FAT. In order to recover the data from the hard disk, it will be necessary to copy the genuine partition sector back to cylinder 0, head 0, sector 1, and to make a copy of the relevant sector from the second copy of the FAT, onto the sector that Stoned has corrupted.

An alternative, and much easier (but more long-winded) method, is as follows. First boot from a clean DOS disk. Then make two backups of the hard disk (the second backup is in case you find that you have a problem restoring the first backup). Then do a low level format of the hard disk, remembering to mark any bad tracks on the bad track map. Many hard disk controllers will trigger a low level format if you load up Debug, and type "G=C800:5" (some controllers might want 6, or CCC instead of 5). Even better, you might have a low level formatting utility (which might be called HDFMT, HDPREP or something like that) that came with your computer, or possibly the diagnostics diskette would have this. There are also programs available that allow low level formatting, such as Disk Manager.

When the disk is formatted, it must be partitioned, using FDISK (some hard disk formatters do this as part of the formatting process). After partitioning the disk, it must be high level formatted using "FORMAT /S/V". Check the disk again with FindVirus, and then restore the backup.

If a large number of diskettes are potentially infected, then you should consider borrowing a hopper-fed diskette cleaning machine, which can handle up to 700 diskettes per hour, sorting them into clean and contaminated bins.

If you have an outbreak of Stoned, then after it is cleared up you could use Inoculate or any other inoculator on all diskettes. This works by putting the Stoned signature (just four harmless bytes) on the boot sector of the diskette. If Stoned sees that signature, it thinks that the diskette is already infected, so doesn't attack it. Inoculate should not be used on 3½-inch diskettes (it won't allow you to) as some versions of DOS will not be able to read inoculated diskettes. You cannot use Inoculate to put the signature on a hard disk, as it would make the hard disk unreadable. Inoculate does not allow you to do this accidentally.

4.4.5 Other Information

The virus is quite small – only about 400 bytes of code. It has been found in the field in the UK, at a number of sites.

4.4.6 Technical Details

Stoned virus is a partition sector virus. On hard disks it hides itself by existing in a place that most people don't even know exists. It puts the displaced partition sector at cylinder 0, head 0, sector 7 on the hard disk. On most hard disks, this is safely before the start of the DOS partition, but on some (about 1 per cent) hard disks, this is in the middle of the FAT and will therefore make a mess of the disk.

On floppy disks, it is a boot sector virus, as floppies don't have a partition sector. On floppy disks, it puts the original boot sector at cylinder 0, head 1, sector 3. On a 360 k floppy, this puts it on the last sector of the directory, and will only cause trouble if there are more than 96 files on the diskette. On a 1.2 Mb floppy, this is the third sector of the directory, and will give big problems if there are more than 32 files on the diskette. Other diskettes can likewise suffer.

4.5 Yale

Other names: Alameda, Merritt
Infects: floppy disks
Classification: boot sector virus

4.5.1 Recognition and Detection

There is no obvious way to recognise Yale, apart from detecting it with FindVirus, or by looking at the boot sector.

4.5.2 How the Virus Copies Itself

Yale is a boot sector virus that affects floppy disks only. It spreads when you accidentally boot or try to boot from an infected diskette. When you replace the diskette, and then press Ctrl-Alt-Del, that keystroke is intercepted by the virus and triggers the infection of the replacement diskette. Thus, only drive A is affected. The original boot sector is moved to track 39, side 0, sector 8; if there is any data there, it will be overwritten.

4.5.3 What the Virus Does

There is most of the code in place for formatting track 39 of the floppy disk, but an essential part is missing in versions that I know about, so the format will not happen. Any data on track 39, side 0, sector 8 will be overwritten, but this would only tend to have data in a fairly full diskette.

4.5.4 How To Get Rid of It

Proceed as for any boot sector virus – boot from a clean DOS diskette by powering off and on again. This is very important – do not just do Ctrl-Alt-Del, as Yale survives this. In fact, it is this sequence that Yale uses to reproduce, as it intercepts the Ctrl-Alt-Del and redefines it.

Next, identify all infected diskettes with FindVirus, copy the data off the infected diskette onto a clean one, and reformat the diskette. Alternatively, you can use any disk sector editor to copy the sector on cylinder 39, head 0, sector 8 onto the boot, overwriting the Yale code.

4.5.5 Other Information

Yale has not yet been seen outside the US. Because of the way it spreads, it isn't likely to be very infectious, and will quite likely never be seen in the UK except as a specimen. It looks as if it is one of the earliest and most primitive viruses.

4.5.6 Technical Details

Yale takes interrupt 9 and replaces it with its own code. This intercepts the Ctrl-Alt-Del keystroke and replaces the boot process with a routine that fakes a reboot by blanking the VDU, beeping and moving the floppy drive heads, before restarting the machine but with its own code still hooked into memory.

4.6 Denzuk

Other names: Venezuelan, Search, Ohio
Infects: floppy diskettes
Classification: boot sector virus

4.6.1 Recognition and Detection

If you have a colour monitor, whenever you reboot an infected machine using Ctrl-Alt-Del before the reboot, you see the Denzuk logo. The Denzuk logo is a graphic, with the words "DEN ZUK" in large red letters. The pixels making up these letters come in from each side until they merge making the words; there is also a symbol to the side that looks rather like a stylised globe.

Denzuk puts a volume label on the diskette, which is "Y.C.1.E.R.P."

4.6.2 How the Virus Copies Itself

Every time you try to read or write a floppy diskette (Denzuk will not infect a hard disk) Denzuk will decrement its infection counter (which is initially set to eight). When the counter reaches zero this triggers the infection process and the counter is set back to two.

4.6.3 What the Virus Does

If Denzuk finds Brain on the diskette it removes Brain and replaces it with itself. It might be thought that Denzuk is actually a helpful virus, in that it kills Brain. This is not so – consider what will happen if Denzuk infects a diskette with more than 40 tracks. The virus uses track 40 to store code and the bitmap of the Denzuk logo, so track 40 would be overwritten, and data could be lost as a result.

Even worse, Denzuk assumes that all diskettes are 360 k diskettes, so when it infects them, it puts a 360 k diskette boot sector on top of the old boot sector. This tells DOS that the diskette has 22 FAT sectors and 7 directory sectors, which is only true for 360 k diskettes. So DOS is not able to read the diskette properly and interprets the directory as part of the FAT, and (depending on what diskette it is) can get the cluster size wrong, and might ignore some of the sectors on each track. In other words, Denzuk infecting a 5¼-inch 1.2 Mb diskette leaves it unreadable, although putting a correct boot sector back in place will rescue most of the data (track 40 head 0 is gone for ever). Other capacity diskettes (other than 360 k) will also have problems.

4.6.4 How To Get Rid of It

Boot from a clean DOS disk; this is a DOS diskette that has come from the manufacturer and has never been write-enabled. This ensures that there is nothing unwanted installed in memory. Use FindVirus to determine which diskettes are infected.

Treatment consists of simply copying all the files off an infected diskette (using "COPY *.*"; do not use Diskcopy or any image copier), and reformatting the diskette. On a 360 k diskette, this would leave the code on track 40, but without the boot sector that links to it, that code is harmless. Alternatively, it is much faster to use UnVirus or any virus removal program to remove the infection from a diskette.

If a large number of diskettes are potentially infected, then you should consider borrowing a hopper-fed diskette cleaning machine, which can handle up to 700 diskettes per hour, sorting them into clean and contaminated bins.

If you have an outbreak of Denzuk then, after it is cleared up, you could use Inoculate or any other inoculator on all diskettes. This works by putting the Denzuk signature on the boot sector of the diskette. If Denzuk sees that signature it thinks that the diskette is already infected so doesn't attack it.

4.6.5 Other Information

I have only seen one infected site in the UK.

There are a couple of text messages in the virus, which are not displayed. These are:

At the beginning:

Welcome to the
C l u b
–The HackerS–
Hackin'
All The Time

At the end:

The HackerS

4.6.6 Technical Details

Denzuk is a boot sector virus. It replaces the original boot sector with its own – this looks very like a normal boot sector, as it has the usual messages "Non-System disk or disk error", "Replace and strike any key when ready" and "Disk Boot failure". It also has the references to IBMBIO.COM and IBMDOS.COM. If your system files are called IO.SYS and MSDOS.SYS, Denzuk doesn't realize this, but it does mean that the boot sector looks normal.

When the boot sector runs, it loads in the rest of the virus, which is located on track 40 (normal 360 k diskettes have tracks numbered 0 to 39), head 0, sectors 33 to 41 (normal tracks are numbered from 1). Putting the virus in this place means that some disk-searching utilities won't find it there. It also means that if you Diskcopy the infected diskette, most of the virus fails to copy. This gives us one simple way to clean up an infection – Denzuk could almost be called a copy-protected virus! If you Diskcopy an infected diskette, the Denzuk boot is copied, but not the rest of Denzuk. If you use COPY or XCOPY to copy the diskette, then the infected boot is left behind also. Of course, you must boot from a known clean diskette before you start.

When Denzuk runs the code that it has loaded in from track 40, it replaces two of the PC's interrupts, 13h (diskette) and 9 (keyboard). A new interrupt is installed, 6Fh, which is the old interrupt 13h; Denzuk uses this as a short way to call the original routine. The new interrupt 9 looks for two keystrokes. On seeing a Ctrl-Alt-Del it calls a routine that displays its logo (if it is running on anything apart from a mono monitor) and then reboots. The other keystroke is Ctrl-Alt-F5, which just triggers a reboot. This is a convenient test to see if you are infected as, on a PC that is not running Denzuk, Ctrl-Alt-F5 does nothing. All other keystrokes are passed on to the original interrupt 9 routine.

Interrupt 13h is used to infect more diskettes. Every time interrupt 13h is called, provided it is referencing one of the two floppy drives (Denzuk will not infect a hard disk), and provided the call is a read, write, verify or format, Denzuk will decrement its infection counter (which is initially set to eight). When the counter reaches zero, this triggers the infection process, and the counter is set back to two.

The infection process works like this. First it reads the sector at cylinder 0, head 0, sector 1. It looks for two bytes that are found in Denzuk and if it finds them, it doesn't infect. If they are absent, it looks for two other bytes which are an old version of Denzuk; if it finds those, it calls the "Find Denzuk Boot" routine, whereby it reads the boot sector from track 40, head 0, sector 33 which is where the original boot is stored. Thus, Denzuk will update you if it finds that you are running an out-of-date version of the virus.

If Denzuk finds Brain (or Ashar) virus on the boot sector (which it does by looking for the 1234h signature of Brain) then it upgrades you from Brain to Denzuk. First, though, it has to go and find the boot sector from where Brain has put it; Brain has three bytes on sector cylinder 0, head 0, sector 1 that tells you where the original boot sector is, and Denzuk decodes these and reads the boot sector.

Whether the diskette was clean or infected by old-Denzuk or Brain, Denzuk now has a copy of the original boot sector. It formats track 40 head 0, and writes its nine sectors there. If this write is successful (some diskette drives may not allow writing beyond track 39) then it replaces the sector at cylinder 0, head 0, sector 1 with its own version of the boot sector. The infection process is now complete. It then scans through the directory to see if there is a volume label there. Brain, you may recall, puts "(c) Brain" as a volume label on the diskette. Denzuk overwrites that with its own label, which is "Y.C.1.E.R.P.", where the "." is character F9h. Denzuk assumes that it is looking at a 360 k diskette, but makes no attempt to ensure that this is the case. This directory scan starts at sector 0, 0, 6, and scans through seven sectors; just right for a 360 k diskette. The meaning of this volume label is obscure.

There is also a generation counter, which keeps track of how many generations have passed; if this is less than three, then Denzuk refrains from its visible signs – the logo is not displayed on reboot, and the volume label is not changed. The specimen that I had was generation 14h. This feature is probably to give it a chance to spread a bit before detecting it becomes easy.

Denzuk puts the Brain signature on the boot sector – this would stop Brain from infecting a Denzuk-infected diskette.

4.7 Lehigh

Other names: none
Infects: COMMAND.COM, any disk, any computer
Classification: COMMAND.COM virus

4.7.1 Recognition and Detection

COMMAND.COM does not grow, but the date/time is changed to the current system time. FindVirus will identify it.

4.7.2 How the Virus Copies Itself

The virus infects COMMAND.COM. When COMMAND.COM is run (this happens every time you boot up), the virus goes memory-resident. Then, whenever you run a program, or do something that causes DOS to look for a file, the virus looks at the currently logged disk to see if there is a file in the root directory called COMMAND.COM. If there is, and it has not already been infected, it infects it.

4.7.3 What the Virus Does

There is an infection counter that counts the number of times (not generations) that the virus has replicated. When the virus creates a copy of itself, this counter is set to zero. Each time the virus replicates it increments the counter; the date/time of COMMAND.COM will be set to the current date/time as it writes the counter back to the file.

After it has copied itself four times it trashes the disk by writing trash (actually, code from the BIOS) to sectors 1 to 32 of the disk. On a floppy, this will be difficult to recover from, as both copies of the FAT and the directory will be overwritten, but on a hard disk, fairly straightforward, as on most hard disks (about 95–99 per cent of disks, as it depends on the layout of the disk, and the DOS version it was formatted under) the virus will not get the second copy of the FAT or the root directory.

After the overwriting has been done the virus will display a string from the BIOS which will probably be nothing that makes sense.

4.7.4 How To Get Rid of It

Boot from a clean DOS disk; this is a DOS diskette that has come from the manufacturer, and has never been write-enabled. This ensures that there is nothing unwanted installed in memory. Use FindVirus to check the disk. If FindVirus identifies COMMAND.COM as being infected, then replace it with a COMMAND.COM from the same version of DOS that you were using before. If you replace it with a COMMAND.COM from a different version of DOS, the disk will no longer be bootable, although if you boot from a diskette it will be accessible. If this happens try to find the correct version of COMMAND.COM. If you can't, and need to completely re-install DOS take a full backup first (preferably make two separate backups using two completely different methods, in case one of them fails to restore for some reason). Then SYS the disk (see your DOS manual) or else reformat the disk using "FORMAT C: /S/V".

If Lehigh has trashed a hard disk copy the first 32 sectors of the second copy of the FAT back over the first copy.

4.7.5 Other Information

This is one of the first viruses. It was first sighted at Lehigh University in the US, and has never been found in the field outside the US. There is another version with a counter of ten which also has not been found outside the US.

4.7.6 Technical Details

The virus uses interrupt 44h to store the original 21h vector. If COMMAND.COM is read-only this will protect it against the virus as it doesn't use DOS to set the file to read/write before trying to infect it. Therefore, a good defence against this particular virus is to make COMMAND.COM read-only using the DOS ATTRIB command (an inoculation program will also do this for you).

Also, this virus doesn't preserve the date/time of COMMAND.COM, nor does it disable DOS's critical error handler, so that if it tries to infect a write-protected diskette, you get the "Write-protect error" message.

The BIOS string displayed after a disk has been trashed is taken from the address FE00:1840. The significance of this is not clear. The virus appends a self-recognition code of one word, 65A9h, to the end of an infected COMMAND.COM, so that it can recognise itself. However, I would recommend that you set the file attribute to read-only, rather than use this self- recognition code.

4.8 405 Virus

Other names: none
Infects: any COM file on any writable DOS device
Classification: direct action file virus

4.8.1 Recognition and Detection

Files smaller than 405 bytes grow to that size; the date and time are unchanged. Programs larger than 405 bytes are unchanged in size, but no longer function.

4.8.2 How the Virus Copies Itself

When you run an infected COM file, the virus will infect another file. It searches through the disk for an uninfected file in order to do so. If a file is read-only it first makes it read/write.

4.8.3 What the Virus Does

Infected programs no longer function.

4.8.4 How To Get Rid of It

Run FindVirus to identify all infected files and delete them. Replace deleted files with clean copies and finish with a final run of Find-Virus.

4.8.5 Other Information

I have only had one report of this virus and because of the immediate damage it does to files it is likely to be very rare. This virus has a lot of major similarities to one that has been published in a book, although it is not just a typed-in version.

4.8.6 Technical Details

405 is a direct action file virus; it does not go TSR. It is the only known overwriting virus that has been found in the field. If the virus tries to infect a write-protected disk or diskette, the DOS message indicating a write-protect error will be seen.

4.9 Vienna Virus

Other names: 648, One-in-Eight, Austrian, DOS62
Infects: any COM file on any writable DOS device
Classification: direct action file virus

4.9.1 Recognition and Detection

COM files grow by 648 bytes. One infection in eight deliberately trashes the file that it infects (it is also known as the One-in-Eight virus). This is done by putting code for a reboot at the beginning of the file (in another variant the code hangs the machine).

4.9.2 How the Virus Copies Itself

Every time an infected file is executed (even if the file is in another subdirectory), the virus searches the current directory for uninfected files, and infects the next available one. It doesn't infect EXE files.

In the original version, the virus searches down the PATH to find an uninfected file; in the variant, it does not.

4.9.3 What the Virus Does

One infection in eight makes the file unusable. Eventually, COM-MAND.COM is infected and then whenever the computer is started up it just keeps rebooting (or, if the virus is the typed-in variant, it hangs).

4.9.4 How To Get Rid of It

If the computer will not boot from its hard disk, boot it from a floppy disk. You can treat it by using FindVirus to search for all instances of the virus. Every infected file that you find you can delete and copy a good file in its place. Alternatively, run a "Remover" that restores the original uninfected file.

Once you have removed all the copies of the virus you can use Inoculate or any other inoculator to mark all files with the mark that it uses to distinguish infected from uninfected files. The virus uses the seconds field of the directory, putting an impossible value (62 seconds) in it.

When you have used Inoculate you can run FindVirus again to check that there are no genuinely infected files around.

4.9.5 Other Information

The source code for this virus has been published in a book with slight modifications. It is commonest in Austria where it has been given several other names by various discoverers.

4.9.6 Technical Details

The virus uses DOS calls to discover the date, time and attribute of the file and, after infection, it sets them back to what they were before to escape detection. COMMAND.COM can be infected; if it is, the virus will certainly be detected; in the main version, the computer will continuously reboot and in the variant it will hang every time it is started up. If the virus tries to infect a write-protected disk or diskette, the DOS message indicating a write-protect error will be seen.

4.10 Datacrime Virus

Other names: 1168
Infects: any COM file on any writable DOS device
Classification: direct action file virus

4.10.1 Recognition and Detection

This affects COM files and grows them by 1168 bytes. There is no other obvious symptom until the trigger date is reached. There is also a version that has an infective length of 1280 bytes.

4.10.2 How the Virus Copies Itself

It scans through the directory tree looking for an uninfected file. It also searches through the different DOS devices in the order C, D, A, B to find an uninfected file. It recognises infected files by setting the last byte of the time field in the directory entry – this is the seconds field, that doesn't display when you do a DIR. When it finds an uninfected file it infects it. Making files read-only is no defence, unless this is done via network permissions. The DOS read-only attribute is set to read/write before the infection and then set back the way it was afterwards. Likewise the date and time (apart from the infected signature, described above). Because of the way that this virus' self-recognition works, a small percentage of files will not get infected.

4.10.3 What the Virus Does

On October 13th (which happened to be a Friday in 1989) and every date thereafter until December 31st when the virus runs it puts up the message "DATACRIME VIRUS RELEASED 1 MARCH 1989" and then does a low level format of the hard disk (if there is one) of cylinder zero, all heads up to head eight (nearly every disk has eight heads or less). On a standard 20 Mb hard disk, this will wipe out the partition, the boot, all of the first copy of the FAT, and much of the second copy. The disk will become unbootable, non-DOS. If you have a full backup you'll have to run FDISK then FORMAT to get it working again. The backups will then have to be checked carefully for the virus.

If you do not have a full backup then much of the data can be salvaged by using the fact that the virus does not necessarily completely wipe out the second copy of the FAT, and might leave the directory unchanged. On disks with other geometries this could differ according to where things are on the disk.

Avoiding Friday the 13th will not help – the low level format is triggered on every day thereafter until the end of the year. The same thing will be triggered every year on October 13th. Searching files looking for the DATACRIME text string won't help, as it is stored in an encrypted form, in order to fool utilities that search for text strings.

4.10.4 How To Get Rid of It

Boot from a clean DOS disk; this is a DOS diskette that has come from the manufacturer, and has never been write-enabled. This ensures that there is nothing unwanted installed in memory (although it does not go TSR, it doesn't treat the critical error handler correctly, and rebooting will fix this). You can then remove Datacrime by using FindVirus to search for all instances of the virus. Every infected file that you find, you can delete and copy a good file in its place.

Once you have removed all the instances of the virus you can use Inoculate or any other inoculator to mark all files with the mark that it uses to distinguish infected from uninfected files.

When you have used Inoculate you can run FindVirus again to check that there are no genuinely infected files around.

4.10.5 Other Information

COMMAND.COM will not become infected, nor will any other file with a "D" as the seventh character. The virus code claims that it was released on March 1st 1989. It is a direct action file virus – there is no TSR code. This is the first really vicious PC virus I've seen, and I can only hope that it doesn't become common. I've been sent a specimen from Holland and so far it hasn't appeared in the UK. If it does, please tell me, as this virus is very dangerous indeed. There is also a version of this virus with the infective length of 1280 bytes.

4.10.6 Technical Details

If the virus tries to infect a write-protected disk or diskette the DOS message indicating a write-protect error will not be seen as the virus intercepts interrupt 24h in order to suppress this. But when it replaces the critical error handler it does so incorrectly and the next critical error that DOS finds could crash the machine.

4.11 Cascade (1701) Virus

Other names: Second Austrian, 1704, Blackjack, Autumn, Waterfall
Infects: any COM file on any writable DOS device
Classification: indirect action file virus

4.11.1 Recognition and Detection

COM files grow by 1701 bytes (in another version, by 1704 bytes). When triggered the letters on the screen gradually crumble into a heap at the bottom of the screen. The trigger is any system date between October and December 1988 inclusive. If the virus tries to infect a write-protected diskette, DOS gives the "Abort, Retry, Ignore" message.

4.11.2 How the Virus Copies Itself

Cascade is very infectious. If you run an infected COM program the virus installs itself into memory. Once it is installed in memory it will infect any program that is run as a COM file, including COM-MAND.COM. It will spread with COM files as they are passed around; these could be parts of DOS such as MODE or FORMAT; most people would see nothing wrong in copying these programs from one computer to another, as almost every computer already has a legal copy of DOS.

The virus does not go memory-resident via the DOS interrupts, so some programs which try to detect viruses going memory-resident may not detect it.

4.11.3 What the Virus Does

At apparently random times the virus triggers the "crumble". The crumble is quite entertaining to watch, although if you weren't expecting it, it would be very alarming. Characters detach themselves from the screen, and fall to the bottom of the display. If they hit a character on the way down, then that character falls instead. Characters speed up as they fall. As each character starts to fall the speaker is clicked, so the whole effect is rather like a hailstorm of characters. Eventually, all the characters end up at the bottom of the screen in a heap, in the correct columns, but the wrong rows.

After the crumble is finished you can carry on working, although this could be difficult as your screen display is unreadable. Most people would reboot half way through the crumble, and lose whatever work they hadn't saved (or possibly worse, as some databases do not take kindly to being interrupted).

The virus takes up 2 k of memory when it goes memory- resident.

4.11.4 How To Get Rid of It

Boot from a clean DOS disk; this is a DOS diskette that has come from the manufacturer and has never been write-enabled. This ensures that Cascade is not installed in memory. You can then remove Cascade by using FindVirus to search for all instances of the virus. Every infected file that you find you can delete, and copy a good file in its place.

Run FindVirus again when you are finished, to make sure that all instances have been found. Alternatively, use a Remover that restores the original uninfected file.

Finally, you should install ChkVirus on all machines that are potentially infectable to provide an early warning of a recurrence of this or another virus.

4.11.5 Other Information

This virus's main claim to fame is the infection of IBM's Network Education Centre at Lehulpe with 1704 virus. Some people consider that this is the most infectious virus around as it can infect COM-MAND.COM, unlike Jerusalem (1813).

In Yugoslavia, a minor variant of 1704 has been found, where the third byte has been changed from EC to CD hexadecimal. FindVirus will still identify it as Cascade.

4.11.6 Technical Details

Cascade hooks interrupt 21h, the DOS function interrupt and 1Ch, the timer tick. It also hooks interrupt 28h, the keyboard wait interrupt. It also checks the BIOS copyright message to see if it is running on an IBM copyright BIOS – if it is, the code seems to quit without doing anything. But there is a bug in the code, and the virus has exactly the same effect on IBMs as on non-IBMs.

If the date is before October 1988, the virus does nothing, apart from spread itself. After October 1988 it begins to trigger at random intervals. The purpose of hooking interrupt 1Ch is that the timer ticks 18.2 times per second. Every timer tick, a random number generator is run. When the right number is generated, Cascade triggers a "crumble" (see above).

The crumble is enabled by any system date between October 1988 and December 1988, or else by the virus going memory-resident when the year is 1980, and the date subsequently being set for 1989 or thereafter. One example of where this can happen is on XTs when COMMAND.COM is infected. Then the infected COMMAND.COM makes the virus go TSR, before the date has been set (so it is 1980). After that, the user, or some utility, sets the date to 1989 and the crumble is then enabled.

The crumble is done in a very sophisticated way. The program uses direct screen writes to animate the characters, and even incorporates a no-snow routine for use on CGA monitors. The crumble works at the same speed, irrespective of the speed of the computer, as it uses a timing loop to measure the CPU speed before it starts.

Infection is also sophisticated. Interrupt 21h is hooked and function 4bh is replaced; all other functions are passed through to the original 21h. A new subfunction is defined – 0FFh. This subfunction is used to return the message that the virus is already installed and so need not be re-installed. This stops a repeated re-installation of the virus from clogging up all of memory, which would soon be noticed by the user.

Subfunction 0 of function 4bh is replaced. The job of this function is to load and execute a program. The virus changes this, so that before a program is loaded, it is infected if it is a COM file and has not previously been infected. The attribute of the file and the date and time are preserved. The virus is encrypted to prevent casual disassembly, and to fool any automatic programs that search for virus characteristics.

When the virus installs itself it doesn't use the DOS services to run the host program and install itself in memory. Instead, it manipulates the Memory Control Blocks and Program Segment Prefixes, and this makes the virus appear to have been installed by a different program. It also means that a program that intercepts the interrupts to detect programs going memory-resident will not trap Cascade.

The DOS critical error is not trapped, and so if the virus tries to infect on write-protected media, the DOS critical error message ("Write-protect error") is displayed.

4.12 Jerusalem (1813) Virus

Other names: Jerusalem, Hebrew University, Israeli, Friday 13th
Infects: any COM or EXE file on any writable DOS device
Classification: indirect action file virus

4.12.1 Recognition and Detection

COM files grow by 1813 bytes (EXE files usually by 1808 bytes, but always by an amount between 1792 and 1808 bytes) without changing their date and time or read/write/hidden attributes. COM files just grow once; EXE files grow each time they are executed. Eventually, an EXE file could get too large to load into memory.

Some EXE files are infected without growing, this is usually because the genuine EXE is followed by overlays in the same file.

Some EXE files are not infected correctly by the virus and fail to run as soon as they are infected. COMMAND.COM does not become infected, probably to help the virus avoid detection. You might also spot the black rectangle or the slowdown (see below).

Here is a screen shot, illustrating the way that files grow by 1813 bytes.

```
C:\S1>dir

    .    <DIR>                        1-01-80      12:05a
    ..   <DIR>                        1-01-80      12:05a
    HELLO COM              57         11-20-88      4:21a

C:\S1>hello
Hello - Copyright S&S Enterprises, 1988

C:\S1>dir

    .    <DIR>                        1-01-80      12:05a
    ..   <DIR>                        1-01-80      12:05a
    HELLO  COM           1870         11-20-88      4:21a
```

4.12.2 How the Virus Copies Itself

When an infected COM or EXE file is executed, the virus goes memory-resident. Each time an EXE program or uninfected COM program is executed thereafter, the virus infects that program.

4.12.3 What the Virus Does

On every Friday 13th, any program that you try to run is deleted. On all dates, 30 minutes after the virus being installed, a standard PC system slows down to a fifth of normal speed; on faster machines the slowdown will not be so noticeable. At the same time, a small black rectangle (if in text mode) opens up, as the portion of screen from row 5, column 5 to row 16, column 16, is scrolled up by two lines. When the virus goes memory-resident, it takes up nearly 2 k of memory.

4.12.4 How To Get Rid of It

Boot from a clean DOS disk; this is a DOS diskette that has come from the manufacturer, and has never been write-enabled. This ensures that Jerusalem is not installed in memory. You can then remove Jerusalem by using FindVirus to search for all instances of the virus. Every infected file that you find you can delete, and copy a good file in its place. Run FindVirus again when you are finished to make sure that all instances have been found. Alternatively, use a Remover that restores the original uninfected file.

Finally, you should install ChkVirus or any other cryptographic checksummer on all machines that are potentially infectable to provide an early warning of a recurrence of this or another virus.

4.12.5 Other Information

This virus got a lot of attention in 1988 in Jerusalem, and again in the UK on January, Friday 13th, 1989. It is probably the most common virus in the City of London, and perhaps even the most common in the world. There are many variants of this virus, and it would seem that other virus authors have used the same or similar code. The best known instance of a Jerusalem infection in the UK was British Rail; also a few computer companies have had an outbreak.

4.12.6 Technical Details

Jerusalem traps interrupt 21h and makes a modification to function 4bh, load and execute a program. Although COM files grow only once, EXE files grow indefinitely, because of what is presumably a bug in the code. After an EXE file has grown sufficiently it will not load and the user will report a problem. Replacing the file makes the problem go away, but as there are almost certainly other infected files around, the problem will come back.

It also hooks interrupt 8 and, after half an hour has passed, it scrolls a window in the bottom left hand corner of the screen. A black rectangle, two rows deep by 11 characters across opens up, and everything above it is scrolled up by two rows. Most people would ignore this, and put it down to some quirk of the computer. Thereafter, the computer does a loop of nothing every time the time-of-day interrupt is invoked, which slows it down considerably. This is irrespective of the date or day of the week, but might have given rise to the stories about the Israeli virus slowing down the computer every Friday and every 13th.

The virus defines a couple of new functions for interrupt 21h. With 0e0h in AH, it returns the version number of the virus (currently version 3). 0ddh is a subroutine that is called by the virus, and 0deh appears to be unused code. Unfortunately, these are functions that are used by Novell.

The virus distinguishes between COM and EXE files on the basis of the file name; if it ends in M, it is treated as a COM file, otherwise it is assumed to be an EXE. This will result in a tiny number of mis-infections, as it is entirely possible to have a misnamed file, since

DOS distinguishes on the basis of the "MZ" signature at the beginning of EXE files.

If the virus goes memory-resident on Friday 13th, then a flag is set; if this flag is set, then any attempt to load and execute a program is intercepted and the file is deleted by the virus, resulting in a "Bad command or filename" message.

The virus traps the DOS critical error handler, so that if it tries to infect a file on write-protected media, there is no give-away "Write-protect error".

4.13 Fu Manchu Virus

Other names: 2086
Infects: any COM or EXE file on any writable DOS device
Classification: indirect action file virus

4.13.1 Recognition and Detection

COM files grow by 2086 bytes; EXE files grow by an amount similar to that. When you do a Ctrl-Alt-Del reboot it clears the screen, slowly types out a message in the middle of the screen, and then does a real reboot. The message is "The world will hear from me again!". If you type Fu Manchu while the virus is resident, it types back "fu manchu virus 3/10/88 - latest in the new fun line!" If you type "Thatcher", "Reagan", "Waldheim" or "Botha", it adds "is a *xyz*", where "*xyz*" is one of four rude words. This is inserted into the keyboard buffer, so would be put into any document or spreadsheet as if the user had typed it.

4.13.2 How the Virus Copies Itself

When an infected COM or EXE file is executed, the virus goes memory-resident. Each time an EXE program or uninfected COM program is executed thereafter, the virus infects that program.

4.13.3 What the Virus Does

Messages are inserted into the keyboard buffer on and after the first of August 1989, as explained above. In addition, the two commonest

English four-letter swear words are censored; if you type them, it backspaces over them. The virus will reboot the computer at random times (see below for more details). When the virus goes memory-resident it takes up just over 2 k of memory.

4.13.4 How To Get Rid of It

Boot from a clean DOS disk; this is a DOS diskette that has come from the manufacturer, and has never been write-enabled. This ensures that the virus is not installed in memory. You can then remove it by using FindVirus to search for all instances of the virus. Every infected file that you find you can delete and copy a good file in its place. Run FindVirus again when you are finished to make sure that all instances have been found.

Finally, you should install ChkVirus or any other cryptographic checksummer on all machines that are potentially infectable, to provide an early warning of a recurrence of this or another virus.

4.13.5 Other Information

There is no dramatic payload in this virus, just the sign-off message and the changes to documents via the keyboard buffer. The sign off message seems to be saying that there may be more from this author. So far there has only been one site reporting it. This report was in the UK and it may be that this is a British virus. Most of the reports of this virus turn out to be either a virus simulator program, or else a false alarm from a scanner that is looking for a rather short signature (which leads to false positives).

4.13.6 Technical Details

This virus works in a very similar way to the Jerusalem virus. When you run an infected COM or EXE file, the virus goes memory-resident. It attaches itself to interrupt 21h, the DOS interrupt, as well as interrupts 8 (timer tick), 9 (keyboard), 16h (keyboard) and 24 (critical error). Interrupt 8 is used to time its "sign-off message" (see below). Interrupt 9 is used to intercept the Ctrl-Alt-Del rebooting keystroke; when it detects this it clears the screen, slowly types out a message in the middle of the screen, and then does a real reboot. The message is "The world will hear from me again!"

When the virus goes memory-resident it sets a timer to a random value between one and fifteen hours. When that timer reaches zero the virus displays its usual sign-off message and reboots the computer.

Interrupt 16h is used to add keystrokes via the keyboard buffer; if the system date is on or after August 1988 whenever you type "Thatcher", "Reagan", "Botha" or "Waldheim", it adds "is a *xyz*", where "*xyz*" is a rude word, different for each. Thus, if a memo is being typed that mentions "Thatcher", Fu Manchu virus will add "is a *xyz*" to the text without the typist doing anything, and unless they are watching the screen it might not get noticed until later. Interrupt 24h is intercepted to prevent the give-away "Abort, Retry, Ignore" message on a write- protected diskette.

Interrupt 21h is used for two purposes; a new function E1h is defined which is used by the virus to find out if it is already in memory. It puts E1h in the AH register and calls interrupt 21h; if E1h is still there on return the virus is not installed, but if the AH register contains 4, then Fu Manchu is already in memory, so it will not re-infect memory. Notice this 4 – in Jerusalem, the same mechanism returns 3. It may be that the author of Fu Manchu considers it to be version 4 of the series that Jerusalem is version 3 of. There are many other similarities between Jerusalem and Fu Manchu; at the very least, the author of Fu Manchu has studied Jerusalem, and possibly was even the author of it, although this does not look likely.

The other purpose that interrupt 21h is used for is infection; the 4bh function (load and execute a program) is what triggers an infection, so that its memory is infected, every program that you run thereafter becomes infected. Unlike Jerusalem, EXE files are infected only once. It avoids infecting COMMAND.COM, probably because there is a widely held belief that COMMAND.COM is a primary target for viruses. COM files grow by 2086 bytes, but EXE files grow by an amount which is close to that, but varies slightly.

Interrupt 24h is trapped so that if an attempt is made to infect a file on write-protected media, there will be no give- away "Write-protect error".

The virus self-recognition code is a bit more complex. In the case of COM files, it looks for six bytes "rEMHOr" at the end of the file. In the case of an EXE file, it looks for the hex bytes 19 and 88 in the header, at offsets 12h and 13h (where the EXE checksum ought to be). Unlike the Jerusalem self- recognition code, the Fu Manchu one works correctly for COM and EXE files, so you don't get the phenomenon of EXE files growing repeatedly. These facts are used in an inoculation program.

4.14 Traceback Virus

Other names: 3066
Infects: any COM or EXE file on any writable DOS device
Classification: indirect and direct action file virus

4.14.1 Recognition and Detection

The only noticeable effect (apart from COM and EXE files growing by 3066 bytes when infected) is a falling letters display, but this is not quite like the Cascade display where letters fall one by one in a hailstorm with sound effects. The Traceback display is silent, and the characters on the screen fall in a slightly different manner. They can also be made to rise up again, by pressing keys until they are all up, or else you can wait for the letters to return.

4.14.2 How the Virus Copies Itself

This has two infection mechanisms – it is an indirect action file virus before December 1988, going memory-resident when an infected program is run, and then infecting any uninfected program run thereafter. After December 1988 it uses that mechanism and also a direct mechanism. With this, every time you run a program it infects a COM file in a subdirectory provided that there is one to infect, and there isn't an infected file higher up in the subdirectory.

4.14.3 What the Virus Does

There is no major damage caused by the virus. When it goes memory-resident it takes up 7 k of memory.

4.14.4 How To Get Rid of It

Boot from a clean DOS disk; this is a DOS diskette that has come from the manufacturer and has never been write-enabled. This ensures that the virus is not installed in memory. You can then remove it by using FindVirus to search for all instances of the virus. Every infected file that you find you can delete, and copy a good file in its place. Run FindVirus again when you are finished to make sure that all instances have been found.

Finally, you should install ChkVirus or any other cryptographic checksummer on all machines that are potentially infectable to provide an early warning of a recurrence of this or another virus.

4.14.5 Other Information

This virus has been found in the UK at a few sites and in Malta.

4.14.6 Technical Details

The virus traps interrupt 24h to suppress the "Abort, Retry, Ignore" message in case a write-protected diskette is used. Next, it sets a counter for one hour. When this time expires the falling letters routine is called.

After setting the counter, it looks for an uninfected file to infect, searching from the root directory down the tree. As usual, it preserves the date, time and attribute of files, and COM files grows by 3066 bytes (EXE by a similar amount).

4.15 Icelandic Virus

Other names: Saratoga, Disk Eater
Infects: any EXE file on any writable DOS device
Classification: indirect action file virus

4.15.1 Recognition and Detection

This is a memory-resident EXE infector – COM files are not infected. It adds around 650 bytes to a file. Infected files are dated with the current system date and time – this is the main way to recognise it. There is also another version with slight differences and a third with greater differences. If the virus tries to infect a write-protected disk you get the DOS critical error message "Write-protect error".

4.15.2 How the Virus Copies Itself

Running an infected EXE program makes the virus go memory-resident, and thereafter, every EXE program that you run is liable to be infected. There is a counter, which means that only every other program (every tenth in the second version) is infected. Unlike almost every other virus, this one doesn't bother about preserving the date/time of infected files, so they will have the date/time that the computer is currently set to.

The virus does not go memory-resident via the DOS interrupts, so some programs which try to detect viruses going memory- resident may not detect it.

There is a third variant of Icelandic which doesn't use interrupt 21h to read and write files, which will mean that many memory-resident virus detectors will not see that activity either, if they assume that all file reads and writes go via interrupt 21h.

4.15.3 What the Virus Does

Every time a file is infected, the virus tries to mark a bad cluster on the hard disk. Because of the way it does this, this attempt will fail until a certain number of files are infected, and only then succeed (see below for details of why this is). After that, the number of bad clusters will increase with the number of infected files. 2 k of memory is used by the virus when it goes memory-resident.

4.15.4 How To Get Rid of It

To get rid of it from an infected system, first boot from a known clean DOS diskette, and run FindVirus (from a write- protected floppy) to spot all infected files. Delete the infected files, and run FindVirus again to make sure.

If there are bad clusters marked in the FAT, these might be the normal bad clusters marked by FORMAT because there is some defect on the disk. If you want to make sure that Icelandic hasn't added to these, then proceed as follows.

Take two full backups of the disk and run FORMAT to give it a high level format (low level is not necessary). This will correct the Icelandic virus mismarking of bad clusters, and leave you with those clusters which are genuinely bad (it is quite normal to have a few, or even a couple of hundred kilobytes in bad sectors). Reload your backup, restore any programs you deleted from clean copies, and run FindVirus again to make sure. Then start checking your floppy diskettes. Icelandic will not have marked any bad clusters, but you could easily have an infected EXE file on a diskette.

Another way to release the pseudo-bad clusters for re-use is to use a disk sector editor to look at the last sector of the FAT, and replace the FFF7h flag with 0000 to signify that the cluster is available.

4.15.5 Other Information

So far, this virus has only been found in Iceland and Saratoga. Inoculate inoculates files against the versions of the Icelandic virus; you cannot inoculate against all as they use different flags in the same position.

The inoculation marks the file so that the virus thinks that the file is already infected and leaves it alone. It does this by putting the four-byte signature at the end of the file (you'll see the file grow by four bytes). This could be useful as part of a major clean-up operation, to stop a re-infection creeping round as fast as you clean up. You cannot inoculate against Jerusalem at the same time as Icelandic as they both use an end-of-file signature. The signatures used are:

"PooT"
44h, 18h, 5fh, 19h

4.15.6 Technical Details

If the currently logged drive is more than 10 Mb in size (most hard disks and cartridge systems) then whenever a file is infected the virus marks one cluster as bad (this usually means 2 k of space becomes unavailable). DOS doesn't usually check the disk for areas going bad (nor does Chkdsk), so if you see an increasing number of bad clusters (unless you are running a utility that tests the disk and marks clusters that are unreadable) then this could be a sign of Icelandic virus.

The clusters are marked bad starting at the far end of the disk (the highest cluster number) and working down as far as cluster number 2048 (it avoids the first nine sectors of the DOS partition). It only marks the first copy of the FAT with these bad clusters, which it does by calling INT 26h to write 0FFF7h into the entry. You may never see any bad sectors, because the virus starts marking bad clusters from the end of the last FAT sector, and these entries might not correspond to an actual cluster on the disk, as there is no requirement that a FAT be a whole number of sectors. Since a bad cluster is marked when an EXE file is infected, and since there is a limited number of EXE files on the disk, this might mean that there are never any bad clusters marked.

Icelandic goes TSR by manipulating the Memory Control Blocks directly, so many memory-resident programs that watch for something going TSR will not spot this. Also, there is a variant of Icelandic which doesn't use interrupt 21h for file reading and writing. Instead, it searches for the interrupt 21h code and makes a far call to the routines there. The purpose of this is to defeat anti-virus software that detects illegal writes to EXE or COM files. This version of Icelandic doesn't mark bad clusters on the hard disk but infects on every tenth program load.

4.16 The SURIV Viruses

Other names: Jerusalem precursors
Infects: COM and EXE files on any writable DOS device
Classification: indirect action file virus

4.16.1 Recognition and Detection

I've grouped these three viruses together, as they have many similarities. At the beginning of the virus, they put the marker "sURIV 1.01", "sURIV 2.01" or "sURIV 3.00", depending on which virus it is. SURIV1 infects COM files, SURIV2 infects EXE files, and SURIV3 infects COM and EXE files.

When a file is infected, its date and time are unchanged. If a disk is write-protected, the error message that DOS would give ("Write-protect error") is suppressed by the virus.

4.16.2 How the Virus Copies Itself

All three viruses go memory-resident when you run an infected program. Then, when you try to run another program, the virus infects that, just like the Jerusalem virus. They do not infect COM-MAND.COM, as the viruses check the filename and avoid COM-MAND.COM.

4.16.3 What the Virus Does

On any April 1st of any year on and after 1988, SURIV1 displays "APRIL 1ST HA HA HA YOU HAVE A VIRUS" and hangs the machine. After April 1st, 1988, it displays "YOU HAVE A VIRUS!!!".

SURIV2 displays the same message on any April 1st and hangs the machine. On all other dates, if the year is 1980 (which probably means that the system date has not been set), approximately one hour after the virus goes memory-resident, it hangs the computer. If it isn't 1980, but is after 1988, and the date is after April 1st and it is a Wednesday, then it will hang the computer an hour after going memory- resident.

SURIV3, on any Friday 13th other than 1987, sets an internal switch and, if that switch is on, every program that you try to run is deleted before you can run it (like Jerusalem virus). On other dates, on years other than 1987, a different action is taken – 30 seconds after the virus goes memory-resident, row 5, column 5 to row 16, column 16 is scrolled up by two lines on the display, and the computer is slowed down thereafter.

4.16.4 How To Get Rid of It

Boot from a clean DOS disk; this is a DOS diskette that has come from the manufacturer, and has never been write-enabled. This ensures that the virus is not installed in memory. You can then remove the virus by using FindVirus to search for all instances of the virus. Every infected file that you find, you can delete, and copy a good file in its place. Run FindVirus again when you are finished, to make sure that all instances have been found.

Finally, you should install ChkVirus or any other cryptographic checksummer on all machines that are potentially infectable to provide an early warning of a recurrence of this or another virus.

4.16.5 Other Information

These viruses have never been found outside Israel. Their main interest is that they look very likely to have been the precursors in the development of the Jerusalem virus. Some of the code in these viruses tends to explain some of the code in Jerusalem, especially code that doesn't appear to have a purpose.

4.16.6 Technical Details

Because these viruses appear to be extinct, there is little point in going into great detail about them. SURIV1 and SURIV2 infect by making a modified copy of the file to a file called TMP$$TMP.COM or TMP$$TMP.EXE, and then deleting the original file and renaming the temporary file to the original name.

4.17 Datacrime II Virus

Other names: none
Infects: any COM or EXE file on any writable DOS device
Classification: direct action file virus

4.17.1 Recognition and Detection

This affects COM files and grows them by 1514 bytes. EXE files grow by about 400 bytes more than that. There is no other obvious symptom until the trigger date is reached. Files are only infected once each.

4.17.2 How the Virus Copies Itself

It scans through the directory tree looking for an uninfected file. It also searches through the different DOS devices in the order C, A, B to find an uninfected file. It recognises infected files by setting the last byte of the time field in the directory entry – this is the seconds field that doesn't display when you do a DIR. When it finds an uninfected file it infects it. Making files read-only is no defence unless this is done via network permissions. The DOS read-only attribute is set to read/write before the infection and then set back the way it was afterwards. Likewise the date and time (apart from the infected signature, described above). Because of the way that this virus self-recognition works, a small percentage of files will not get infected. The setting of the time byte is slightly different to Datacrime.

4.17.3 What the Virus Does

On October 13th (which happened to be a Friday in 1989) and every date thereafter until December 31st (except for Mondays), when the virus runs it puts up the message "* DATACRIME II VIRUS *" and then does a low level format of the hard disk (if there is one) of cylinder zero, all heads up to head eight (nearly every disk has eight heads or less). On a standard 20 Mb hard disk, this will wipe out the partition, the boot, all of the first copy of the FAT, and much of the second copy. The disk will become unbootable, non-DOS. If you have a full backup, you'll have to run FDISK then FORMAT to get it working again. The backups will then have to be checked carefully for the virus.

If you do not have a full backup, then much of the data can be salvaged by using the fact that the virus does not necessarily completely wipe out the second copy of the FAT, and might leave the directory unchanged. On disks with other geometries this could differ according to where things are on the disk. Please note – this virus is not a "Friday 13th" virus, it is an "October 13th" virus. Also, avoiding Friday the 13th will not help – the low level format is triggered on every day thereafter until the end of the year. The same thing will be triggered every year on October 13th. Searching files looking for the DATACRIME text string won't help as it is stored in an encrypted form in order to fool utilities that search for text strings.

4.17.4 How To Get Rid of It

Boot from a clean DOS disk; this is a DOS diskette that has come from the manufacturer, and has never been write-enabled. This ensures that there is nothing unwanted installed in memory (although it does not go TSR, it doesn't treat the critical error handler correctly, and rebooting will fix this). You can then remove Datacrime by using FindVirus to search for all instances of the virus. Every infected file that you find you can delete, and copy a good file in its place.

Once you have removed all the instances of the virus, you can use Inoculate or any other inoculator to mark all files with the mark that it uses to distinguish infected from uninfected files.

When you have used Inoculate you can run FindVirus again to check that there are no genuinely infected files around.

4.17.5 Other Information

COMMAND.COM will become infected, but any file with "B" as the second letter of the filename (such as IBMBIO.COM and IBMDOS.COM) will be left alone. It is a direct action file virus – there is no TSR code.

4.17.6 Technical Details

If the virus tries to infect a write-protected disk or diskette, the DOS message indicating a write-protect error will not be seen, as the virus intercepts interrupt 24h in order to suppress this. But when it replaces the critical error handler, it does so incorrectly and the next critical error that DOS finds could crash the machine.

The virus is encrypted, apart from the first few dozen bytes, to avoid detection by programs looking for the kind of operations that a virus does.

4.18 Ogre

Other names: Computer Ogre, Disk Killer
Infects: the boot sector of any writable diskette or hard disk
Classification: boot sector virus

4.18.1 Recognition and Detection

If the virus triggers (see below) then recognition is easy. Another method of recognising it is the 8 k of memory lost (so a 640 k machine will show 647 168 bytes of memory instead of 655 360 bytes). A third way is if you look at the boot sector using Peeka, it will be full of program code, without the usual messages like "Not a system disk".

You can detect infected diskettes by running Chkdsk (which comes with DOS). If you get 3 k of bad sectors on a 360 k diskette, that's a sign of Ogre (Brain and Ashar give the same), as FORMAT marks an entire track (5 k on a 360 k diskette) as bad if it finds a defect. Likewise on other sizes of diskette; one track is the minimum that should be marked as bad, except of course for zero bad. You can also use FindVirus to detect Ogre. On a hard disk, Ogre doesn't use bad sectors, so can't be detected that way.

4.18.2 How the Virus Copies Itself

When you boot from an infected diskette, the virus goes memory-resident; this is true whether the diskette is a boot disk or not. So the usual thing is for someone to have an infected data diskette, which they leave in drive A when they shut down. Next day when they start up the computer it attempts to boot from that diskette; if it isn't a system diskette, you see the message "Not a system disk. Please insert a system disk and retry" or a similar message. If that diskette was infected the virus is now in memory, and when you continue the boot, it remains there.

While it is in memory, any disk that you access is liable to be infected. If you access the diskette (whether read or write) and the diskette is write-enabled then Ogre will replace the boot sector with its own code, move the boot sector further up the disk, add the rest of the Ogre code, and mark these sectors as bad in the FAT. But there is a bug (or perhaps it is deliberate) in the virus; instead of marking the sectors it has used as bad, it marks a different group. Ogre also infects hard disks.

4.18.3 What the Virus Does

If you leave your computer on for 48 hours, and access the hard disk during the following hour, the virus triggers. It clears the screen and puts up "Disk Killer - Version 1.00 by COMPUTER OGRE 04/01/1989" in black characters on a white background. Then in yellow on green it says "Warning !!", and two lines down "Don't turn off the power or remove the diskette while Disk Killer is Processing!" Then in bright red, and blinking, on black it says "PROCESSING".

By the time you see that and react to it, it will be too late as the disk will be inaccessible. You might decide to switch off in spite of what Ogre has told you, but even if you do, the disk will have been made unreadable by then, and your best course will be to re-initialise the disk and restore the latest backups.

4.18.4 How To Get Rid of It

Boot from a clean DOS disk; this is a DOS diskette that has come from the manufacturer, and has never been write-enabled. This ensures that there is nothing unwanted installed in memory. Use FindVirus to determine which diskettes are infected.

Treatment consists of simply copying all the files off an infected diskette (using "COPY *.*"; do not use Diskcopy or any image copier), and reformatting the diskette (see below for details). Remember that Ogre might have written itself onto one (or more) of the files. This would not make the file infectious, but would mean that if it were a program it would not run, and if it were data, the data would be corrupted.

If a large number of diskettes are potentially infected, then you should consider borrowing a hopper-fed diskette cleaning machine, which can handle up to 700 diskettes per hour, sorting them into clean and contaminated bins.

If you have a major outbreak of Ogre on a large site, then while you clear it up you should use Inoculate or any other inoculator on all diskettes. This works by putting the Ogre signature (just two harmless bytes) on the boot sector of the diskette. If Ogre sees that signature, it thinks that the diskette is already infected, so doesn't attack it. This means that if you use a moving line method to clear out Ogre, you can't have a re-infection following the demarcation line.

In the case of a hard disk, you could use a disk sector editor. Find the original boot sector (it will be in the bad sectors) and copy it back to the place where it should be, at Logical Sector Number zero. I would recommend that you take a full backup before doing this, as if you get it wrong, you could make your disk inaccessible.

An alternative, and much easier method, is as follows. First boot from a clean DOS disk. Then make two backups of the hard disk (the second backup is in case you find that you have a problem restoring the first backup). With most versions of DOS, SYS will replace the boot sector, and you can use FindVirus to check that this has worked.

This leaves the body of the Ogre code in between the partition and the boot sector, but since there is nothing to load it in, it is perfectly harmless. If in spite of that, you wish to get rid of it, then the simplest way is a low level format of the hard disk.

4.18.5 Other Information

It was first sighted in the US, but I have also had a case in Ealing near London. Floppy disks are not infected correctly, and Ogre can write its code into a file on the diskette, not using the bad sectors that it creates.

Ogre is more infectious than Italian virus, as it can infect 80286 and 80386 machines, which Italian cannot.

4.18.6 Technical Details

If the computer is left on for 48 hours, and not accessed during the next hour, then the trigger is deferred for 255 hours, at which point a disk access will have the same effect. In order to do this, it hooks interrupt 8, the timer tick.

To copy itself onto other diskettes, Ogre goes memory-resident at boot up, occupying 8 k of memory at the top of memory, and changing the byte 413h to reflect 8 k less than the computer has. It hooks interrupt 13h, and attempts to infect on read accesses to a disk.

When Ogre infects a hard disk, it writes the code into the sectors immediately preceding the boot sector.

4.19 Typo

Other names: none
Infects: the boot sector of any writable diskette or hard disk except 80286 or 80386 machines
Classification: boot sector virus

4.19.1 Recognition and Detection

If you look at the boot sector using a disk sector editor, it will be full of program code without the usual messages like "Not a system disk".

You can detect infected diskettes by running Chkdsk (which comes with DOS). If you get 1 k of bad sectors, that's a good sign of Typo (or Italian virus), as FORMAT marks an entire track (5 k on a 360 k diskette) as bad if it finds a defect. You can also use FindVirus to detect Typo.

4.19.2 How the Virus Copies Itself

When you boot from an infected diskette, the virus goes memory-resident; this is true whether the diskette is a boot disk or not. So the usual thing is for someone to have an infected data diskette, which they leave in drive A when they shut down. Next day when they start up the computer, it attempts to boot from that diskette; if it isn't a system diskette, you see the message "Not a system disk. Please insert a system disk and retry" or a similar message. If that diskette was infected, the virus is now in memory, and when you continue the boot, it remains there.

While it is in memory, any disk that you access is liable to be infected. If you access the diskette (whether read or write) and the diskette is write-enabled then Typo will replace the boot sector with its own code, move the boot sector further up the disk, add the rest of the Typo code, and mark these sectors as bad in the FAT. Typo also infects hard disks.

4.19.3 What the Virus Does

It installs a routine that replaces the normal printer handler routine. It sets a counter to 50, and decrements it each time a character is printed (unless it is an escape, in which case it increases it by five). When the counter reaches zero, it does a typo. A typo consists of a character substitution from the following:

18CKGJMNOU36VW27ckgjmnou49vw

So 1 is substituted for 8 and vice versa, C for K and so on. It also does a substitution on some of the high order bytes:

80h, 92h, 9ah, 88h, 97h, 8bh, 85h, 8fh

This is more meaningful when the Hebrew character set is used.

4.19.4 How To Get Rid of It

Boot from a clean DOS disk; this is a DOS diskette that has come from the manufacturer, and has never been write-enabled. This ensures that there is nothing unwanted installed in memory. Use FindVirus to determine which diskettes are infected.

Treatment consists of simply copying all the files off an infected diskette (using "COPY *.*"; do not use Diskcopy or any image copier), and reformatting the diskette (see below for details). Alternatively, you can use UnVirus or any virus removal program to remove the infection from a diskette; UnVirus is a lot faster.

If a large number of diskettes are potentially infected, then you should consider borrowing a hopper-fed diskette cleaning machine, which can handle up to 700 diskettes per hour, sorting them into clean and contaminated bins.

If you have an outbreak of Typo, then while you clear it up you should use Inoculate or any other inoculator on all diskettes. This works by putting the Typo signature (just two harmless bytes) on the boot sector of the diskette. If Typo sees that signature, it thinks that the diskette is already infected, so doesn't attack it. You cannot inoculate against Italian and Typo on the same diskette, as they use different signatures in the same place.

In the case of a hard disk, you could use a disk sector editor. Find the original boot sector (it will be in the bad sectors) and copy it back to the place where it should be, at Logical Sector Number zero. I would recommend that you take a full backup before doing this, as if you get it wrong, you could make your disk inaccessible. You could then patch the FAT to mark the bad sectors as usable. I have not provided a utility to do this, as there are so many different layouts of hard disk to cope with.

An alternative, and much easier method, is as follows. First boot from a clean DOS disk. Then make two backups of the hard disk (the second backup is in case you find that you have a problem restoring the first backup). With most versions of DOS, SYS will replace the boot sector, and you can use FindVirus to check that this has worked, but this still leaves you with the 2 k in bad sectors; this is now quite harmless, and can be ignored. Alternatively, you can format the hard disk using "FORMAT /S/V" and restore the backup; this has the advantage of reclaiming the fake bad sectors.

4.19.5 Other Information

It was first sighted in Israel. It is based on Italian virus, and the infective code is very similar indeed.

This is a very insidious virus. Printers often give problems, and so do printer cables. A lot of time will be wasted trying to fix a hardware fault before the virus is discovered. Likewise, a lot of genuine printer problems will be blamed on this virus.

4.19.6 Technical Details

See Italian virus. Like Italian, Typo does not work on 80286 and 80386 machines; if you boot from an infected floppy, the machine hangs.

4.20 Big Italian

Other names: none
Infects: the boot sector of any writable diskette or hard disk
Classification: boot sector virus

4.20.1 Recognition and Detection

Once every half hour, if you are accessing the disk, the bouncing diamond is triggered. The diamond bounces off the edges of the screen and passes through any text, with replacement after it. Sometimes this doesn't work properly, and screen displays are slightly messed up. If you look at the boot sector using a sector editor, it will be full of program code without the usual messages like "Not a system disk".

You can detect infected diskettes by running Chkdsk (which comes with DOS). If you get 1 k of bad sectors, that's an almost sure sign of Italian, as FORMAT marks an entire track (5 k on a 360 k diskette) as bad if it finds a defect. You can also use FindVirus to detect Big Italian.

The moving diamond is much larger than that of the ordinary Italian virus.

4.20.2 How the Virus Copies Itself

When you boot from an infected diskette, the virus goes memory-resident; this is true whether the diskette is a boot disk or not. So the usual thing is for someone to have an infected data diskette, which they leave in drive A when they shut down. Next day when they start up the computer, it attempts to boot from that diskette; if it isn't a system diskette you see the message "Not a system disk. Please insert a system disk and retry" or a similar message. If that diskette was infected, the virus is now in memory, and when you continue the boot, it remains there.

While it is in memory any disk that you access is liable to be infected. If you access the diskette (whether read or write) and the diskette is write-enabled then Italian will replace the boot sector with its own code, move the boot sector further up the disk, add the rest of the Big Italian code, and mark these sectors as bad in the FAT. Big Italian also infects hard disks.

4.20.3 What the Virus Does

The bouncing diamond display is the main outcome of the virus. In addition, infected diskettes lose 1 k of space to the fake bad sectors that Big Italian creates (hard disks lose one cluster, which usually means 2 k). Attempts to infect slows the computer down, although not noticeably.

4.20.4 How To Get Rid of It

Boot from a clean DOS disk; this is a DOS diskette that has come from the manufacturer, and has never been write-enabled. This ensures

that there is nothing unwanted installed in memory. Use FindVirus to determine which diskettes are infected. Treatment consists of simply copying all the files off an infected diskette (using "COPY *.*"; do not use Diskcopy or any image copier), and reformatting the diskette (see below for details). Alternatively, you can use UnVirus or any virus removal program to remove the infection from a diskette; UnVirus is a lot faster.

If a large number of diskettes are potentially infected, then you should consider borrowing a hopper-fed diskette cleaning machine, which can handle up to 700 diskettes per hour, sorting them into clean and contaminated bins.

If you have an outbreak of Big Italian, then while you clear it up you should use Inoculate or any other inoculator on all diskettes. This works by putting the Italian signature (just two harmless bytes) on the boot sector of the diskette. If Big Italian sees that signature, it thinks that the diskette is already infected, so doesn't attack it.

In the case of a hard disk, you could use a disk sector editor. Find the original boot sector (it will be in the bad sectors) and copy it back to the place where it should be, at Logical Sector Number zero. I would recommend that you take a full backup before doing this, as if you get it wrong, you could make your disk inaccessible. You could then patch the FAT to mark the bad sectors as usable. I have not provided a utility to do this, as there are so many different layouts of hard disk to cope with.

An alternative, and much easier method, is as follows. First boot from a clean DOS disk. Then make two backups of the hard disk (the second backup is in case you find that you have a problem restoring the first backup). With most versions of DOS, SYS will replace the boot sector, and you can use FindVirus to check that this has worked, but this still leaves you with the 2 k in bad sectors; this is now quite harmless, and can be ignored. Alternatively, you can format the hard disk using "FORMAT \S\V" and restore the backup; this has the advantage of reclaiming the fake bad sectors.

4.20.5 Other Information

Clearly, someone has taken a disassembly of the Italian virus, made some changes, and re-assembled it.

4.20.6 Technical Details

Italian fails to infect 80286 and 80386 machines, because of a bug in the virus. But this virus, Big Italian, will infect such machines.

4.21 Virus-B

Other names: Friday 13th, 423
Infects: any COM file on any writable DOS device
Classification: direct action file virus

4.21.1 Recognition and Detection

There are two main variants; some researchers classify these as two viruses, as the differences are rather large. In the original version, files grow by 1399 bytes, then on second, third, etc. infection, grow by 976 bytes. Whenever an infected application is run, the following message comes up:

> WARNING!!!! THIS PROGRAM IS INFECTED WITH VIRUS-B!
> IT WILL INFECT EVERY .COM FILE IN THE CURRENT SUBDIRECTORY!

and the computer beeps. In the other version this message has been removed, and COM files grow by 423 bytes once only. The larger version is actually the concatenation of two viruses into one file.

4.21.2 How the Virus Copies Itself

It is a direct action file virus. Every time an infected file is executed (even if the file is in another subdirectory), the virus searches the current directory for uninfected files, and infects all available ones. It doesn't infect EXE files. It avoids COMMAND.COM.

4.21.3 What the Virus Does

On every Friday 13th, each time you run an infected program, the program is deleted after it is loaded into memory and executed. Other uninfected COM files in the subdirectory are still infected.

4.21.4 How To Get Rid of It

If the computer will not boot from its hard disk, boot it from a floppy disk. You can treat it by using FindVirus to search for all instances of the virus. Every infected file that you find, you can delete, and copy a good file in its place.

4.21.5 Other Information

This virus is thought to have been written as a demo virus.

4.21.6 Technical Details

The virus doesn't make read-only files into read/write, and doesn't preserve the date/time of the file. If it tries to infect a write-protected diskette, you will see the DOS critical error message, "Write-protect error writing drive x, Abort, Retry, Ignore".

4.22 Dark Avenger

Other names: none
Infects: any non-tiny COM or EXE file on any writable DOS device
Classification: indirect action file virus

4.22.1 Recognition and Detection

COM files grow by 1800 bytes, EXE files by a similar amount, subject to rounding up to a multiple of 16. Probably the likeliest give-away for this virus is the way it tries very hard to write to write-protected diskettes, although there is no "Abort, Retry, Ignore" message.

4.22.2 How the Virus Copies Itself

It is an indirect action file virus. When you run an infected COM or EXE file, it goes memory-resident. Thereafter, a number of actions can trigger an infection. The virus makes files read/write and resets the attribute after infection. It also preserves the date and time of files. It only infects files if they are larger than about 1800 bytes.

If you copy a file, the source and target are both infected. If you read a file, it is infected, so if a program looks at all the files on a disk, that will infect all the files. If you change the attribute of a file, that will infect it. Loading and executing a file infects it, just like Jerusalem virus. Because of all these infection mechanisms, it is a very infectious virus.

4.22.3 What the Virus Does

It writes a sector that starts "Eddie lives...somewhere in time!" to a random sector on the hard disk, at intervals. This sector might not land on anything, or it might overwrite part of a program or some data. The damage done is therefore quite subtle.

4.22.4 How To Get Rid of It

Boot from a clean DOS disk; this is a DOS diskette that has come from the manufacturer, and has never been write-enabled. This ensures that Dark Avenger is not installed in memory. You can then remove Dark Avenger by using FindVirus to search for all instances of the virus. Every infected file that you find, you can delete, and copy a good file in its place. Run FindVirus again when you are finished, to make sure that all instances have been found.

If you want to replace the boot sector with a clean copy, you can take a full backup, and then use SYS C: to do this.

Finally, you should install ChkVirus or any other cryptographic checksummer on all machines that are potentially infectable, to provide an early warning of a recurrence of this or another virus.

4.22.5 Other Information

There is a message that says "This program was written in the city of Sofia (C) 1988-89 Dark Avenger". There is also a string "Diana P.". Neither of these strings are used. The virus only works on DOS 3 and above.

4.22.6 Technical Details

This virus does an end run around the disk interrupts. So any program that checks to see if anything is using interrupt 13h or 40h will be fooled. To do this, it attempts to replace interrupts 13h (disk and diskette) and 40h (diskette). It also replaces interrupt 24h (critical error) with its own, to suppress the "Abort, Retry, Ignore" message when it tries to infect a write-protected disk. This doesn't work properly, and you can get a number of these messages if diskettes are write-protected.

In spite of carefully doing the end run round 13h and 40h, it does not attempt to avoid using interrupt 26h to write to the disk, so any TSR monitoring program that hooks that interrupt will stand a chance of spotting it.

It also replaces interrupt 27h (terminate and stay resident) with its own version that doesn't let other programs use this method to go TSR, and replaces interrupt 21h. It also traps the DOS calls to get or set interrupt 21h and 27h, and if any program tries to do this, it pretends that it has been done, but doesn't do it.

It uses the boot sector to store data; every time an infected program is run, it increments a counter which is the last byte of the OEM label on the boot (byte 0ah), and zeros the four most significant bits. When this byte is zero (every 16th time), it adds 40h to the word at offset 8 on the boot. If the word at offset 8 is less than the number of sectors on the volume, it writes a sector that starts "Eddie lives...somewhere in time!" to the sector that it has calculated on the disk.

4.23 Vacsina

Other names: none
Infects: any non-tiny COM or EXE file on any writable DOS device
Classification: indirect action file virus

4.23.1 Recognition and Detection

EXE files are converted to COM files, and in the process they grow by a hundred bytes or so (132 is typical). The conversion is only done to files less than 63 k, as COM files cannot be larger than that. The conversion is done to the file format, but not to the file name, so there is no filename change.

COM files are infected, growing by 1207 to 1213 bytes. Only files that are 1206 bytes or larger are infected. When a COM file is infected, the computer beeps. The file's date is not preserved – that's the most likely way that this virus will be spotted. When it infects a file it accesses drive A, even if the infected program doesn't.

4.23.2 How the Virus Copies Itself

It is an indirect action file virus. When you run an infected COM or EXE file, it goes memory-resident. Thereafter, any time you load a COM or EXE file, that file is infected. Read-only files are set to read/write and it then resets the attribute after infection. EXE files are infected in two stages – first the conversion to COM, and then the COM infection. EXE files are not in themselves infectious though – only COM files contain the code that goes memory-resident.

4.23.3 What the Virus Does

There is no payload to this virus, other than the beep when it infects a COM file.

4.23.4 How To Get Rid of It

Boot from a clean DOS disk; this is a DOS diskette that has come from the manufacturer, and has never been write-enabled. This ensures that Vacsina is not installed in memory. You can then remove Vacsina by using FindVirus to search for all instances of the virus. Every infected file that you find, you can delete, and copy a good file in its place. Run FindVirus again when you are finished, to make sure that all instances have been found.

Finally, you should install ChkVirus or any other cryptographic checksummer on all machines that are potentially infectable, to provide an early warning of a recurrence of this or another virus.

4.23.5 Other Information

The virus is named after the string VACSINA that is found in each copy of it. But it isn't clear how this virus could be considered a vaccinator in any sense. There are many other versions of this virus.

4.23.6 Technical Details

The string VACSINA is a file name of a file that it looks for on drive A. If it finds it, it opens the file using an FCB call (interrupt 21h, function 0fh). The file is left open as it does the infection, and when the infection terminates normally, the file is closed using an FCB call interrupt 21h, function 10h. I cannot see the purpose of this call, unless it was something to do with debugging.

The virus author makes extensive use of the DOS function 45h, duplicate a file handle. This is done for error handling, and is not a feature of any other virus so far.

4.24 Mix1

Other names: none
Infects: any non-tiny EXE file on any writable DOS device
Classification: indirect action file virus

4.24.1 Recognition and Detection

This is a virus with a lot of interesting effects, any of which might be noticed. The most obvious is the garbling of serial and parallel port information; the garble is quite noticeable.

In late generation infections (see below for details) the virus displays a bouncing ball, the lower case letter "o", which bounces off the sides of the screen like a ping pong ball. It is not deflected by letters on the screen (unlike Italian virus) but does replace letters that it passes over. The bouncing ball display comes up 60 minutes after the virus goes memory-resident.

Also in late generation infections, after 50 minutes the keyboard handler is replaced with a routine that always turns off Caps Lock, and always switches Num Lock on. Also, if you reboot at that time it triggers the video display.

The virus doesn't disable the "Abort, Retry, Ignore" message, so that if it tries to infect a write-protected diskette, it gives that message.

Only EXE files are infected, and they grow by 1620 or so bytes. Files are not infected unless they are greater than 8192 bytes.

4.24.2 How the Virus Copies Itself

It is an indirect action file virus. When you run an infected EXE file, it goes memory-resident. Thereafter, any time you load an EXE file, that file is infected. Read-only files are set to read/write and it then resets the attribute after infection. The memory-resident part of the virus is in high conventional memory, consuming 2048 bytes.

4.24.3 What the Virus Does

The main effect is the garbling of the parallel and serial ports, which will affect modems and printers. It uses a simple table; here is the translation for letters (numbers are unaffected):

```
abcdefghijklmnopqrstuvwxyz becomes
ebsdapghejklmnufqrctovwxyz
ABCDEFGHIJKLMNOPQRSTUVWXYZ becomes
BECDAPGHYJKLMNUFQRSTOVWXIZ
```

So, for example, "Bad command or file name" becomes "Eed summend ur pela nema".

4.24.4 How To Get Rid of It

Boot from a clean DOS disk; this is a DOS diskette that has come from the manufacturer, and has never been write-enabled. This ensures that Mix1 is not installed in memory. You can then remove Mix1 by using FindVirus to search for all instances of the virus. Every infected file that you find, you can delete, and copy a good file in its place. Run FindVirus again when you are finished, to make sure that all instances have been found.

If the outbreak is on a large site, you can use Inoculate or any other inoculator to prevent a re-infestation as you clean up.

Finally, you should install ChkVirus or any other cryptographic checksummer on all machines that are potentially infectable, to provide an early warning of a recurrence of this or another virus.

4.24.5 Other Information

This virus is modelled after the Icelandic viruses, but the virus author has put everything that he can think of into the payload. It was first detected in Israel in August 1989.

4.24.6 Technical Details

There is a counter in the virus, which counts the number of infections since the virus went memory-resident, and this counter is written out to each infected file. If the counter is greater than 5, then when such a late generation instance of the virus goes TSR, it replaces the timer tick (interrupt 8) and the keyboard handler (interrupt 9), as well as interrupt 14h (serial) and interrupt 17h (parallel). It is the replacement of interrupts 8 and 9 that eventually triggers the bouncing "o" display, the Caps Lock and Num Lock twiddling, and the reboot display. This doesn't work properly, and on a CGA, just triggers typical CGA snow.

To go memory-resident, the virus uses Memory Control Blocks directly, instead of using the DOS interrupts to do so.

4.25 Fumble

Other names: none
Infects: any COM file on any writable DOS device
Classification: direct action file virus

4.25.1 Recognition and Detection

This virus makes you seem to hit the wrong key, but only rarely. COM files grow by 867 bytes.

The virus doesn't disable the "Abort, Retry, Ignore" message, so that if it tries to infect a write-protected diskette, it gives that message. However, it does preserve date/time, and the file's attribute (it temporarily sets it to read/write in order to infect it).

4.25.2 How the Virus Copies Itself

It is a direct action file virus. When you run an infected COM file, it infects every other uninfected COM file in that subdirectory. It detects whether a file is infected or not by looking for the characters "V1" immediately after the original infected program. On odd days (the first, third, fifth, etc. of each month) it does not infect.

4.25.3 What the Virus Does

The virus replaces the keyboard handler, interrupt 16h. If it is in place, it occasionally replaces the key that is typed with the key immediately to the right (actually, it is a bit more complicated than this, see below).

4.25.4 How To Get Rid of It

Boot from a clean DOS disk; this is a DOS diskette that has come from the manufacturer, and has never been write-enabled. This ensures that Fumble is not installed in memory. You can then remove Fumble by using FindVirus to search for all instances of the virus. Every infected file that you find, you can delete, and copy a good file in its place. Run FindVirus again when you are finished, to make sure that all instances have been found.

Finally, you should install ChkVirus or any other cryptographic checksummer on all machines that are potentially infectable, to provide an early warning of a recurrence of this or another virus.

4.25.5 Other Information

This virus has only ever been found on one site.

4.25.6 Technical Details

The virus defines a new function for interrupt 16h, function 0ddh. If interrupt 16h is called with that in the AH register, then it returns with 0ddh in the AL register. The virus uses this to determine whether it is already installed. The fumble table used is:

```
12345687790-=\~!@#$%^&*()_+|qwertyuiop()(asdfghjkl;
zxcvbnm,./QWERTYUIOP{}ASDFGHJKL:";ZXCVBNM<>?.
```

The way the table is used is each character is replaced by the character on the right.

The fumble only activates if you type at better than six characters per second (approximately 60 wpm). If you type at that speed, after not using the keyboard for five seconds, you get a fumble. There is code in the virus that should gradually decrease that five second gap, but it doesn't work correctly.

4.26 Dbase

Other names: none
Infects: any COM file on any writable DOS device
Classification: indirect action file virus

4.26.1 Recognition and Detection

COM files grow by 1864 bytes, and 1884 bytes are subtracted from the top of conventional memory, which would be shown up by Chkdsk.

The virus doesn't disable the "Abort, Retry, Ignore" message, so that if it tries to infect a write-protected diskette, it gives that message. However, it does preserve date/time, and the file's attribute (it temporarily sets it to read/write in order to infect it).

.DBF files are garbled (see below for details). The virus creates a hidden file in the root directory called C:\BUGS.DAT. The way you are most likely to detect this virus is if you copy a file with the extension DBF to an uninfected computer, and then you find that a database that is fine on the infected computer, is garbled on the clean one.

4.26.2 How the Virus Copies Itself

It is an indirect action file virus. When you run an infected COM file, part of the virus goes memory-resident. Then, when you run another COM program, it infects that from the memory- resident part.

4.26.3 What the Virus Does

It intercepts the DOS functions to create, open, read, write and close a file. If the file does not have the DBF extension, it ignores it (DBF is a common extension for database files). If it does have a DBF extension, it garbles it.

The garble is very simple – it just interchanges pairs of bytes. It is equally easy to ungarble a garbled file, by writing a program that swaps pairs of bytes back again. I have written such a program, and it is available free of charge to any registered user of the Anti-Virus Toolkit who has been affected by this virus. It isn't on the Toolkit diskette, as the virus has only ever been seen on one site.

The virus creates a hidden file C:\BUGS.DAT that contains the list of garbled files. If you create a .DBF file (whether you start up a new database, or copy a file, or make a backup to a file with this name) three months after the BUGS.DAT file is created, then a damage routine is triggered. The same thing happens if the system date is three months before the date of BUGS.DAT.

The first thing to say is that the damage routine doesn't actually work. This is because of a bug in it. But if it had worked, it would have written garbage over the first 256 sectors on the hard disk, overwriting the boot, both copies of the FAT, and the whole directory. It does this to every device attached to the computer, starting at device D, and working up to device Z. On most computers there is no drive D, and the system will just hang, with no damage done. On networks, the direct write to the device will be disallowed by the network software. So the only time this routine will work is if there is a local drive D.

4.26.4 How To Get Rid of It

Boot from a clean DOS disk; this is a DOS diskette that has come from the manufacturer, and has never been write-enabled. This ensures that Dbase is not installed in memory. You can then remove Dbase by using FindVirus to search for all instances of the virus. Every infected file that you find, you can delete, and copy a good file in its place. Run FindVirus again when you are finished, to make sure that all instances have been found.

Finally, you should install ChkVirus or any other cryptographic checksummer on all machines that are potentially infectable, to provide an early warning of a recurrence of this or another virus.

4.26.5 Other Information

This virus has only ever been found on one site. It seems to be targeted, as it only attacks .DBF files.

4.26.6 Technical Details

To determine whether the virus is already memory-resident, it puts 0fb0ah in the AX register, and calls interrupt 21h. If the interrupt returns with 0afbh in the AX register, then the virus was already installed.

The virus traps DOS interrupt 21h, functions 6ch (DOS 4 create file extended), 5bh (create new file), 3ch (create file), 3dh (open file), 3fh (read file), 40h (write to file) and 3eh (close file). It also traps 4bh, and uses this as the trigger to infect a file.

4.27 Virdem

Other names: none
Infects: any COM file on drive A
Classification: direct action file virus

4.27.1 Recognition and Detection

Small (less than 11 k) COM files grow by 2559 bytes. Larger files grow by 1336 bytes. Infected programs ask you to guess a number before running the program (if you guess correctly).

4.27.2 How the Virus Copies Itself

It is an direct action file virus. When you run an infected COM file, the next uninfected program becomes infected – the first COM file in the root directory is avoided.

4.27.3 What the Virus Does

When you run a program, the virus asks you to guess a number between 0 and n where n is the generation number of the virus plus one. If you guess correctly, the program runs – if not, it returns to DOS.

4.27.4 How To Get Rid of It

Use FindVirus to search for all instances of the virus. Every infected file that you find, you can delete, and copy a good file in its place. Run FindVirus again when you are finished, to make sure that all instances have been found.

Finally, you should install ChkVirus or any other cryptographic checksummer on all machines that are potentially infectable, to provide an early warning of a recurrence of this or another virus.

4.27.5 Other Information

This virus was written as a demonstration virus, by Ralf Burger. As it only infects files on the A drive, and it announces its presence so clearly, it is unlikely to spread accidentally.

4.27.6 Technical Details

It only infects on drive A. It doesn't intercept interrupt 24h, so a write-protected diskette will give the game away with an "Abort, Retry, Ignore" message. Read-only files are set to read/write, infected and then not set back to read-only. The virus self-recognition code is two NOP instructions at the beginning of the file, which is not likely to be found in a normal file.

4.28 Denzuk I

Other names: Ohio
Infects: floppy diskettes
Classification: boot sector virus

4.28.1 Recognition and Detection

Whenever you reboot an infected machine using Ctrl-Alt-Del, before the reboot, you see the Denzuk I logo. The Denzuk I logo is a box with the words "(c) 1988, The HACKERS Technology Bandung 40254 Indonesia". See also the section on Denzuk.

4.28.2 How the Virus Copies Itself

Every time you try to read a floppy diskette in drive A or B (Denzuk I will not infect a hard disk), Denzuk I will decrement its infection counter (which is initially set to two). When the counter reaches zero this triggers the infection process and the counter is set back to two. Since most accesses of floppy disks are in fact multiple accesses, this means that Denzuk I will infect every writable diskette that is accessed.

4.28.3 What the Virus Does

If Denzuk I finds Brain on the diskette it removes Brain and replaces it with itself. It might be thought that Denzuk I is actually a helpful virus in that it kills Brain. This is not so: consider what will happen if Denzuk I infects a diskette with more than 40 tracks. The virus uses track 40 to store code and the Denzuk I logo so track 40 would be overwritten and data could be lost as a result.

Even worse, Denzuk I assumes that all diskettes are 360 k diskettes, so when it infects them it puts a 360 k diskette boot sector on top of the old boot sector. This tells DOS that the diskette has 22 FAT sectors and 7 directory sectors, which is only true for 360 k diskettes. So DOS is not able to read the diskette properly, and interprets the directory as part of the FAT, and (depending on what diskette it is) can get the cluster size wrong, and might ignore some of the sectors on each track. In other words, Denzuk I infecting a 5¼-inch 1.2 Mb diskette leaves it unreadable, although putting a correct boot sector back in place will rescue most of the data (track 40 head 0 is gone for ever). Other capacity diskettes (other than 360 k) will also have problems.

4.28.4 How To Get Rid of It

Boot from a clean DOS disk; this is a DOS diskette that has come from the manufacturer, and has never been write-enabled. This ensures that there is nothing unwanted installed in memory. Use FindVirus to determine which diskettes are infected.

Treatment consists of simply copying all the files off an infected diskette (using "COPY *.*"; do not use Diskcopy or any image copier), and reformatting the diskette. On a 360 k diskette, this would leave the code on track 40, but without the boot sector that links to it that code is harmless. Alternatively, it is much faster to use UnVirus or any virus removal program to remove the infection from a diskette.

If a large number of diskettes are potentially infected you should consider borrowing a hopper-fed diskette cleaning machine, which can handle up to 700 diskettes per hour, sorting them into clean and contaminated bins.

If you have an outbreak of Denzuk I, then after it is cleared up you could use Inoculate or any other inoculator on all diskettes. This works by putting the Denzuk I signature on the boot sector of the diskette. If Denzuk I sees that signature it thinks that the diskette is already infected, so doesn't attack it.

4.28.5 Other Information

I have only seen infected sites in Australia. There, Denzuk I (which should more properly be called Denzuk II) is quite clearly a previous version of the virus called Denzuk, as there are several additional features in Denzuk I that are not present in Denzuk and the proof is that Denzuk I automatically upgrades instances of Denzuk.

It has been suggested that the "Y.C.1.E.R.P." text string inside Denzuk which is used as the replacement volume label in Denzuk I, is an amateur radio call sign in Indonesia.

This is the text message in the virus, which is not displayed:

```
Now... You Are Inside Virus
!           CONGRATULATION    -----------
            VIRUS 1.0                       (C) 1988 by
         The Hackers                          Society
      ----------------                      Y C 1 E R P
         0 D 8 7 2 0 9                      D E N Z U K O
      ----------------                      Jl Ancol Timur
            XII/10
      Bandung  40254                          Indonesia
      ----------------                         Hackin'
         All The Time                       ----------------
```

4.28.6 Technical Details

Denzuk I is a boot sector virus. It replaces the original boot sector with its own – this looks very like a normal boot sector as it has the usual messages "Non-system disk or disk error", "Replace and strike any key when ready" and "Disk boot failure". It also has the references to the system files.

The virus installs itself into 7 k of high memory and patches the byte 413h to reserve this memory. When the boot sector runs it loads in the rest of the virus which is located on track 40 (normal 360 k diskettes have tracks numbered 0 to 39), head 0, sectors 33 to 41 (normal tracks are numbered from 1). Putting the virus in this place means that some disk-searching utilities won't find it there. It also means that if you Diskcopy the infected diskette most of the virus fails to copy. This gives us one simple way to clean up an infection – Denzuk I could almost be called a copy-protected virus! If you Diskcopy an infected diskette the Denzuk I boot is copied but not the rest of Denzuk I. If you use COPY or XCOPY to copy the diskette then the infected boot is left behind also. Of course, you must boot from a known clean diskette before you start. UnVirus or any virus removal program is a much faster way to get rid of Denzuk.

When Denzuk I runs the code that it has loaded in from track 40, it replaces two of the PC's interrupts: 13h (diskette) and 9 (keyboard). A new interrupt is installed, 6Dh, (Denzuk II uses 6Fh) which is the old interrupt 13h; Denzuk I uses this as a short way to call the original routine. The new interrupt 9 looks for two keystrokes. On seeing a Ctrl-Alt-Del, it calls a routine that displays its logo and then reboots. The other keystroke is Ctrl-Alt-F5, which just triggers a reboot. This is a convenient test to see if you are infected, as on a PC that is not running Denzuk Ctrl-Alt-F5 does nothing. All other keystrokes are passed on to the original interrupt 9 routine.

Interrupt 13h is used to infect more diskettes. Every time interrupt 13h is called, provided it is referencing one of the two floppy drives (Denzuk I will not infect a hard disk), and provided the call is a read, write, verify or format, Denzuk I will decrement its infection counter (which is initially set to two). When the counter reaches zero this triggers the infection process and the counter is set back to two.

The infection process works like this. First it reads the sector at cylinder 0, head 0, sector 1. It looks for two bytes that are found in Denzuk I, and if it finds them it doesn't infect.

If Denzuk I finds Brain (or Ashar) virus on the boot sector (which it does by looking for the 1234h signature of Brain) then it upgrades you from Brain to Denzuk I. First, though, it has to go and find the boot sector from where Brain has put it; Brain has three bytes on sector cylinder 0, head 0, sector 1 that tells you where the original boot sector is and Denzuk I decodes these and reads the boot sector.

Whether the diskette was clean or Brain infected Denzuk I now has the original boot sector. It formats track 40, head 0, and writes its six sectors there. If this write is successful (some diskette drives may not allow writing beyond track 39) then it replaces the sector at cylinder 0, head 0, sector 1 with its own version of the boot sector. The infection process is now complete.

Denzuk I puts the Brain signature on the boot sector – this would stop Brain from infecting a Denzuk-infected diskette.

4.29 Yankee Doodle

Other names: none, but see also Vacsina
Infects: any non-tiny COM or EXE file on any writable DOS device
Classification: indirect action file virus

4.29.1 Recognition and Detection

COM files are infected, growing by 2772 to 2900 bytes (see below for details of how this works). Only files that are 33 bytes or larger are infected. Date and time are preserved. The most likely way that this virus will be detected is when it plays Yankee Doodle at 5 p.m. You can confirm an infection by setting the clock to 16:59:30 (using the DOS TIME command) and waiting for a short while.

4.29.2 How the Virus Copies Itself

It is an indirect action file virus. When you run an infected COM or EXE file, it goes memory-resident. Thereafter, any time you load a COM or EXE file, that file is infected. Read-only files are set to read/write and it then resets the attribute after infection. The critical error handler is disabled while infecting to avoid a give-away "Abort, Retry, Ignore" message on write-protected disks.

4.29.3 What the Virus Does

At 5.00 p.m. (16:59:53, to be precise), the 27h version of the virus plays Yankee Doodle. The 2ch version of the virus doesn't play it every 5 p.m.

With version 27h, COM files grow by an amount which can be calculated as follows: round up the file size to the next number divisible by 16, then add 2772, so files grow by between 2772 and 2787 bytes.

With version 2ch, COM files grow by an amount which can be calculated as follows: round up the file size to the next number divisible by 16, then add 2885, so files grow by between 2885 and 2900 bytes.

4.29.4 How To Get Rid of It

Boot from a clean DOS disk; this is a DOS diskette that has come from the manufacturer, and has never been write-enabled. This ensures that Yankee Doodle is not installed in memory. You can then remove Yankee Doodle by using FindVirus to search for all instances of the virus. Every infected file that you find you can delete and copy a good file in its place. Run FindVirus again when you are finished to make sure that all instances have been found.

Finally, you should install ChkVirus or any other cryptographic checksummer on all machines that are potentially infectable to provide an early warning of a recurrence of this or another virus.

4.29.5 Other Information

Because of the similarity to Vacsina, and the two somewhat different versions of Yankee Doodle, with provisions for version numbers and upgrades, it looks as if we can expect several versions of this virus. Indeed, some 16 versions are known. It has been found in the UK.

4.29.6 Technical Details

COM files less than 33 bytes and greater than x bytes (x = 62 182 for version 27h, 62 070 for version 2ch, 62 866 for Vacsina) bytes are not infected. This is because the way that Yankee Doodle runs an infected file is by patching in memory the first 32 bytes of the original program back to the pre-infected version; the upper limit is because COM files must not be greater than 64 k because of the segmentation of the 8088.

The virus uses interrupt 21h, functions c5h and c6h. Novell also uses these functions for semaphores and lock mode, so there will be problems running this virus on a Novell network. C6h is used for a Yankee Doodle version number check and c5h is not used by the virus, merely reprogrammed. It looks like these interrupts are used for debugging the virus.

This virus makes use of the same in-memory flags as Vacsina. At 0:c5h to 0:c7h it puts 7fh, 39h, 27h. Vacsina puts 7fh, 39h, 05h at the same place, and uses that as a test to see if it is already loaded in memory.

Furthermore, it uses a very similar self-recognition string in the file. Yankee Doodle has f4h, 7ah, xxh, 00h at the end of the file. Yankee Doodle uses the f4h, 7ah as the self- recognition code, and the byte xx is probably a version number (it is the same as the byte at 0:c7h). Vacsina puts f4h, 7ah, 05h, 00h at the end of the file, and uses the first three of those four bytes as the self-recognition code.

If you have a file infected with Vacsina, or with a version of Yankee Doodle 22h or lower, versions 27h and 2ch upgrade your old version. At offset 12h into an infected COM file, you can find the original length of the uninfected file, in paragraphs.

In common with many other viruses Yankee Doodle goes memory-resident without using DOS calls to do it in order to evade detection. When the virus goes memory-resident, it occupies: 2896 bytes = b5h paragraphs (27h version) or 3008 bytes = bch paragraphs (2ch version).

The virus author makes use of the DOS function 45h, duplicate a file handle. This is done for error handling, and is not a feature of any other virus so far, apart from Vacsina.

4.30 Alabama

Other names: none
Infects: any EXE file on any writable DOS device
Classification: indirect action file virus

4.30.1 Recognition and Detection

EXE files are infected, growing by 1560 bytes. Date and time are preserved. The most likely way that this virus will be detected, is by the display, which is:

CSOFTWARE COPIES ARE PROHIBITED BY
INTERNATIONAL LAW
xxxxx 00000012
xxxxxxxxxxx Box 1055 Tuscambia ALABAMA USA

where xxx represents unreadable bytes, and 00000012 is a generation counter.

This display triggers when the hour changes after the virus goes memory-resident and the computer then hangs. You can confirm an infection by setting the clock to 12:59:30 (using the DOS TIME command) and waiting for a short while.

4.30.2 How the Virus Copies Itself

It is an indirect action file virus. When you run an infected EXE file it goes memory-resident. Thereafter, any time you load a COM or EXE file, the next uninfected file in the current subdirectory is infected. Read-only files are set to read/write and it then resets the attribute after infection. The critical error handler is disabled while infecting to avoid a give-away "Abort, Retry, Ignore" message on write-protected disks.

4.30.3 What the Virus Does

When the hour changes, the display (see above) is triggered and the computer hangs. On a colour monitor, the message is red and surrounded by a blinking red double-line box. If the computer is rebooted, the virus survives the reboot (see below for details of how).

4.30.4 How To Get Rid of It

Boot from a clean DOS disk; this is a DOS diskette that has come from the manufacturer, and has never been write-enabled. Be sure to do the boot by powering off, and then on again, as Alabama will survive a Ctrl-Alt-Del. This ensures that Alabama is not installed in memory. You can then remove Alabama by using FindVirus to search for all instances of the virus. Every infected file that you find you can delete and copy a good file in its place. Run FindVirus again when you are finished to make sure that all instances have been found.

Finally, you should install ChkVirus or any other cryptographic checksummer on all machines that are potentially infectable, to provide an early warning of a recurrence of this or another virus.

4.30.5 Other Information

As of January 1990 this virus has not been found in the UK. It has version numbers in two places: once as used in the display (the version I have is 10) and once in the code (the version I have is 678).

Any files starting with DEBU or SYMD aren't infected, but are modified in such a way as to make them unusable. This is obviously aimed at DEBUG and SYMDEB.

If the virus is installed in memory, COPY doesn't work properly, and neither will many other operations that involve opening files. For example, if you copy a file from floppy disk to the hard disk, the file is copied, but is given the name of the first .EXE file on the floppy. So if multiple files are copied you only get the last one, as each is copied on top of the previous one.

4.30.6 Technical Details

This virus is most interesting for the way it stores itself in memory, and for the way it survives Ctrl-Alt-Del.

Every other virus examined so far either uses DOS functions to go memory-resident, or else manipulates the Memory Control Blocks to do so. Alabama doesn't do either of these; it simply copies itself into high memory, and hopes that nothing overwrites it. The advantage of this is that it is impossible to spot in memory by memory mapping programs; the disadvantage is that it will get overwritten by something sooner or later. But this disadvantage doesn't matter too much as long as it survives long enough to reproduce itself.

The virus traps interrupt 9, the interrupt that services keystrokes. When it detects that the Del key has been released, and that the Ctrl and Alt keys are down, it goes into its survival routine.

It installs a routine on the timer tick, interrupt 1ch, which counts down 500 ticks (27 seconds). It then puts the screen back and forth between graphics and text mode 15 times and calls interrupt 19h. This causes the usual reboot but without resetting the interrupts. DOS is then loaded, and then when the counter reaches 500, the virus is then re-installed on interrupt 21h, so that infections can continue. When this is done, interrupt 1ch is then set to a "return", which means that anything that was installed on the timer tick is no longer there.

The virus self-recognition code on files is the same as 648 (Vienna) virus; a value of 62 in the seconds field of the directory entry. The self-recognition code in memory is zero in the first four bytes of memory, addresses 0:0 to 0:3. This is the divide-by-zero interrupt, and this means that the machine will crash if this happens. There are other ways that this virus can hang the machine: if the replacement interrupt 21h handler is overwritten in memory by data, when it is executed the machine will stop.

Interrupt 24h is replaced temporarily on each infection to suppress the DOS critical error message if the disk is write-protected. The virus makes extensive use of FCBs in the infection process to read and write files, but it also uses handle calls to manipulate attributes. The date/time is preserved – it uses FCBs to discover the date/time, but handles to reset it.

4.31 Ghostballs

Other names: none
Infects: any COM file on any writable DOS device
Classification: direct action file virus

4.31.1 Recognition and Detection

COM files are infected, growing by 2351 bytes. Date and time are preserved. The most likely way that this virus will be detected is by the bouncing ball display (as per Italian virus), but this is quite misleading.

4.31.2 How the Virus Copies Itself

It is a direct action file virus. When you run an infected COM file it looks for the next uninfected file in that subdirectory, and infects it. Read-only files are set to read/write and it then resets the attribute after infection. Likewise, date and time are preserved in the usual way. The critical error handler is not disabled while infecting, so there could be a give-away "Abort, Retry, Ignore" message on write-protected disks. The virus leaves alone files less than 10 bytes and more than 64 000 bytes.

4.31.3 What the Virus Does

When an infected application is run, the virus tries to read the boot sector of the diskette in drive A. If this attempt is successful, it drops what is almost a copy of Italian virus (the version called Big Italian, but using character 7, as per ordinary Italian) onto the boot sector. It isn't quite a copy of Italian as all the infecting code has been removed (replaced by NOPs). It doesn't create bad sectors on the diskette in the way that Italian does.

4.31.4 How To Get Rid of It

Boot from a clean DOS disk; this is a DOS diskette that has come from the manufacturer and has never been write-enabled. This is not really necessary for this virus, but is good practice in general when virus-hunting. You can then remove Ghostballs by using FindVirus to search for all instances of the virus. Every infected file that you find, you can delete, and copy a good file in its place. Run FindVirus again when you are finished to make sure that all instances have been found.

Finally, you should install ChkVirus or any other cryptographic checksummer on all machines that are potentially infectable to provide an early warning of a recurrence of this or another virus.

It isn't necessary to remove the non-infective Italian code on the diskettes that Ghostballs has put it on, but if you want to you can use UnVirus or any virus removal program for this, choosing the Italian option.

4.31.5 Other Information

It isn't very infectious, so it is entirely possible that it won't be seen very widely. In the code, there is the message "GhostBalls, Product of Iceland Copyright (c) 1989, 4418 and 5F19". This is never displayed. These are the two pseudonyms of the Icelandic virus authors, from whom came Icelandic virus and possibly others.

It isn't clear why the authors decided to make the Italian that is dropped non-infective. If they had made it infective, it would have been very difficult to tell an outbreak of Ghostballs from real Italian, and every time the apparent Italian virus had been eradicated, it would have broken out again because of the drop by Ghostballs.

4.31.6 Technical Details

This virus is partly Vienna (648) virus, and partly Italian virus. The infective code is that of the Burger book version of Vienna. The part of the Vienna virus that overwrites the first five bytes of one in eight files, has been NOPed out. When an infected application is run, if a 360 k diskette is in drive A and writable, it drops a version of Italian onto the boot sector, and puts the body of the code onto track 39, head 1, sectors 8 and 9. This is non-infectious, but has all the bouncing ball code. It isn't the original Italian – it is the version that was modified in Iceland to work on 286 and 386 machines. There is one interesting difference – XOR AX,AX assembles as 33h, c0h, whereas in the original it assembles as 31h, c0h. Similarly XOR, DX,DX. Obviously the author has changed assemblers.

The virus uses far calls to the BIOS code to write the non- infectious Italian virus to the diskette; this means that it will not be trapped by "active monitor" anti-virus programs that watch the interrupts for unauthorised disk accesses.

The virus self-recognition code on files is the same as 648 (Vienna) virus; a value of 62 in the seconds field of the directory entry.

4.32 765 Virus

Other names: Perfume
Infects: any COM file on any writable DOS device
Classification: indirect action file virus

4.32.1 Recognition and Detection

COM files are infected, growing by 765 bytes. Attribute, date and time are preserved. The most likely way that this virus will be detected is when the infected file has been run 80 times (see below).

4.32.2 How the Virus Copies Itself

When you run an infected COM file, the virus goes memory-resident. Thereafter, whenever you load and execute a program the virus in memory checks to see if it is a COM file and (if on a diskette) whether the diskette is write-enabled. If so, it stores the attribute of the file and sets it to read/write; this is so that it can restore the attribute after infection. Likewise, date and time are preserved in the usual way.

4.32.3 What the Virus Does

When infecting a file, it puts four bytes at the end of the file. The first two are the virus self-recognition code ("VI") and the second two are a counter, which it initialises to zero. Thereafter, every time the COM file is run, it increments the counter by one, and when it reaches 80 (or more) it triggers the password routine.

The password routine works like this. When you run a program that has the counter at 80 or more, a message is put up on the screen before the program is run. If you type as a response "4711" then the program continues to run; if you type anything else the virus puts up a second message and terminates the program with a return code of 1.

In the sample of the virus that I have the message has been replaced by nulls. Possibly, the first message is a request for the password, and the second is a message saying that you got it wrong. By coincidence, 4711 is a famous perfume.

4.32.4 How To Get Rid of It

Boot from a clean DOS disk; this is a DOS diskette that has come from the manufacturer and has never been write-enabled. You can then remove 765 by using FindVirus to search for all instances of the virus. Every infected file that you find you can delete and copy a good file in its place. Run FindVirus again when you are finished to make sure that all instances have been found.

Finally, you should install ChkVirus or any other cryptographic checksummer on all machines that are potentially infectable to provide an early warning of a recurrence of this or another virus.

4.32.5 Other Information

A version with messages has been found in Germany.

4.32.6 Technical Details

The virus takes up 1024 bytes in memory when resident. It uses an interesting technique to discover whether a diskette is write-protected – where other viruses replace interrupt 24h with a dummy critical error handler, this one uses interrupt 13h to attempt to write to the device if it is physical device number 0 or 1. This won't work for external floppy drives if they are a physical device number greater than 1. The most interesting part of this is that the write is to cylinder 0, head 0, sector 0, which doesn't exist, as sectors start from 1. The technique appears to work.

765 has a call to see if it is already in memory. This is interrupt 21h, function 0bh, with 56 ("V") in the AL register. If the call returns with 4952 ("IR") in the AX register then the virus was already in memory.

There isn't an inoculator for 765. As well as checking the two bytes near the end of the file it also looks at the first byte of the file, to see if it is a CALL rather than the more usual JMP.

765 refrains from infecting any file that is greater than fc00h (64 512) bytes long in order to avoid making a COM file longer than 64 k.

4.33 Lisbon Virus

Other names: none
Infects: any COM file on any writable DOS device
Classification: direct action file virus

4.33.1 Recognition and Detection

COM files grow by 648 bytes. One infection in four deliberately trashes the file that it infects. If it tries to infect write-protected media, you'll get an "Abort, Retry, Ignore" message.

4.33.2 How the Virus Copies Itself

It is a direct action file virus. Every time an infected file is executed (even if the file is in another subdirectory), the virus searches the current directory for uninfected files and infects the next available one. It doesn't infect EXE files.

4.33.3 What the Virus Does

One infection in four makes the file unusable. Eventually, COM-MAND.COM is infected, and then whenever the computer is started up it just hangs. It does this by putting the five character "@AIDS" at the start of the file.

4.33.4 How To Get Rid of It

If the computer will not boot from its hard disk, boot it from a floppy disk. You can treat it by using FindVirus to search for all instances of the virus. Every infected file that you find you can delete and copy a good file in its place.

Once you have removed all the copies of the virus, you can use Inoculate or any other inoculator to mark all files with the mark that it uses to distinguish infected from uninfected files. The virus uses the seconds field of the directory, putting an impossible value (62 seconds) in it.

When you have used Inoculate you can run FindVirus again to check that there are no genuinely infected files around.

4.33.5 Other Information

This is a very small modification of the Vienna or 648 virus. The source code (or a disassembly) of this was published in a book.

4.33.6 Technical Details

The virus uses DOS calls to discover the date, time and attribute of the file and, after infection, it sets them back to what they were before to escape detection. COMMAND.COM can be infected; if it is, the virus will certainly be detected; the computer will hang every time it is started up. If the virus tries to infect a write-protected disk or diskette, the DOS message indicating a write-protect error will be seen. Files larger than 64 000 or less than 10 bytes are not infected.

4.34 W13 Virus

Other names: none
Infects: any COM file more than 256 bytes on any writable DOS device
Classification: direct action file virus

4.34.1 Recognition and Detection

COM files grow by 534 bytes in version A, 507 in version B. If it tries to infect write-protected media, you'll get an "Abort, Retry, Ignore" message. One easy way to notice this virus is if the date of a COM file is the 13th month.

4.34.2 How the Virus Copies Itself

It is a direct action file virus. Every time an infected file is executed (even if the file is in another subdirectory), the virus searches the current directory for uninfected files and infects the next available one. It doesn't infect EXE files.

4.34.3 What the Virus Does

There is no payload to this virus.

4.34.4 How To Get Rid of It

You can treat it by using FindVirus to search for all instances of the virus. Every infected file that you find you can delete and copy a good file in its place.

Once you have removed all the copies of the virus you can use Inoculate or any other inoculator to mark all files with the mark that it uses to distinguish infected from uninfected files. The virus uses the months field of the directory, putting an impossible value (13th month) in it.

When you have used Inoculate, you can run FindVirus again to check that there are no genuinely infected files around.

4.34.5 Other Information

This is a modification of the Vienna or 648 virus. The source code (or a disassembly) of this was published in a book.

4.34.6 Technical Details

The virus uses DOS calls to discover the date, time and attribute of the file, and after infection, it sets them back to what they were before, to escape detection. COMMAND.COM can be infected.

If the virus tries to infect a write-protected disk or diskette the DOS message indicating a write-protect error will be seen. Files larger than 64 000 or less than 256 bytes not infected. The 507 version is the same as the 534 version, but tidied up a bit.

4.35 Oropax

Other names: none
Infects: any COM file on any writable DOS device
Classification: indirect action file virus

4.35.1 Recognition and Detection

COM files grow by between 2756 and 2806 bytes in such a way that the file size is divisible by 51. If it tries to infect write-protected media, you'll get an "Abort, Retry, Ignore" message. This is highly unlikely to happen though (see below).

On almost all (see technical details) computers, one in four times that Oropax goes memory-resident, it plays a tune every few minutes. This is the main way the virus will be noticed.

4.35.2 How the Virus Copies Itself

When an infected file is executed the virus goes memory-resident. When a subdirectory is created or removed, or a file is created, opened for writing, deleted or renamed, Oropax infects the next uninfected file in the current subdirectory. It doesn't infect EXE files.

4.35.3 What the Virus Does

One in four times that Oropax goes memory-resident a counter is started. Five minutes later Oropax plays the first tune. It then cycles through its repertoire of three tunes, playing one every few minutes. The three tunes are: *Stars and Stripes For Ever*, usually sung with the words "Hurrah for the red, white and blue" (this is a Sousa march); *Symphony No. 40* by Mozart; and *The Blue Danube* by Strauss. These three tunes are all on the DOS Supplemental diskette that comes with DOS 2 from IBM; perhaps this is where the author got them. By coincidence, Yankee Doodle is also one of those tunes.

4.35.4 How To Get Rid of It

First, switch the computer off, and then after a few seconds on again, booting from a known clean DOS diskette (which is a diskette that has come from the manufacturer and has always been write-protected). You can then use FindVirus to search for all instances of the virus. Every infected file that you find you can delete and copy a good file in its place.

4.35.5 Other Information

Oropax is a virus that has been reported for a long time, but not seen by very many people – virus researchers used to speak about the "Legendary Oropax". The variable number of bytes added to the file will make identification a bit harder but the music makes it very easy. Oropax is a brand of German earplugs; this is how the virus got its name.

4.35.6 Technical Details

The virus uses DOS calls to discover the date, time and attribute of the file and, after infection, it sets them back to what they were before to escape detection. COMMAND.COM can be infected.

If the virus tries to infect a write-protected disk or diskette, the DOS message indicating a write-protect error will be seen. But this is not going to happen, as the infection is only triggered by activities that are going to write to the disk anyway. Files larger than 61 981 bytes will not be infected.

The virus self-recognition is partly the fact that the file size is divisible by 51. This makes the searching for an uninfected file very fast, as it can be done by just referencing the directory entries without opening the file. To confirm the infection, Oropax looks for a byte f1h in the fourth byte of an infected program.

The tune-playing criterion is quite complicated. The date must be on or after 1 May 1987. A random number generator is used to trigger one time in four. The machine ID at ffff:e must be fc, fd, fe or ff. This eliminates the PS/2 model 30 and 80, and the convertible, and some XTs; it also eliminates some compatible PCs which use other machine IDs. Then, eight minutes after the virus goes TSR, it plays its first tune. After another eight minutes, it plays the second, and after another eight minutes, the third. It then cycles through its repertoire again.

Oropax intercepts interrupts 8, 20h, 21h and 27h. Interrupt 8 is used to play the music (it is only installed if the conditions for playing the music have been met), and interrupt 21h to trigger additional infections. Functions 13h, 16h, 17h, 39h, 3ah, 3ch, 3dh (subfunction 01),

41h, 43h and 56h are all trapped, and trigger the infection of the next uninfected file in the current subdirectory. Notice that function 4bh, load and execute, does not trigger an infection. To find out whether it is already in memory, Oropax puts 33e0h into the AX register and calls interrupt 21h. If the interrupt returns with ffh in AL the virus isn't present in memory.

4.36 Twelve Tricks

Other names: none
Affects: partition records
Classification: trojan

4.36.1 Recognition and Detection

This is a trojan, not a virus, but is included here because it does leave part of itself on every affected hard disk.

The trojan consists of a program (more about this aspect later) which you run; running the program, as well as the obvious things that the program is expected to do, also replaces the partition record (also called the Master Boot Record, or MBR) on your hard disk with its own version. This can easily be recognised by inspecting the hard disk at cylinder 0, head 0, sector 1, which can be done with a disk sector editor such as Peeka. If the partition has this trojan in place, it will contain the following text near the beginning:

SOFTLoK V3.0 SOFTGUARD SYSTEMS INC
2840 St. Thomas Expwy, suite 201
Santa Clara, CA 95051 (408)970-9420

At this point, let me state that I believe that the company mentioned above has nothing whatsoever to do with the trojan; perhaps the trojan author has a grudge against them.

4.36.2 How the Trojan Installs Itself

The trojan uses a far call to the hard disk BIOS code in order to plant this partition. To do this, it must know the location in memory of the entry point; it tries five different ones, one of which is the one documented in the IBM PC-XT technical reference manual, and the other four are presumably fairly common alternatives.

The purpose of planting the trojan with a far call is, I believe, to escape detection by active monitor programs that protect a computer by monitoring the interrupt table, and preventing unauthorised writes to system areas on the hard disk. Since Twelve Tricks doesn't use an interrupt to plant the MBR, such programs won't be able to prevent it. I tested this using Flushot, probably the most successful of the active monitors, and Twelve Tricks went straight through it – the same would be true, I think, of any other active monitor.

4.36.3 What the Trojan Does

When the MBR is run, which is every time you boot from the hard disk, Twelve Tricks copies 205 (d7h) bytes of itself onto locations 0:300h to 0:3d6h. This overwrites part of the interrupt vector table, but it is a part that doesn't get used very much. This means that these d7h bytes are memory-resident without having to use any of the TSR calls of DOS, and without having to reserve part of high memory. Reserving part of high memory is the usual ploy used by boot sector viruses, but the drawback of that route is that you might notice that a few kilobytes from your 640 k has disappeared (Chkdsk would reveal this). The method used by Twelve Tricks would not show up as a loss from your 640 k.

When the computer is started up, a random number generator determines which of the Twelve Tricks will be installed. It does the installation by replacing one of the interrupt vectors with a vector that points to the Twelve Tricks' own code, and then chains on to the original code. The Twelve Tricks are:

1. Insert a random delay loop in the timer tick, so that 18.2 times per second, the computer executes a loop that is randomly between 1 and 65 536 long (different each time it is executed). This slows the machine down, and makes it work rather jerkily.

2. Insert an End-Of-Interrupt in the timer tick. This interferes with the servicing of hardware interrupts, so for example, the clock is stopped, TSRs that depend on the timer tick don't work, and the floppy motor is permanently on.

3. Every time a key is pressed or released, the timer tick count is incremented by a random number between 0 and 65 535. This has a variety of effects; programs sometimes won't run, when you type "TIME" you get "Current time is divide overflow", and copying files sometimes doesn't work.

4. Every time interrupt 0dh is executed, it will only do the routine three times out of four. Interrupt 0dh is used on PCs and XTs for the fixed disk, on ATs for the parallel port.

5. Every time interrupt 0eh is executed it will only do the routine three times out of four. Interrupt 0eh is used for the floppy disk.

6. Every time interrupt 10h is called (this is the video routine), insert a delay loop that is randomly between 1 and 65 536 long (different each time it is executed). This slows the video down, and makes it work rather jerkily and/or slowly.

7. Every time the video routine to scroll up is called, instead of the requested number of lines being scrolled, the entire scrolling window is blanked.

8. Every time a request is made to the diskette handler, it is converted into a write request. This means that the first time you try to read or write to a diskette, whatever happens to be in the buffer will be written to the diskette, and will probably overwrite the boot sector, FAT or directory, as these must be read before anything else can be done. If you try to read a write-protected diskette, you get "Write-protect error reading drive A". If you do a DIR of a write-enabled diskette, you get "General Failure", and if you inspect the diskette using a sector editor, you'll find that the boot and FAT have been zeroed or overwritten.

9. Every time interrupt 16h is called (read the keyboard) the keyboard flags (Caps Lock, Num Lock, Shift States, etc.) are set randomly before the keystroke is returned. This means that at the DOS prompt, the keyboard will only work occasionally. Programs that poll interrupt 16h will be unusable. Holding down the Del key will trigger a Ctrl-Alt-Del.

10. Everything that goes to the printer is garbled by xoring it with a byte from the timer tick count.

11. Every letter that is sent to the printer has its case reversed by xoring it with 20h. Also, non-alpha characters are xored, so a space becomes a null, and line feeds don't feed lines.

12. Whenever the Time-Of-Day interrupt (1ah) is executed, it will do an End-Of-Interrupt instead. This means that you can't set the system clock, and the time is set permanently to one value.

These are the twelve tricks. In addition there are two more things that the trojan does. It uses a random number generator; one time out of 4096 it does a low level format of the track that contains the active boot sector; this will also destroy part of the first copy of the FAT. You can recover from this by creating a new boot sector and copying the second copy of the FAT back over the first copy. After it does the format it will display the message "SOFTLoK ..." as above, and hang the computer.

If it doesn't do the format, it makes a random change to a random word in one of the first 16 sectors of the FAT, which will make a slight and increasing corruption in the file system. This is perhaps the worst of the things that it does as it will cause an increasing corruption of the files on the disk.

4.36.4 How To Get Rid of It

It's easy to get rid of Droppers; just delete them and replace them with a clean copy. If you find the string above in the MBR or in memory at 0:38b, you need to boot from a clean DOS diskette and replace the partition record. DO NOT use FDISK to do this unless you are prepared for FDISK to zero your FAT and directory; you will lose all your data that way. One way would be to do a file-by-file backup, low-level format to get rid of the trojan MBR, then FDISK FORMAT and restore your backup. I would recommend doing two backups using as many different methods as possible if you use this route, in case one of them fails to restore.

The other way to replace the partition is to run a program that drops a clean partition record onto the MBR, but doesn't change the partitioning data. A program to do this is available; should you need it, please ask.

If the FAT is corrupted, it is likely that the second copy of the FAT is likewise corrupted, as DOS will update the second copy each time it makes a change to the first copy. You should start by copying each file off the disk, and examining it to see if it is intact. If not, you will have to go to your backups.

After removing Twelve Tricks, I would recommend running Chkdsk /F to restore your FAT to self-consistency.

4.36.5 Other Information

The whole of the MBR is used for the code. Most normal MBRs don't use more than half the space, and a number of other programs have started using this space, for example Disk Manager and the Western Digital WDXT-Gen controllers (but the Dropper doesn't work on the WDXT-Gen). This means that the Dropper might cause an immediate problem in some circumstances.

The main damage done, however, will be in the impression that this trojan creates that your hardware is suffering from a variety of faults which usually go away when you reboot (only to be replaced by other faults). Also, the FAT gets progressively corrupted.

So far, this has been reported in Surrey, England. It was noticed because it made a disk using Speedstor to control it non-bootable. Disks that are controlled in the normal way remain bootable. I would be grateful if any sightings could be reported to me, especially if the Dropper program is different from the one I have examined; I would also like a specimen of it.

It has subsequently been noticed in two different files in the US; it was noticed because a virus finder program was being run.

4.36.6 Technical Information

The program that drops the trojan was, in the specimen that I first analysed, a hacked version of CORETEST, a program to benchmark hard disk performance. The file is CORETEST.COM, it is version 2.6 (dated 1986 in the copyright message), had a length of 32 469 bytes, and it was timestamped 6-06-86, 9:44. When I looked in more detail at this program I found some interesting things.

It looks as if the original CORETEST program was an EXE file and the trojan author prepended his code to it. This code consists of some relocation stuff, then a decryptor, to decrypt the following 246h bytes. The decryption is a double xor with a changing byte. Those 246h bytes, when run, examine the memory to try to find one of five sets of hard disk handler code (presumably corresponding to five BIOSs). When it finds one of them (I have identified the first one as being the IBM XT BIOS) it plants the trojan MBR in place, using a far call to the BIOS code. The trojan MBR is 200h of the 246h bytes. The trojan is patched so that it also does disk accesses using a far call to the same location. Finally, the prepended trojan passes control to the original program. I call the combination of the prepended code, plus the original program, the Dropper.

The main purpose of the encryption, I would guess, is to evade detection by programs that check code for bombs and trojans. There are no suspicious strings or interrupt calls in the code until it is decrypted at run time.

This is not a virus, but a trojan. However, it is unlikely that all the patching to the original program was done by hand – it is far more likely that the trojan author wrote a prepender program (I would call this the Prepender), to automatically attach his code to the target executable. If this is the case then there are two consequences. The first is that he might have trojanised other programs besides the ones that I have examined. In other words, there might be other Droppers around besides the one I have examined. The second is that if that is the case, we cannot rely on the encryption having the same seed each time, as the Prepender might change the seed each time it operates. So it would be unsafe to search files for the encrypted MBR.

Indeed, a further possibility exists. The Prepender program might have been placed into circulation, and people running it would unwittingly be creating additional Droppers. There is absolutely no evidence to suggest that that is actually the case, but I would ask anyone who detects this Dropper in one of their files to also examine all the others.

4.37 Zero Bug

Other names: Zero Eater
Infects: any COM file on any writable DOS device
Classification: indirect action file virus

4.37.1 Recognition and Detection

COM files are infected, growing by 1536 bytes. Attribute, date and time are preserved. The most likely way that this virus will be detected is when the display is triggered (see below). But, if the virus is in memory, you don't see the increased file size, as the virus conceals this.

4.37.2 How the Virus Copies Itself

When you run an infected COM file, the virus goes memory-resident. Thereafter, whenever you copy a COM file it infects the copy. Because it is infecting on a write, it doesn't need to check that the media is writable, or disable the critical error handler. It stores the attribute of the file and sets it to read/write; this is so that it can restore the attribute after infection. Likewise, date and time are preserved in the usual way.

4.37.3 What the Virus Does

When it triggers, you get an interesting screen display. A face (ASCII character 1) eats all the zeros. It starts at the top left hand corner, and works its way from left to right, and goes slowly down the screen. As it goes, each zero on the screen is "eaten" and replaced by a space.

4.37.4 How To Get Rid of It

Boot from a clean DOS disk; this is a DOS diskette that has come from the manufacturer, and has never been write-enabled. You can then remove Zero Bug by using FindVirus to search for all instances of the virus. Every infected file that you find you can delete and copy a good file in its place. Run FindVirus again when you are finished to make sure that all instances have been found.

Finally, you should install ChkVirus or any other cryptographic checksummer on all machines that are potentially infectable, to provide an early warning of a recurrence of this or another virus.

4.37.5 Other Information

As of March 1990, this virus has not been found in the UK.

4.37.6 Technical Details

Zero Bug uses the same self-recognition code as Vienna (648) virus; it sets the time field in the directory to 62 seconds. When you do a DIR to look at files, any file with this flag has 600h bytes subtracted from the size. This was probably done to hide the virus.

The virus goes TSR using interrupt 27h, so many active monitors will spot this. It uses 700h bytes, so memory mappers will see it.

The virus uses interrupt 1ch for the display, and captures interrupt 21h for various purposes. It replaces functions 11h and 12h, the Find First File and Find Next, used by DOS to look at directories. If one of those is being called, and an infected file is being examined, it subtracts the 600h bytes from the length. It does not trap functions 4eh or 4fh, the handle calls to find file sizes. It defines a function 60h for interrupt 21h, which it uses for its own purposes, to run the original program.

The display only triggers if the machine was booted from the hard disk; it looks for the string "COMSPEC=C:" in memory. The virus also puts the two bytes "ZE" at offset 3 and 4 from the start of the file.

4.38 Sylvia

Other names: none
Infects: any COM file on any writable DOS device
Classification: direct action file virus

4.38.1 Recognition and Detection

COM files are infected, growing by 1332 bytes. Attribute, date and time are preserved. When an infected file is run, the virus spends a lot of time searching for a file to infect; there is a lot of disk activity.

4.38.2 How the Virus Copies Itself

When you run an infected COM file the virus infects the first un-infected file that it finds. It avoids infecting IBMBIO.COM, IBMDOS.COM and COMMAND.COM, presumably to avoid detection. Before it writes, it disables the critical error handler to suppress any possible "Abort, Retry, Ignore" message. It stores the attribute of the file and sets it to read/write; this is so that it can restore the attribute after infection. Likewise, date and time are preserved in the usual way.

It tries to infect four more files each time an infected program is run.

4.38.3 What the Virus Does

There is a message in the virus which it doesn't display. However, if you look at the code, you see that the following would be displayed if there were code to do so:

```
      This
          program
             is
                 infected
                    by
                       a
                          HARMLESS
                             Text-Virus V2.1

      Send a FUNNY postcard to : Sylvia Verkade, 1
                                 Duinzoom 36b,
                                 3235 CD Rockanje
                                 The Netherlands.

      You might get an ANTIVIRUS program.....
```

The virus checksums this message every time it runs, and if it finds that the message has been altered, it displays:

FUCK YOU LAMER!!!!
system halted...

and then it hangs the system.

4.38.4 How To Get Rid of It

Boot from a clean DOS disk; this is a DOS diskette that has come from the manufacturer, and has never been write-enabled. You can then remove Sylvia by using FindVirus to search for all instances of the virus. Every infected file that you find you can delete and copy a good file in its place. Run FindVirus again when you are finished to make sure that all instances have been found.

Finally, you should install ChkVirus or any other cryptographic checksummer on all machines that are potentially infectable, to provide an early warning of a recurrence of this or another virus.

4.38.5 Other Information

As of March 1990, this virus has not been found in the UK. The named person does exist, but has no idea who might have written the virus.

4.38.6 Technical Details

Sylvia uses "He" at offset 17ah in the file as a self-recognition code. It disables the critical error handler to avoid the "Abort, Retry, Ignore" message on write-protected media. It is one of the few viruses that infects a file by making an infected copy then deleting the original.

4.39 Tenbytes

Other names: 1554
Infects: any COM or EXE file on any writable DOS device
Classification: indirect action file virus

4.39.1 Recognition and Detection

COM files are infected, growing by 1554 to 1569 bytes. Attribute, date and time are preserved. This virus could be recognised by the way it corrupts files between September and December (see below). EXE files grow by 1514 to 1529 bytes.

4.39.2 How the Virus Copies Itself

When you run an infected file, the virus goes memory-resident. Thereafter, it infects every program that you run, provided it is at least 1000 bytes (COM files) or 1024 bytes (EXE files). Before it infects, it disables the critical error handler to suppress any possible "Abort, Retry, Ignore" message. It stores the attribute of the file and sets it to read/write; this is so that it can restore the attribute after infection. Likewise, date and time are preserved in the usual way.

4.39.3 What the Virus Does

Every year, in the months of September, October, November and December, the trojan is triggered. The effect of this is, whenever DOS does a write to a file, the first ten bytes to be written are omitted, and ten bytes of garbage are added at the end of the write. This is done for all writes, whether it is for an entire file or part of a file. The effect of this will be a progressive corruption of files, including backups. Data files as well as programs are affected by the corruption.

4.39.4 How To Get Rid of It

Boot from a clean DOS disk; this is a DOS diskette that has come from the manufacturer, and has never been write-enabled. You can then remove Tenbytes by using FindVirus to search for all instances of the virus. Every infected file that you find you can delete and copy a good file in its place. Run FindVirus again when you are finished to make sure that all instances have been found.

Finally, you should install ChkVirus or any other cryptographic checksummer on all machines that are potentially infectable to provide an early warning of a recurrence of this or another virus.

4.39.5 Other Information

This virus was posted to Usenet after being converted to a printable format using UUENCODE, a standard way to transfer binaries. The person posting the message explained that he had found this on his disk, and wanted information about it. The message was potentially available to millions of readers of Usenet news. Of course, they would have had to make a deliberate act of decoding it to turn it back into runnable code, so there was no immediate danger. However, this does mean that copies of the virus are freely available.

4.39.6 Technical Details

Tenbytes prevents the use of Debug or similar debuggers to step through the code by defining replacements for interrupt 1 and interrupt 3. It goes TSR in an interesting way; the virus copies the memory-resident part up to 9800:0, but doesn't attempt to reserve memory for it. This has the disadvantage that any other program may use this memory, and if it does, the next time that an interrupt 21h is called the computer will almost certainly crash. But the advantage of this method of going TSR is that it will not be detected by any of the programs that watch for programs going TSR nor will it be spotted by any memory mapper. So for the small price of occasionally crashing a user's machine (and, of course, the virus will only work on machines with at least 640 k of memory), the memory-resident part will be very hard for virus checkers to find, unless they are looking for this particular virus.

When the virus is copying itself it sets the ES register to 8 as a signal not to corrupt its own copying.

The virus self-recognition code for COM files is 2eh, 01h as bytes 2 and 3 from the start of a file. For EXE files, it is that the checksum bytes at offset 12h and 13h in the EXE header, is the negative of the bytes at offset 2 and 3, which is the file length mod 512.

The length added to the file is worked out as follows. For COM files, you round the length up to be divisible by 16, then add 1554. If this comes to more than 64 k it doesn't infect; nor does it if the original file is less than 1000 bytes.

4.40 Sunday

Other names: none
Infects: any COM or EXE file on any writable DOS device
Classification: indirect action file virus

4.40.1 Recognition and Detection

COM files grow by 1636 bytes (EXE files by a similar amount) without changing their date and time or read/write/hidden attributes.

Some EXE files are not infected correctly by the virus, and fail to run as soon as they are infected. COMMAND.COM does not become infected, probably to help the virus avoid detection.

4.40.2 How the Virus Copies Itself

When an infected COM or EXE file is executed the virus goes memory-resident. Each time an uninfected program is executed thereafter the virus infects that program.

4.40.3 What the Virus Does

Because of a major bug in the virus it does very little.

4.40.4 How To Get Rid of It

Boot from a clean DOS disk; this is a DOS diskette that has come from the manufacturer, and has never been write-enabled. This ensures

that Sunday is not installed in memory. You can then remove Sunday by using FindVirus to search for all instances of the virus. Every infected file that you find you can delete and copy a good file in its place. Run FindVirus again when you are finished to make sure that all instances have been found.

Finally, you should install ChkVirus or any other cryptographic checksummer on all machines that are potentially infectable to provide an early warning of a recurrence of this or another virus.

4.40.5 Other Information

This virus is extremely similar to Jerusalem. Bytes 3 and 4 are "sU", just like in Jerusalem and the Suriv viruses. But the five-bytes self-recognition code is different; it is c8, f7, e1, ee, e7, which is "Hwang" with the high bit set (could this be the author's name?).

It looks at the day-of-week when it goes memory-resident and if this is seven, it sets a flag. The timer tick decrements a counter which is initially set to 7e90h (this would be exactly 30 minutes if the timer ticked at 18 per second, but as it ticks at 18.2, it is slightly less). When the counter reaches zero, the following text is put up on the screen "Today is SunDay! Why do you work so hard? All work and no play make you a dull boy! Come on ! Let's go out and have some fun!". The counter is then reset to 7e90h so that the message will appear about every 30 minutes. Also, it deletes every program that you try to run.

However, there is a bug in this. The day-of-week is never 7; on Sunday it is 0. So the flag is never set, and none of the above ever happens on all the versions of DOS that I've looked at. Of course, it may be that the author intended that the virus should never trigger, in which case it is a feature not a bug.

4.40.6 Technical Details

Sunday traps int 21h and makes a modification to function 4bh, load and execute a program. It changes three bytes in the interrupt vector table, 0:3fch to 0:3feh. But it doesn't use these bytes.

The virus defines a couple of new functions for int 21h. With 0ffh in AH, it returns the version number of the virus (currently version 4). 0ddh is a subroutine that is called by the virus to run the original program.

The virus distinguishes between COM and EXE files on the basis of the file name; if it ends in "M" it is treated as a COM file, otherwise it is assumed to be an EXE. This will result in a tiny number of mis-infections, as it is entirely possible to have a misnamed file, since DOS distinguishes on the basis of the "MZ" signature at the beginning of EXE files.

The virus traps the DOS critical error handler, so that if it tries to infect a file on write-protected media, there is no give-away "Write-protect error".

4.41 Stupid

Other names: none
Infects: COM files on any writable DOS device
Classification: indirect action file virus

4.41.1 Recognition and Detection

COM files are infected, growing by 583 bytes. Attribute, date and time are not preserved.

4.41.2 How the Virus Copies Itself

When you run an infected COM file, the virus goes memory-resident. Thereafter, whenever you open a file the virus in memory infects the first COM file in the subdirectory.

4.41.3 What the Virus Does

This virus has no self-recognition code, so files grow indefinitely. Sooner or later, running an infected file will crash the computer.

4.41.4 How To Get Rid of It

Boot from a clean DOS disk; this is a DOS diskette that has come from the manufacturer and has never been write-enabled. You can then remove the virus by using FindVirus to search for all instances of it. Every infected file that you find you can delete and copy a good file in its place. Run FindVirus again when you are finished to make sure that all instances have been found.

Finally, you should install ChkVirus or any other cryptographic checksummer on all machines that are potentially infectable to provide an early warning of a recurrence of this or another virus.

4.41.5 Other Information

It is unlikely ever to become common, as it lacks many of the features that an infectious virus needs.

4.41.6 Technical Details

This is another virus that needs 640 k to run as it copies itself up to 9800:0. It defines a new interrupt, number 70h, which is the original interrupt 21h. Interrupt 21h calls the virus, provided it is calling function 3dh or 0fh (open a file).

4.42 Vcomm

Other names: none
Infects: any EXE file on any writable DOS device
Classification: direct action file virus

4.42.1 Recognition and Detection

EXE files are infected, growing by between 637 and 1148 bytes. Attribute, date and time are preserved. The most likely way that this virus will be detected is when it is run on a mono monitor. The first time any disk access is attempted after that, the machine will hang. On a CGA monitor, the virus causes a slight "snow" effect.

4.42.2 How the Virus Copies Itself

When you run an infected EXE file the virus searches the current directory for an uninfected file. If it finds one it infects it. It stores the attribute of the file and sets it to read/write; this is so that it can restore the attribute after infection. Likewise, date and time are preserved in the usual way. If the diskette is write-protected, you'll see a DOS "Write-protect error".

4.42.3 What the Virus Does

The virus installs a small routine that converts all disk writes to reads. This means that as long as it is in memory you cannot create, copy, change or delete a file.

4.42.4 How To Get Rid of It

Boot from a clean DOS disk; this is a DOS diskette that has come from the manufacturer and has never been write-enabled. You can then remove Vcomm by using FindVirus to search for all instances of the virus. Every infected file that you find you can delete and copy a good file in its place. Run FindVirus again when you are finished to make sure that all instances have been found.

Finally, you should install ChkVirus or any other cryptographic checksummer on all machines that are potentially infectable, to provide an early warning of a recurrence of this or another virus.

4.42.5 Other Information

Because of the way that it hangs mono systems it is likely to be easily noticed. Also, the infection mechanism means that it isn't very infectious.

4.42.6 Technical Details

The virus doesn't go memory-resident. The routine to convert writes to reads is installed at 0bffe:0, in video memory, and takes 17h bytes. This means that memory mappers will not find it, but it could be overwritten by a video write. However, it is unlikely that a program will use this corner of memory, and if it does, it just means that next time a disk is accessed the machine will crash. The routine intercepts interrupt 13h, and converts function 3 to 2, and 0bh to 0ah.

The string "*.EXE" is needed to search for files to infect. In the file it is encrypted by subtracting one from each byte ")- DWD".

While the virus is in the middle of infecting an EXE file it renames it to have no extension. So, if the computer hangs in the middle of an infection you won't be left with a partly-infected EXE file. The increase in file size can be calculated thus: round the original program up to a multiple of 512 bytes, then add 637. The virus self-recognition code consists of a check that the first four bytes to be executed match those of the virus.

4.43 More Versions of Cascade (1704)

Other names: Second Austrian, 1704, Blackjack, Autumn, Waterfall
Infects: any COM file on any writable DOS device
Classification: indirect action file virus

4.43.1 Recognition and Detection

Section 4.11 describes the 1701 and 1704 viruses. There are four additional variants of this virus.

4.43.2 How the Virus Copies Itself

All the versions of Cascade use the same copying mechanism.

4.43.3 What the Virus Does

At apparently random times, the virus triggers the "crumble" (see Section 4.11). One of the versions does a low level format of track zero instead.

4.43.4 How To Get Rid of It

Boot from a clean DOS disk; this is a DOS diskette that has come from the manufacturer and has never been write-enabled. This ensures that Cascade is not installed in memory. You can then remove Cascade by using FindVirus to search for all instances of the virus. Every infected file that you find you can delete and copy a good file in its place. Run FindVirus again when you are finished to make sure that all instances have been found.

Finally, you should install ChkVirus or any other cryptographic checksummer on all machines that are potentially infectable to provide an early warning of a recurrence of this or another virus.

4.43.5 Other Information

The main 1701 and 1704 versions are described in Section 4.11. In Yugoslavia, a minor variant of 1704 has been found, where the third byte has been changed from EC to CD hexadecimal. This will stop the virus from working properly. This is called 17Y4.

1704-B looks for IBB where the main versions look for IBM. Also, the date tests have been changed, so that instead of triggering during October to December 1988 it triggers during August to December all years except 1993.

Also omitted is the routine whereby if the virus goes memory-resident when the year is 1980, and the year is then changed to 1989 or after, the crumble is triggered. There are a few other minor changes.

1704-C has the same IBB change as 1704-B and the other details are changed in the same way. The only difference between this and 1704-B is a minor change in the decryption routine and a minor change to the display routine.

1704-Format is another IBB version, with the same change in the date test, except that the month referred to is October, not August. Instead of triggering a screen display, a low level format of heads 0 to 8 on track 0 is done, followed by a beep that continues indefinitely.

4.43.6 Technical Details

As for the main versions (see Section 4.11).

4.44 Syslock

Other names: Macho, 3551
Infects: any COM or EXE file on any writable DOS device
Classification: direct action file virus

4.44.1 Recognition and Detection

COM and EXE files are infected, growing by between 3551 and 3566 bytes; you can calculate this by rounding up the size of the COM file to be a multiple of 16, and then adding 3551. Attribute, date and time are preserved. The infection happens with a small probability each time you run an infected file. Syslock searches through the disk, and might be noticed because of the unusual amount of disk accesses.

4.44.2 How the Virus Copies Itself

When you run an infected file the virus searches the current drive for an uninfected file. It searches through all subdirectories and picks a directory at random. It then picks a file at random in that subdirectory to infect. It stores the attribute of the file and sets it to read/write; this is so that it can restore the attribute after infection. Likewise, date and time are preserved in the usual way. If the diskette is write-protected you'll see a DOS "Write-protect error".

4.44.3 What the Virus Does

If "SYSLOCK=@" is in the environment the virus does nothing, not even infecting (hence the name). Otherwise, it works its way down the disk, 32 sectors at a time, converting each occurrence of "Microsoft" to "Macrosoft" (or "Machosoft" in the Macho variant).

4.44.4 How To Get Rid of It

Boot from a clean DOS disk; this is a DOS diskette that has come from the manufacturer and has never been write-enabled. You can then remove Syslock by using FindVirus to search for all instances of the virus. Every infected file that you find you can delete and copy a good file in its place. Run FindVirus again when you are finished to make sure that all instances have been found.

Finally, you should install ChkVirus or any other cryptographic checksummer on all machines that are potentially infectable to provide an early warning of a recurrence of this or another virus.

4.44.5 Other Information

This virus has been found in the UK. It looks for a DOS subdirectory off the root, and if it finds it, it creates a hidden, system file called "KEYB.PCM", which is two bytes long. It uses this to mark the point it has got to in changing "Microsoft" to "Macrosoft". At offset 2 in the file there is a generation counter.

4.44.6 Technical Details

The virus doesn't go memory-resident which is surprising in such a large virus. The virus is encrypted and decrypts itself at runtime. It uses a different encryption scheme each time it replicates, using a key generated by a random number generator that uses the system clock.

The virus self-recognition code for EXE files is b67ch at offset 12h–13h (where the checksum is). For COM files it is 39h, 28h, 46h, 03h, 03h, 01h at offset 10h.

If there is no DOS subdirectory off the root it cannot create the KEYB.PCM file and doesn't do the "Microsoft" to "Macrosoft" conversion.

4.45 Saturday 14th

Other names: Durban
Infects: any COM or EXE file on any writable DOS device
Classification: indirect action file virus

4.45.1 Recognition and Detection

COM and EXE files are infected, growing by between 669 and 684 bytes; you can calculate this by rounding up the size of the file to be a multiple of 16, and then adding 669. The attribute of the file is preserved, but date and time are not preserved. This means that infected files will have the current system date, which is the way they are likely to be noticed.

The virus uses one of the interrupts that Novell uses, so it will not co-exist with a Novell network.

4.45.2 How the Virus Copies Itself

When you run an infected file, the virus goes memory-resident. Thereafter, every time an uninfected program is loaded the virus infects it. It then picks a file at random in that subdirectory to infect. It stores the attribute of the file and sets it to read/write; this is so that it can restore the attribute after infection. But date and time are not preserved. If the diskette is write-protected, you won't see a DOS "Write-protect error", because the virus suppresses this.

4.45.3 What the Virus Does

On every Saturday 14th it writes 100 sectors of rubbish to the first sectors of drives D, C, B and A, in that order. This will overwrite the boot sector, the FAT and the root directory, on most disks. On larger disks it might only overwrite the boot and the FAT. In any case, the best way to recover after this has happened is to restore a current backup; failing that, a proper data recovery might be required.

This virus demonstrates that it is not wise to set your system clock one day forward on Friday 13th as an anti-virus precaution.

4.45.4 How To Get Rid of It

Boot from a clean DOS disk; this is a DOS diskette that has come from the manufacturer, and has never been write-enabled. You can then remove Saturday 14th by using FindVirus to search for all instances of the virus. Every infected file that you find you can delete and copy a good file in its place. Run FindVirus again when you are finished to make sure that all instances have been found.

Finally, you should install ChkVirus or any other cryptographic checksummer on all machines that are potentially infectable to provide an early warning of a recurrence of this or another virus.

4.45.5 Other Information

This virus has many resemblances to Jerusalem virus; it was almost certainly written by someone who had examined it.

4.45.6 Technical Details

The virus discovers whether it is already in memory by doing an interrupt 21h function 0deh. If 0dfh comes back in ah, it was in memory, otherwise it copies itself to the top of memory, patches the last Memory Control Block to protect itself against being overwritten, and so goes memory-resident. This should evade most active monitoring systems that watch for programs going TSR.

This function of interrupt 21h is used by Novell for the "Set Broadcast Mode" call; if you run this virus on a Novell network the network won't function properly. The virus traps interrupt 21h, and on seeing an attempt to use function 4bh (load and execute a program) it infects the program being loaded.

This is one of the viruses that puts its loader at the beginning of the file, and copies the original program chunk to elsewhere in memory, replacing it back at runtime.

The virus self-recognition code is at the end of infected files; the last four bytes are "ECVt", although the "t" is not part of the recognition. Could "ECV" be the author's initials?

It is very economical to get a memory-resident COM and EXE infector into 669 bytes; it is rather surprising that the author has omitted to preserve the date and time of files on infection.

4.46 June 16th

Other names: Pretoria
Infects: any COM file on any writable DOS device
Classification: direct action file virus

4.46.1 Recognition and Detection

COM files are infected, growing by 879 bytes (or growing to 1758 if they would end up less than that size). Date and time are preserved, but the virus is very visible, as every time an infected program is run the virus scans the whole directory tree, looking for uninfected files to infect, and infecting any it finds.

It scans the current drive, unless there is a command tail (for example, Chkdsk C:) in which case it scans the drive referred to.

4.46.2 How the Virus Copies Itself

When you run an infected file, every COM file on the default disk is infected (or else on the drive referred to in the command). This is the first virus to do this.

It makes the attribute of the file read/write to infect it and doesn't set it back the way it was. But date and time are preserved. If the diskette is write-protected you'll see a DOS "Write-protect error".

4.46.3 What the Virus Does

On every June 16th, it scans through the root directory of the drive it has been looking at. It reads each sector one at a time, and converts any file name it finds to the name "ZAPPED.", with the attribute of a normal file (so subdirectories are no longer subdirectories).

To recover from this (if you don't have a current backup), you have to use a disk sector editor to edit the sectors one at a time, converting the subdirectory attributes back to 10h. File names in subdirectories are not altered.

4.46.4 How To Get Rid of It

Boot from a clean DOS disk; this is a DOS diskette that has come from the manufacturer, and has never been write-enabled. You can then remove June 16th by using FindVirus to search for all instances of the virus. Every infected file that you find you can delete and copy a good file in its place. Run FindVirus again when you are finished to make sure that all instances have been found.

Finally, you should install ChkVirus or any other cryptographic checksummer on all machines that are potentially infectable to provide an early warning of a recurrence of this or another virus.

4.46.5 Other Information

This virus is unlikely to become widespread as the infective process is so noticeable.

4.46.6 Technical Details

The virus self-recognition code is the bytes 0e5h, 095h at locations 7 and 8 bytes offset from the start of the file. This is an encrypted virus, encrypted by xoring each byte with 0a5h.

4.47 Aids

Other names: none
Infects: any non-small COM file on any writable DOS device
Classification: direct action file virus

4.47.1 Recognition and Detection

COM files are overwritten, and become 13 952 bytes if they are less than that. The original program no longer works at all. On colour screens the virus hangs the system.

4.47.2 How the Virus Copies Itself

When you run an infected file, it looks for an uninfected COM file in the current subdirectory, and infects it.

4.47.3 What the Virus Does

Programs no longer work.

4.47.4 How To Get Rid of It

Boot from a clean DOS disk; this is a DOS diskette that has come from the manufacturer, and has never been write-enabled. You can then remove it by using FindVirus to search for all instances of the virus. Every infected file that you find you can delete and copy a good file in its place. Run FindVirus again when you are finished, to make sure that all instances have been found.

Finally, you should install ChkVirus or any other cryptographic checksummer on all machines that are potentially infectable to provide an early warning of a recurrence of this or another virus.

4.47.5 Other Information

This virus is unlikely to ever spread, as the infective process is so noticeable. This virus is nothing to do with the "Aids Information Diskette", a Trojan that was mailed to several thousand users in mid-December 1989. That diskette was a trojan, not a virus.

4.47.6 Technical Details

This virus was written in Turbo Pascal version 3, and it was compiled to run only on monochrome screens. It overwrites files that it infects so that they no longer work. It scarcely deserves to be called a virus.

4.48 4096

Other names: Century, 4K, Frodo
Infects: any executable file on any writable DOS device
Classification: indirect action file virus

4.48.1 Recognition and Detection

Executable files are infected, growing by 4096 bytes. Attribute, date and time are preserved. This virus is highly unlikely to be detected, as it hides itself very well. However, the virus has become corrupted at some point in its travels, and on September 22nd and thereafter it will become more visible (see below for details).

4.48.2 How the Virus Copies Itself

When you run an infected file, the virus goes memory-resident. Thereafter it will infect an executable file if you do one of a variety of operations, such as copying it.

It stores the attribute of the file and sets it to read/write; this is so that it can restore the attribute after infection. Likewise, date and time are preserved in the usual way. If the diskette is write-protected, it will suppress the "Write- protect error".

4.48.3 What the Virus Does

The virus is intended to install a small routine on the partition sector of hard disks, and on the boot sector of any diskette in drive A. When you boot from such a disk, you get a display in large letters made out of block characters that says "FRODO LIVES!", and there is a display like a neon sign around the edge of the screen. This installation is intended to happen on September 22nd and every day thereafter until December 31st. The hard disk is inaccessible, although this is reversible by putting a valid partition record back in place.

In all the instances of the virus that I've seen, the routine to drop this into place is corrupted, and the machine will hang when the routine is called. However, I have seen two versions, and in one this is less corrupt than in the other. Presumably there is a fully operational copy somewhere.

4.48.4 How To Get Rid of It

Removal of 4096 has to be done carefully and systematically. Boot from a clean DOS disk; this is a DOS diskette that has come from the manufacturer, and has never been write-enabled. This is especially vital for this virus, as it will conceal itself completely from any anti-virus program, and it is memory-resident. You should also make certain that you don't run any software that could possibly have become infected.

You can then remove 4096 by using FindVirus to search for all instances of the virus. Every infected file that you find, you can delete, and copy a good file in its place. Run FindVirus again when you are finished, to make sure that all instances have been found. I would suggest that you use the option in FindVirus to check all files, not just executable ones; this will also detect instances where the virus has written itself into data files.

A hopper-fed diskette checker may be useful if a large number of diskettes need looking at.

Finally, you should install ChkVirus or any other cryptographic checksummer on all machines that are potentially infectable, to provide an early warning of a recurrence of this or another virus. Again, it is really important that the run of ChkVirus be done after booting from a known clean diskette, and that ChkVirus be run from a write-protected floppy diskette. If you run ChkVirus (or any other anti-virus software) while this virus is in memory, the virus will filter out all the virus code, and the software will see a clean file.

4.48.5 Other Information

This virus has been found in a number of places. It is very infectious indeed, and spreads very rapidly.

4.48.6 Technical Details

This is a large virus; it is large because it is doing a lot. The main feature of this virus is that it hides itself quite thoroughly.

As a result it has been called a "stealth" virus. When an infected application is run, the virus goes memory-resident, trapping interrupt 21h. It checks for the following functions:

- 30h: the DOS version check. This triggers the boot replacement routine, if it is September 22nd to December 31st
- 11h, 12h, 4eh, 4fh: look for directory entry

- 14h, 21h, 27h, 3fh: read file
- 23h: file size
- 0fh, 3dh: open file
- 3eh: close file
- 3ch: create file
- 3fh: read file
- 40h: write file
- 42h: seek position in file
- 57h: get/set file date/time
- 4bh: load and execute a program
- 48h: allocate memory

In addition, it makes use of the DOS undocumented functions 32h, 37h, 51h and 52h.

By trapping those DOS functions, it ensures that if you use DOS to open and read a file, it can filter out any of the virus bytes, and present only the bytes of the original file.

The virus self-recognition is to add 100 years to the file date; this will not be noticed, even if the virus is not in memory, as DOS only shows you the last two years. If the virus is in memory, then any program looking at the date gets given the original one.

The virus goes memory-resident by direct manipulation of the Memory Control Block chain, in order to evade programs that monitor this activity.

Because of this self-hiding, it is vitally important that all work on infected systems be done after booting from a clean DOS diskette, and all software run on the system must be known to be clean. If an infected program is run, then all executables accessed thereafter will be infected, and this fact will not be noticed by the anti-virus software.

4.49 Chameleon

Other names: 1260
Infects: any COM file on any writable DOS device
Classification: direct action file virus

4.49.1 Recognition and Detection

COM files are infected, growing by an amount that is approximately 1260 bytes. Attribute, date and time are preserved. This virus is unlikely to be detected, as there is no payload. However, if it tries to infect on a write-protected diskette, you'll see the "Write-protect error" message from DOS.

4.49.2 How the Virus Copies Itself

When you run an infected file, the virus searches the directory for an uninfected file, and infects it. It stores the attribute of the file and sets it to read/write; this is so that it can restore the attribute after infection. Likewise, date and time are preserved in the usual way.

4.49.3 What the Virus Does

The virus has no payload. It is based on the book version of 648 virus (Vienna) but the Vienna trojan is omitted.

4.49.4 How To Get Rid of It

Boot from a clean DOS disk; this is a DOS diskette that has come from the manufacturer, and has never been write-enabled. You can then remove the virus by using FindVirus to search for all instances of it. Every infected file that you find, you can delete, and copy a good file in its place. Run FindVirus again when you are finished, to make sure that all instances have been found. I would suggest that you use the option in FindVirus to check all files, not just executable ones.

Finally, you should install ChkVirus or any other cryptographic checksummer on all machines that are potentially infectable, to provide an early warning of a recurrence of this or another virus.

4.49.5 Other Information

This virus has not been seen in the field.

4.49.6 Technical Details

I think that this virus has been written especially for virus researchers. There is no payload, and it is very resistant to anti-virus techniques.

First, the virus is encrypted; this is nothing new, as this idea was pioneered by 1701. When you decrypt it, you find that some parts of the code have a second encryption, which is decrypted at runtime by calling interrupt 3, the one-byte interrupt. But if you single step through the code using Debug, the decryption is disabled, because the virus also uses the single step interrupt.

When this second decryption is broken, you can then write a program to implement it. But that doesn't work, as there are some dummy interrupt 3s that don't get called, and so don't decrypt anything. I ended up using a hexadecimal calculator to decrypt the code.

It is only then that it becomes possible to disassemble the virus, and then you discover the other interesting feature. It is not possible to use the standard search-string technique to locate instances of the virus, as the longest reliable search- string is just two bytes long. The virus uses a different key to do its encryption each time it copies itself, so only the decryptor/loader part is in clear, just like 1701 virus. But it has another trick – the decryptor code is variable; as the virus copies itself, it uses a random number generator to intersperse the parts of the decryptor with instructions that do nothing useful (and do nothing to prevent the decryption). It also makes the code appear in random order, again, subject to the needs of making the decryption actually work.

The decryptor is divided into three parts. First is the setup code; this consists of three instructions to load the registers. These instructions can appear in any order, and can be interspersed with five other instructions that have no effect. The virus picks from these eight instructions until it has all of the necessary three.

The second part of the decryptor is the two XORs. Again, there are five unnecessary instructions, and the virus picks at random from these seven (and a NOP) until the three instructions that are needed are in place. The third part of the decryptor increments the registers before doing the next iteration of the loop. Again, there are two necessary instructions plus a NOP, and five unnecessary instructions, and all of these can appear in any order.

It uses the same virus self-recognition code as Vienna (62 seconds in the date/time field). It also tries to avoid infecting files that are too large or too small, but there is a bug in the code, and it just avoids infecting files that are exactly 0ah or 0f800h bytes long.

It has been necessary to rewrite a number of anti-virus programs that depend on using search-strings, in order to deal with this virus.

4.50 Eddie 2

Other names: 651
Infects: any executable file on any writable DOS device
Classification: indirect action file virus

4.50.1 Recognition and Detection

COM files are infected, growing by 651 bytes. Attribute, date and time are preserved. This virus is unlikely to be detected, as it hides itself well.

4.50.2 How the Virus Copies Itself

When you run an infected file, the virus goes memory-resident. Thereafter it will infect an executable file if you run it.

It sets the attribute of the file to read/write. This is so that it can restore the attribute after infection. Date and time are preserved in the usual way. If the diskette is write- protected, it will suppress the "Write-protect error".

4.50.3 What the Virus Does

There is no payload in this virus.

4.50.4 How To Get Rid of It

Boot from a clean DOS disk; this is a DOS diskette that has come from the manufacturer, and has never been write-enabled.

You can then remove Eddie 2 by using FindVirus to search for all instances of the virus. Every infected file that you find, you can delete, and copy a good file in its place. Run FindVirus again when you are finished, to make sure that all instances have been found. I would suggest that you use the option in FindVirus to check all files, not just executable ones; this will also detect instances where the virus has written itself into data files.

A hopper-fed diskette checker may be useful if a large number of diskettes need looking at.

Finally, you should install ChkVirus or any other cryptographic checksummer on all machines that are potentially infectable, to provide an early warning of a recurrence of this or another virus.

4.50.5 Other Information

This virus is called Eddie 2 because the string "Eddie lives" can be found in the code – this is not displayed by the virus. It may be a reference to Dark Avenger virus, or to the same thing that Dark Avenger is referring to.

When it checks for whether a file is in the EXE format, it looks for "ZM" as the first two bytes, as well as "MZ".

4.50.6 Technical Details

This is a very small virus for one that is a memory-resident COM and EXE infector. It also hides the increase in file size, by trapping interrupt 21h functions 11h and 12h. It avoids small files and large ones; it won't infect a file smaller than 651 bytes or COM files larger than 64 375 bytes.

The virus "Are you in memory?" call is an interrupt 21h, with 0a55ah in AX. If the virus was in memory, 5aa5h is returned in AX. The virus doesn't use DOS services to go memory-resident, or even the MCB chain. It simply copies itself into high memory, and hopes that nothing overwrites it. Of course, if some program does use this memory, it will crash the system.

4.51 Print Screen Virus

Other names: none
Infects: any boot sectors on hard and floppy disks
Classification: boot sector virus

4.51.1 Recognition and Detection

The computer triggers a print screen every now and then.

4.51.2 How the Virus Copies Itself

When you boot from an infected diskette, the virus goes memory-resident; this is true whether the diskette is a boot disk or not. So the usual thing is for someone to have an infected data diskette, which they leave in drive A when they shut down. Next day when they start up the computer, it attempts to boot from that diskette; if it isn't a system diskette, you see the message "Not a system disk. Please insert a system disk and retry" or a similar message. If that diskette was infected, the virus is now in memory, and when you continue to boot it remains there.

While it is in memory, any disk that you access is liable to be infected. If you access the diskette (whether read or write) and the diskette is write-enabled then Print Screen virus will replace the boot sector with its own code, and move the boot sector further up the disk.

4.51.3 What the Virus Does

The first screen dump to the printer is triggered after 32 floppy disk BIOS accesses – this means just a few user accesses. Thereafter the screen dump is triggered every 255 accesses (again, this means BIOS access; only a fraction of that number of user accesses, as each user access means multiple BIOS calls).

This screen dump could cause problems if the printer is not connected or is offline.

4.51.4 How To Get Rid of It

Boot from a clean DOS disk; this is a DOS diskette that has come from the manufacturer, and has never been write-enabled. This ensures that there is nothing unwanted installed in memory. Use FindVirus to determine which diskettes are infected.

Treatment consists of simply copying all the files off an infected diskette (using "COPY *.*"; do not use Diskcopy or any image copier), and reformatting the diskette (see below for details). Alternatively, you could use UnVirus or any virus removal program to remove it from diskettes.

If a large number of diskettes are potentially infected, then you should consider borrowing a hopper-fed diskette cleaning machine, which can handle up to 700 diskettes per hour, sorting them into clean and contaminated bins.

If you have an outbreak of Print Screen, then after it is cleared up you should use Inoculate or any other inoculator on all diskettes. This works by putting the virus's self- recognition code (just two harmless bytes) on the boot sector of the diskette. If the virus sees that signature, it thinks that the diskette is already infected, so doesn't attack it.

In the case of a hard disk, there is likely to be logical damage to files or to the FAT. I would recommend the following procedure, unless you know what you are doing with a disk sector editor.

First boot from a clean DOS disk. Then make two backups of the hard disk (the second backup is in case you find that you have a problem restoring the first backup – defective diskettes are always possible). With most versions of DOS, SYS will replace the boot sector, and you can use FindVirus to check that this has worked. But this will not repair any logical damage (see below).

Alternatively, you can format the hard disk using "FORMAT /S/V" and restore the backup; this has the advantage of reclaiming the fake bad sectors.

4.51.5 Other Information

This virus was found during a routine sweep of some diskettes from India. The bugs in this virus are the worst I've seen; the author has assumed that all hard disks are laid out like a 4-head, 17 sector-per-track, 20 Mb disk under DOS 3, and various problems will happen with other shapes and sizes of disk.

The virus also appears to be very derivative from three older boot sector viruses, Brain, Italian and Stoned.

4.51.6 Technical Details

When the virus infects, it replaces interrupt vector 13h with its own version, revectoring the old routine to interrupt 6dh, which is the interrupt that Brain virus uses. It goes memory- resident using the same method as Italian virus, reserving 2 k by subtracting 2 from location 413h, and copying itself into high memory.

It moves the original boot sector. On a floppy diskette, it moves it to cylinder 0, head 1, sector 3, which is the last directory sector on a 360 k floppy. Unfortunately, other types of floppy disk are laid out differently, and so a 1.2 Mb diskette, for example, will have the third directory sector overwritten. This is the same method, and the same bug, as is used by Stoned virus.

On a hard disk, it moves the original boot sector to cylinder 1, head 3, sector 13. This is the last directory sector on a 20 Mb hard disk (the commonest type in the field). But on other capacities of disk, this would be in a different place. For example, a 32 Mb hard disk has 46 extra FAT sectors, so this would be in the middle of the second copy of the FAT. Likewise, there would be various other problems on various other sizes of disk. The virus does not make any checks of the disk before doing this write.

Even though the original boot is stored in a fixed place, the virus stores the location of the boot, and refers to these stored values in order to load the original boot. It resembles Italian virus in the way it does this.

After 32 BIOS reads of the disk (including hard and floppy), the virus uses interrupt 5 to trigger a screen dump. Thereafter it does a screen dump every 255 BIOS reads.

4.52 Taiwan

Other names: none
Infects: any COM file on any writable DOS device
Classification: direct action file virus

4.52.1 Recognition and Detection

COM files are infected, growing by 708 bytes (or to 1416 bytes if they are smaller than 708). Attribute, date and time are preserved. Program loading is slowed by the long directory search for an uninfected file.

4.52.2 How the Virus Copies Itself

When you run an infected file, the virus searches the disk, through all directories, for an uninfected file, and infects it. If a diskette is write-protected, it will not suppress the "Write-protect error" when it tries to infect.

4.52.3 What the Virus Does

On the eighth day of any month, the trojan is triggered. This displays the message "Greetings from National Central University !Is today sunny?" and it waits for a key to be pressed. Before displaying that message, it writes garbage to the first 320 sectors of the hard disk, starting at the boot sector, overwriting the two copies of the FAT and the root directory. This is done to the current drive (which would usually be drive C) and to drive D.

4.52.4 How To Get Rid of It

Boot from a clean DOS disk; this is a DOS diskette that has come from the manufacturer, and has never been write-enabled. You can then remove Taiwan by using FindVirus to search for all instances of the virus. Every infected file that you find, you can delete, and copy a good file in its place. Run FindVirus again when you are finished, to make sure that all instances have been found.

Finally, you should install ChkVirus or any other cryptographic checksummer on all machines that are potentially infectable, to provide an early warning of a recurrence of this or another virus. You can use Inoculate to prevent files from getting this virus in future.

4.52.5 Other Information

It may be that the author intended that the second drive to be overwritten should be drive C, not D.

4.52.6 Technical Details

The message is encoded in the virus by XORing it with 0adh. The virus self-recognition code is 62 in the seconds field of the time stamp, just as in Vienna virus and others.

The virus replaces the interrupt 16h keyboard handler while it is infecting, with a handler that just returns the letter "g".

4.53 December 24th Virus

Other names: Icelandic
Infects: any EXE file on any writable DOS device
Classification: indirect action file virus

4.53.1 Recognition and Detection

This is a memory-resident EXE infector – COM files are not infected. Files grow as follows: round the file size up to the next multiple of 16, then add 848. So files grow between 848 and 863 bytes. 2 k of memory is used.

4.53.2 How the Virus Copies Itself

Running an infected EXE program makes the virus go memory-resident, and thereafter every EXE program that you run is liable to be infected. There is a counter, which means that only every tenth EXE program run is infected. Date and time are preserved.

The virus does not go memory-resident via the DOS interrupts, so some programs which try to detect viruses going memory- resident may not detect it. Instead, it manipulates the MCBs directly.

Nor does it use interrupt 21h to read and write files, which will mean that many memory-resident virus detectors will not see that activity either, if they assume that all file reads and writes go via interrupt 21h. Instead, it searches memory for the DOS kernel, and makes far calls to that.

4.53.3 What the Virus Does

If the virus goes memory-resident on December 24th, it displays "Gleileg jAl" instead of running your program.

4.53.4 How To Get Rid of It

To get rid of it from an infected system, first boot from a known clean DOS diskette, and run FindVirus (from a write- protected floppy) to spot all infected files. Delete the infected files, and run FindVirus again, to make sure.

4.53.5 Other Information

So far, this virus has only been found in Iceland and Saratoga. Inoculate inoculates files against the virus. The inoculation marks the file so that the virus thinks that the file is already infected, and leaves it alone. It does this by putting the four-byte signature at the end of the file (you'll see the file grow by four bytes). This could be useful as part of a major clean-up operation, to stop a re-infection creeping round as fast as you clean up.

You cannot inoculate against Jerusalem at the same time as Icelandic, as they both use an end-of-file signature. The signature used is: 44h, 18h, 5fh, 19h.

4.53.6 Technical Details

This virus is a development of the Icelandic series. The signature (44h, 18h, 5fh, 19h) is the same, and the code is very similar.

The in-memory self-recognition code is similar, also. Where the Icelandic viruses use the value 0ffh at location 0:37fh to indicate that they are in memory, December 24th uses 0feh at 0:37eh.

One big difference between December 24th and the older Icelandic viruses is that date and time are preserved, and the DOS critical error handler is disabled, to avoid the "Abort, Retry, Ignore" message. But there is a bug in the code here, and it doesn't restore the original interrupt 24h handler. If there is a critical error, the machine is likely to hang.

December 24th goes TSR by manipulating the Memory Control Blocks directly, so many memory-resident programs that watch for something going TSR will not spot this. Also, it doesn't use interrupt 21h for file reading and writing. Instead, it searches for the int 21h code, and makes a far call to the routines there. The purpose of this is to defeat anti-virus software that detects illegal writes to EXE or COM files.

4.54 Number of the Beast

Other names: NotB, V512, 666
Infects: any COM file on any writable DOS device
Classification: indirect action file virus

4.54.1 Recognition and Detection

COM files are infected, but they don't grow. Attribute, date and time are preserved. This virus is highly unlikely to be detected, as it hides itself very well. Some of the DOS utilities give inappropriate error messages.

4.54.2 How the Virus Copies Itself

When you run an infected file, the virus goes memory-resident. Thereafter it will infect a COM file if you do one of a variety of operations, such as copying it, executing it or reading it.

4.54.3 What the Virus Does

This virus has no payload – it appears to have been written as an exercise in using the internals of DOS. However, if you do not have the virus in memory, and copy an infected file, the copy is likely not to work.

4.54.4 How To Get Rid of It

Removal of NotB has to be done carefully and systematically. Boot from a clean DOS disk; this is a DOS diskette that has come from the manufacturer, and has never been write-enabled. This is especially vital for this virus, as it will conceal itself completely from any anti-virus program if it is memory- resident. You should also make certain that you don't run any software on the machine that could possibly have become infected.

You can then remove NotB by using FindVirus to search for all instances of the virus. Every infected file that you find, you can delete, and copy a good file in its place. Run FindVirus again when you are finished, to make sure that all instances have been found. I would suggest that you use the option in FindVirus to check all files, not just executable ones; this will also detect instances where the virus has written itself into data files.

A hopper-fed diskette checker may be useful if a large number of diskettes need looking at.

Finally, you should install ChkVirus or any other cryptographic checksummer on all machines that are potentially infectable, to provide an early warning of a recurrence of this or another virus. Again, it is really important that the run of ChkVirus be done after booting from a known clean diskette, and that ChkVirus be run from a write-protected floppy diskette. If you run ChkVirus (or any other anti-virus software) while this virus is in memory, the virus will filter out all the virus code, and the software will see a clean file.

4.54.5 Other Information

The virus is "signed" with the signature "666" at the end; hence the name. There are six versions of it.

4.54.6 Technical Details

This is an extremely interesting virus. It uses a lot of undocumented features of DOS to work.

It starts off by checking to see what DOS it is running under. If this has the minor version 30 or above (for example, DOS 3.30, 3.31, etc.) then it calls interrupt 2fh to get the address of the original interrupt 13h (before DOS was loaded). This means that it has the address of the disk interrupt, before any anti-virus active monitor program is loaded, which means that the active monitor won't notice what it is doing.

Next, it checks to see if it is in memory using a fast method and a slower way; it looks at one word of memory, and if that is correct, it checks the whole 512 bytes. If the virus is already in memory, the original program is run, otherwise the virus goes memory-resident.

This virus goes memory-resident in a most unusual way – it takes over one of DOS's buffers, and marks it as unavailable by DOS. So memory checkers will not see it in memory. To do this, it uses a large number of undocumented features of DOS. It uses interrupt 52h, the list of lists, to discover where the DOS buffers are, and it changes the pointer to the first buffer so that it points to the second one instead – that gives it the 512 bytes it needs. It uses the top of memory as its work space (which will just mean that COMMAND.COM will have to reload itself).

At this point, the virus has taken over interrupt 21h, and every time a program is loaded or a file is read or closed, the virus does extra work. When a file is read, the virus filters out the virus code, so that cryptographic checksummers and virus finders only see the original file. It is particularly important to boot from a clean DOS disk when looking for this virus.

On the disk, the virus replaces the first sector of the file with its own 512 bytes; files must be at least 512 bytes long to be infected. The 512 bytes that were at the start of the original file are copied to the end of the file. But the file is not increased in length, the 512 bytes are put into the slack space at the end of the file, between the end of the file and the end of the cluster, where they will not be apparent. Also, files must be less than 63 k to be infected. If there isn't enough slack space in the last cluster, the file isn't infected.

It uses two methods to recognise itself in a file, a fast way and a certain method. The fast way is to change the seconds field to 62; this means that it can check files without having to open and read the file. If it finds that a file isn't infected this way, it infects it. But if it finds that the file has the 62 seconds marker, it then checks the first 512 bytes of the file, comparing byte for byte, to see if it really is infected, or if it has just had the time field changed. So you can't inoculate against this virus.

The virus doesn't make DOS calls to manipulate the file it is infecting. Instead, it finds the system File Control Block (FCB) by using an undocumented DOS call, and then the virus manipulates it directly. So, for example, it opens the file as read-only, but then changes the FCB to make it writable.

If you copy an infected file while the virus is in memory, you will get a working, but infected, copy. If you copy the file before the virus has gone memory-resident, then the 512 bytes in the slack space will be left behind, so part of the file will be missing. If you run this copy, the whole of the virus is there, so the virus will go memory-resident, and infect subsequent programs loaded (probably starting with COMMAND.COM). But the program will not work.

At one point in the infection process, the virus copies itself into the upper half of the Interrupt Vector Table (0:200 to 0:3ff). This could cause a problem if there are any processes using these interrupts.

Because of this self-hiding, it is vitally important that all work on infected systems be done after booting from a clean DOS diskette, and all software run on the system must be known to be clean. If an infected program is run, then all executables accessed thereafter will be infected, and this fact will not be noticed by the anti-virus software.

4.55 Devil's Dance

Other names: none
Infects: any COM file on any writable DOS device
Classification: indirect action file virus

4.55.1 Recognition and Detection

When you reboot you get the following message, displayed on a textured background:

> Have you ever danced with the devil under the weak light of the moon?
> Pray for your disk!
> TheJoker …
> Ha Ha Ha Ha Ha Ha Ha Ha Ha Ha

The virus adds 941 bytes to an infected file, but it usually does multiple infections of files. The file's date and time are not preserved, which is rather noticeable. Because the COM files keep on growing, they will eventually exceed the 64 k limit of a COM file. At that time, when you load the program you will get the following message from DOS:

> Program too big to fit in memory

4.55.2 How the Virus Copies Itself

When you run an infected file, the virus goes memory-resident. Thereafter it will infect a COM file if you execute it.

4.55.3 What the Virus Does

Every time you reboot, you get the message above displayed slowly on the screen. If you reboot after the virus has gone memory-resident and you have entered a few thousand keystrokes, after displaying this message it overwrites your partition record with garbage. This means that when you next start up the computer, it will seem to have no hard disk. After a few keystrokes, each character displayed on the screen is in a different colour.

4.55.4 How To Get Rid of It

Boot from a clean DOS disk; this is a DOS diskette that has come from the manufacturer, and has never been write-enabled. You can then remove Devil's Dance by using FindVirus to search for all instances of the virus. Every infected file that you find, you can delete, and copy a good file in its place. Run FindVirus again when you are finished, to make sure that all instances have been found.

Finally, you should install ChkVirus or any other cryptographic checksummer on all machines that are potentially infectable, to provide an early warning of a recurrence of this or another virus.

4.55.5 Other Information

The virus is "signed' with the signature "Drk" in memory, to prevent multiple memory usage.

4.55.6 Technical Details

This virus uses direct manipulation of MCBs to go memory-resident. It hooks interrupt 9 to intercept the Ctrl-Alt-Del keystroke. The virus uses interrupt 11h to determine what monitor is attached, but uses them incorrectly. Also, there doesn't appear to be any attempt to determine whether a file is already infected, so files continue to grow indefinitely. When a COM file is bigger than 64 k, it will fail to load.

4.56 More Versions of Vienna

Other names: VHP
Infects: any COM file on any writable DOS device
Classification: direct action file virus

4.56.1 Recognition and Detection

COM files between 10 and 64 000 bytes are infected, growing by a number of bytes that depends on the version. Attribute, date and time are preserved.

4.56.2 How the Virus Copies Itself

When you run an infected file, the virus searches the disk for an uninfected file, and infects it. It first looks at the current subdirectory, and then down the path. If a diskette is write-protected, it will not suppress the "Write-protect error" when it tries to infect; other versions do suppress this.

4.56.3 What the Virus Does

On some versions, one file in eight has a trojan patched into the first five bytes. This damage can be either a reboot, or a low level format (see below). It marks infected files by putting a figure of 62 into the seconds field of the date/time stamp.

4.56.4 How To Get Rid of It

Boot from a clean DOS disk; this is a DOS diskette that has come from the manufacturer, and has never been write-enabled. You can then remove the virus by using FindVirus to search for all instances of the virus. Every infected file that you find, you can delete, and copy a good file in its place. Run FindVirus again when you are finished, to make sure that all instances have been found.

Finally, you should install ChkVirus or any other cryptographic checksummer on all machines that are potentially infectable, to provide an early warning of a recurrence of this or another virus. You can use Inoculate to prevent files from getting this virus in future.

4.56.5 Other Information

648 (Vienna, Austrian) virus was published in a freely available book. It reached Bulgaria in this form, and was then worked on by various programmers, creating new versions.

The viruses described below are all nearly functionally equivalent to the original, but there seems to have been several attempts to reduce the byte-count of the virus.

4.56.6 Technical Details

648 version The far jump at the end has become corrupted, so that instead of jumping to the location that causes a reboot, it jumps to a random place. There is also a version with this location correct.

627 version If you assemble the disassembly with MASM, it optimises the code slightly by omitting unnecessary zeros. This reduces the virus size to 627 bytes. In this version, a bug has been introduced and the one-in-eight routine has been disabled, so the damage routine is never called.

623 version A critical error handler has been added, so that DOS will no longer give any "Write-protect error" if it tries to infect a write-protected diskette. The damage routine has been re-enabled, and changed to a far jump to c800:0. This is perhaps intended to be a low level format, but in fact will try to execute the BIOS signature, and the computer will probably hang.

435 version This is very much smaller, because the stack is used for storage instead of local variables in the virus. The critical error handler is still there, but the damage routine is changed to a jump to c800:5, which is the low level format routine on many hard disk controllers. However, this is not as bad as it sounds, as the routine on the controller asks a number of questions before it does the format.

367 version The virus is essentially the same as 435, but the jump is changed to c800:6 (this is the location used by OMTI controllers for the low level format routine), and there is a cunning coding trick that allows an area of code to be used in multiple roles, saving bytes.

353 version As 367, with a few more optimisations.

348 version As 353, more optimisations.

4.57 Pixel Virus

Other names: none
Infects: any COM file on any writable DOS device
Classification: direct action file virus

4.57.1 Recognition and Detection

COM files are infected, growing them by a number of bytes that depends on the version. Attribute, date and time are preserved in some versions, not in others.

4.57.2 How the Virus Copies Itself

When you run an infected file, the virus searches the disk for an uninfected file, and infects it. It only looks at the current subdirectory, and it infects all the files in it. If a diskette is write-protected, it will not suppress the "Write- protect error" when it tries to infect.

4.57.3 What the Virus Does

There is a counter that keeps track of the generation number of the virus. After the fifth generation, when you run an infected file there is a 50 per cent probability of getting the following message: "Program sick error:Call doctor or buy PIXEL for cure description".

4.57.4 How To Get Rid of It

Boot from a clean DOS disk; this is a DOS diskette that has come from the manufacturer, and has never been write-enabled. You can then remove the virus by using FindVirus to search for all instances of the virus. Every infected file that you find, you can delete, and copy a good file in its place. Run FindVirus again when you are finished, to make sure that all instances have been found.

Finally, you should install ChkVirus or any other cryptographic checksummer on all machines that are potentially infectable, to provide an early warning of a recurrence of this or another virus. You can use Inoculate or any other inoculator to prevent files from getting this virus in future.

4.57.5 Other Information

This virus was allegedly published in a Greek computer magazine, as a program in Basic; when you run the program, it creates a COM file which is the virus. It reached Bulgaria in this form, and was then worked on by various programmers, creating new versions.

The viruses described below are all nearly functionally equivalent to the original, but seem to have been attempts to reduce the byte-count of the virus.

4.57.6 Technical Details

847 version This is the original version. The virus self-recognition code is "IV" in bytes 3 and 4 in the file. If a file is read-only, it will not infect it.

345 version The main difference is that in the 847 version, there is a major bug concerning the length of the virus, so that what is copied is far too long. 345 corrects this bug. The VSC is now at bytes 2 and 3.

299 version Date and time are preserved by the virus, and the virus uses the default DTA instead of defining a local one, which economises on byte-count.

4.58 NJH

Other names: none
Infects: the partition sector of hard disks, the boot sector of floppies
Classification: partition sector virus

4.58.1 Recognition and Detection

If this infects a hard disk, it makes it inaccessible. Memory is reduced by 2 k at the top, to make space to store the virus.

4.58.2 How the Virus Copies Itself

When you boot from an infected diskette, the virus goes memory-resident; this is true whether the diskette is a boot disk or not. So the usual thing is for someone to have an infected data diskette, which they leave in drive A when they shut down. Next day when they start up the computer it attempts to boot from that diskette; if it isn't a system diskette, you see the message "Not a system disk. Please insert a system disk and retry" or a similar message. If that diskette was infected the virus is now in memory, and when you continue the boot, it remains there.

While the virus is in memory, any disk that you access is liable to be infected. If you access the diskette with a read and the diskette is write-enabled then NJH will replace the boot sector with its own code and move the boot sector further up the disk.

4.58.3 What the Virus Does

No intentional damage is done. But because the place that NJH stores the original boot sector does not change according to the kind of diskette it infects, it causes problems on 1.2 Mb floppies if they have more than 32 files, by overwriting the directory entries for files 33 to 48, and would also cause problems on 3½-inch diskettes. There is a test in the virus to avoid infecting hard disks, but there is a bug in the test and it infects all hard disks, making them inaccessible.

4.58.4 How To Get Rid of It

You can use FindVirus to detect NJH, and a sector editor will confirm it, since the partition sector (boot sector on diskettes) has the distinctive message.

Boot from a clean DOS disk; this is a DOS diskette that has come from the manufacturer, and has never been write-enabled. This ensures that there is nothing unwanted installed in memory. Use FindVirus to determine which diskettes are infected. Treatment consists of simply copying all the files off an infected diskette (using "COPY *.*"; do not use Diskcopy or any image copier), and reformatting the diskette (see below for details). Alternatively, you can use UnVirus or any virus removal program to remove the infection from a diskette; UnVirus is a lot faster.

In the case of a hard disk, you could use a disk sector editor. Find the original partition sector (it will be at cylinder 0, head 1, sector 3), and copy it back to the place where it should be, at Physical Sector Number zero (0, 0, 1). Unfortunately, by putting the original boot sector at (0, 1, 3), NJH will have overwritten one of the FAT sectors.

So you will also have to copy the good version of that FAT sector from the second copy of the FAT to the first copy.

If you have a good set of backups, then you can use an alternative, and much easier (but more long winded) method. First boot from a clean DOS disk. Then do a low level format of the hard disk, remembering to mark any bad tracks on the bad track map. Many hard disk controllers will trigger a low level format if you load up Debug, and type "G=C800:5" (some controllers might want 6, or CCC instead of 5). Even better, you might have a low level formatting utility (which might be called HDFMT, HDPREP or something like that) that came with your computer, or possibly the diagnostics diskette would have this on. There are also programs available that allow low level formatting, such as Disk Manager and Speedstor.

When the disk is formatted, it must be partitioned using FDISK (some hard disk formatters do this as part of the formatting process). After partitioning the disk, it must be high level formatted using "FORMAT /S/V". Check the disk again with FindVirus, and then restore the backup.

If a large number of diskettes are potentially infected, then you should consider borrowing a hopper-fed diskette cleaning machine, which can handle up to 700 diskettes per hour, sorting them into clean and contaminated bins.

If you have an outbreak of NJH, then after it is cleared up you could use Inoculate or any other inoculator on all diskettes. This works by putting the NJH signature (just two harmless bytes) on the boot sector of the diskette. If NJH sees that signature, it thinks that the diskette is already infected, so doesn't attack it.

4.58.5 Other Information

The virus is quite small – only about 400 bytes of code. It has been found in the field in the UK, at an academic site. There is a message on the boot sector of infected diskettes that doesn't get displayed: "virse program messge Njh to Lbc".

The virus also puts on the diskette the bytes that inoculate against Brain and also Italian virus, so clearly the virus author had access to the code of these. The virus self- recognition code is "Eh" as bytes 6 and 7.

4.58.6 Technical Details

NJH virus is a partition sector virus on hard disks. On floppy disks it is a boot sector virus, as floppies don't have a partition sector. On floppy disks it puts the original boot sector at cylinder 0, head 1, sector 3. On a 360 k floppy this puts it on the last sector of the directory, and will only cause trouble if there are more than 96 files on the diskette. On a 1.2 Mb floppy this is the third sector of the directory, and will give big problems if there are more than 32 files on the diskette. Other diskettes can likewise suffer. There is a test in the virus to stop it copying itself to hard disks; it tests to see if the physical device number is greater than 1 (hard disks are 128, 80h). But the test is wrongly coded, and although it won't copy itself to drives 2 to 127, it will infect device 128 and above.

Because the virus author thought that hard disks would not be infected, no provision was made for treating them differently. So on hard disks, the original partition record is copied to cylinder 0, head 1, sector 3, and this (on most hard disks) is the second sector of the first copy of the FAT.

4.59 EDV

Other names: none
Infects: the partition sector of hard disks, the boot sector of floppies
Classification: partition sector virus

4.59.1 Recognition and Detection

Hard disks become non-bootable, although accessible. Memory is not reduced by the virus. The damage routine is very noticeable.

4.59.2 How the Virus Copies Itself

When you boot from an infected diskette, the virus goes memory-resident; this is true whether the diskette is a boot disk or not. So the usual thing is for someone to have an infected data diskette, which they leave in drive A when they shut down. Next day when they start up the computer, it attempts to boot from that diskette; if it isn't a system diskette, you see the message "Not a system disk. Please insert a system disk and retry" or a similar message. If that diskette was infected the virus is now in memory, and when you continue the boot, it remains there.

While the virus is in memory, any disk that you access is liable to be infected. If you access the diskette and the diskette is write-enabled then EDV will replace the boot sector with its own code and move the boot sector further up the disk.

4.59.3 What the Virus Does

While the virus is in memory, it counts the number of diskettes that it infects. After it infects the sixth diskette, the damage routine is triggered (the count starts again if the computer is rebooted).

The damage routine writes garbage over the first and second hard disk, then over the first four floppy diskette drives. In practice, this will mean all drives, on most computers. The garbage is written onto cylinders 0 and 1, heads 0 to 3. This will overwrite the partition, the boot, both copies of the FAT and the directory, on most disks.

It then displays "That rings a bell, no ? From Cursy".

4.59.4 How To Get Rid of It

You can use FindVirus to detect EDV, and a sector editor will confirm it, since the partition sector (boot sector on diskettes) has the distinctive message "MSDOS Vers. E.D.V.".

Boot from a clean DOS disk; this is a DOS diskette that has come from the manufacturer, and has never been write-enabled. This ensures that there is nothing unwanted installed in memory. Use FindVirus to determine which diskettes are infected.

Treatment consists of simply copying all the files off an infected diskette (using "COPY *.*"; do not use Diskcopy or any image copier), and reformatting the diskette. Alternatively, you can use UnVirus or any virus removal program to remove the infection from a diskette; UnVirus is a lot faster.

In the case of a hard disk, you could use a disk sector editor. Find the original partition sector (it will be at cylinder 39, head 1, sector 8), and copy it back to the place where it should be, at Physical Sector Number zero (0, 0, 1). Unfortunately, by putting the original boot sector at (39, 0, 8), EDV will have partly overwritten a file or sub-directory.

If you have a good set of backups, then you can use an alternative, and much easier (but more long winded) method. First boot from a clean DOS disk. Then do a low level format of the hard disk, remembering to mark any bad tracks on the bad track map. Many hard disk controllers will trigger a low level format if you load up Debug, and type "G=C800:5" (some controllers might want 6, or CCC instead of 5). Even better, you might have a low level formatting utility (which might be called HDFMT, HDPREP or something like that) that came with your computer, or possibly the diagnostics diskette would have this on. There are also programs available that allow low level formatting, such as Disk Manager and Speedstor.

When the disk is formatted it must be partitioned, using FDISK (some hard disk formatters do this as part of the formatting process). After partitioning the disk, it must be high level formatted using "FORMAT /S/V". Check the disk again with FindVirus, and then restore the backup.

If a large number of diskettes are potentially infected then you should consider borrowing a hopper-fed diskette cleaning machine, which can handle up to 700 diskettes per hour, sorting them into clean and contaminated bins.

If you have an outbreak of EDV, then after it is cleared up you could use Inoculate or any other inoculator on all diskettes. This works by putting the EDV signature (just two harmless bytes) on the boot sector of the diskette. If EDV sees that signature, it thinks that the diskette is already infected, so doesn't attack it.

4.59.5 Other Information

The virus is quite small – only about 400 bytes of code. It has been found in the field in the UK, but was first found in the US.

EDV also installs a replacement keyboard handler that will, under certain circumstances, simply hang the machine. The circumstance that it is looking for is a certain relationship between the segment registers CS, DS and ES.

4.59.6 Technical Details

EDV virus is a partition sector virus on hard disks. On floppy disks it is a boot sector virus, as floppies don't have a partition sector. It puts the original boot sector at cylinder 39, head 1, sector 8. On a 320 k floppy, this puts it on the last sector of the disk; DOS 1.1 formats diskettes this way. So sector 39, 1, 8 is guaranteed to exist on anything except a single sided floppy.

When it goes memory-resident, it searches memory from E800h downwards in increments of 1000h, omitting B800h (as this is screen memory). It does this by writing 1881h to the location, and reading it back. So, for example, if there is RAM memory at D800h, it will use that. If it doesn't find any memory above the 640 k, it will put itself at 9800h.

When it is copied to that location, it makes no attempt to protect itself from being overwritten by another program; the intent is that it will make copies of itself before that happens. When it does, the computer will hang when it accesses a disk drive.

The virus self-recognition is "EV" in bytes 510 and 511 on the disk boot sector. The message that it displays is not visible; it is encrypted by subtracting 5 from each byte.

If the virus is in memory, it tries to hide the virus on the disk. If you try to read sector 0, 0, 1, the virus reads the original boot sector at 39, 1, 8 and substitutes that, so the disk looks normal. If you try to read sector 39, 1, 8, it appears to be unreadable. The virus detects the attempt to read that sector, and returns an error code 1 to the calling program, which will be interpreted as "Sector not found" or a similar error message by the reading program.

The substitution of the boot sector doesn't work reliably; it is sometimes possible to do a BIOS read that shows you the infected sector.

4.60 Eight Tunes

Other names: none
Infects: any executable file on any writable DOS device
Classification: indirect action file virus

4.60.1 Recognition and Detection

COM files between 8177 and 63 310 bytes are infected, growing by 1971 bytes. EXE files greater than 8177 are infected. Attribute, date and time are preserved.

4.60.2 How the Virus Copies Itself

When you run an infected file, the virus goes memory-resident. Thereafter it infects each program that you run. If a diskette is write-protected, you will not see the "Write-protect error" when it tries to infect; the virus suppresses this.

4.60.3 What the Virus Does

When a file is first infected, the virus stores the current date as the number of days since January 1st 1984. When you run an infected file and the system date is 91 days or more after that, it chooses a tune from a repertoire of eight, and plays it – this happens about 30 minutes afterwards. The tune most likely to be recognised is "Auld Lang Syne", the others are "Nobody knows the trouble I've seen", four German rambling songs, a series of random notes, and the interrupt 8 handler re-interpreted as music.

After it has played the first tune, it waits for a few minutes and repeats the choice of a random tune, and thereafter continues to play a tune every few minutes.

4.60.4 How To Get Rid of It

Boot from a clean DOS disk; this is a DOS diskette that has come from the manufacturer, and has never been write-enabled. You can then remove the virus by using FindVirus to search for all instances of the virus. Every infected file that you find, you can delete, and copy a good file in its place. Run FindVirus again when you are finished, to make sure that all instances have been found.

Finally, you should install ChkVirus or any other cryptographic checksummer on all machines that are potentially infectable, to provide an early warning of a recurrence of this or another virus. You can use Inoculate to prevent files from getting this virus in future.

4.60.5 Other Information

This virus was first found in Germany, as a result of an initiative by a magazine.

4.60.6 Technical Details

The virus does the in-memory self-recognition in a similar way to 1813; it puts 0e00fh into AX and calls interrupt 21h. If AX returns with 4c31 then the virus was already in memory. The on-disk self-recognition is to compare 13 bytes near the end of the file, with the same bytes in the virus.

The virus uses MCB manipulation to go memory-resident, to avoid detection.

While the virus is in memory, every time a program is loaded the following happens. The virus looks at memory location 0:1c2h, (the segment for interrupt 70h, which services IRQ8, the real-time clock). It looks at the location in memory that has this as the segment, and 103h as the offset, and if it finds 0bah there, it zeros offset 156h. In any case, it calls interrupt 21h with 0ff0fh in AX, and zeros AX if it doesn't contain 101h. Interrupt 21h function ffh will do a warm boot on some computers.

4.61 Dark Avenger 3

Other names: V2000
Infects: any executable file on any writable DOS device
Classification: indirect action file virus

4.61.1 Recognition and Detection

Files larger than 1958 bytes are infected, growing by 2000 bytes. Attribute, date and time are preserved.

4.61.2 How the Virus Copies Itself

When you run an infected file, the virus goes memory-resident. Thereafter it infects each program that you run. It also infects if you open, rename or get the attribute of a file. If a diskette is write-protected, you will not see the "Write-protect error" when it tries to infect; the virus suppresses this.

4.61.3 What the Virus Does

When a program containing a copyright message from Vesselin Bontchev is run, the system hangs. Vesselin is a Bulgarian virus researcher.

4.61.4 How To Get Rid of It

Boot from a clean DOS disk; this is a DOS diskette that has come from the manufacturer, and has never been write-enabled. You can then remove the virus by using FindVirus to search for all instances of the virus. Every infected file that you find, you can delete, and copy a good file in its place. Run FindVirus again when you are finished, to make sure that all instances have been found.

Finally, you should install ChkVirus or any other cryptographic checksummer on all machines that are potentially infectable, to provide an early warning of a recurrence of this or another virus.

4.61.5 Other Information

This virus was first found in Bulgaria. It is "signed" with the signature "666", the same as 512 virus – it also uses many of the ideas in that virus. The text "Copy me - I want to travel" is in the virus, but not displayed.

4.61.6 Technical Details

The virus uses several tricks to use the interrupt 13h from before any anti-virus software was installed. It uses an undocumented DOS call if it is running under DOS 3.31 or above, it looks for the firmware of two controllers and it checks interrupt 40h to see if it is the original firmware routine. If it finds anything this way, it substitutes it for the one that is currently in place. Some of this code is very like Dark Avenger.

The virus does the in-memory self-recognition in a similar way to 512; it checks one word in memory, and if that is correct it checks the whole area where the virus should be, byte for byte. To go TSR, it manipulates the MCB chain directly, to avoid detection.

It uses other undocumented features of DOS – for example, to discover what drive a file is on, and to get the parameters of that drive.

This is the only virus known so far that sets the DOS verify off before infecting, and resets it back the way it was afterwards.

If the virus is in memory, then it conceals its presence on disk; if you do a DIR, the file sizes appear to be the same, as the virus intercepts DOS functions 11h and 12h. The on-disk self-recognition code is 62 in the seconds field of the file date/time. If the virus is in memory, it also conceals the 62 in the seconds field, replacing it with a zero.

4.62 Virus-90

Other names: none
Infects: any COM file on drives A or B
Classification: direct action file virus

4.62.1 Recognition and Detection

Files grow by 857 bytes. Attribute, date and time are preserved. If the diskette is write-protected, the "Write-protect error" is suppressed.

4.62.2 How the Virus Copies Itself

When you run an infected file, the virus looks for the next uninfected COM file in the directory, and infects it. Whenever you run an infected program, it first displays "Infected! " before running the program.

4.62.3 What the Virus Does

When an infected file is run on the 9th, 18th or 27th of the month, a display is triggered. The display consists of white bars moving down the screen from the top – after a period of this, the computer is rebooted.

4.62.4 How To Get Rid of It

Boot from a clean DOS disk; this is a DOS diskette that has come from the manufacturer, and has never been write-enabled. You can then remove the virus by using FindVirus to search for all instances of the virus. Every infected file that you find, you can delete, and copy a good file in its place. Run FindVirus again when you are finished, to make sure that all instances have been found.

Finally, you should install ChkVirus or any other cryptographic checksummer on all machines that are potentially infectable, to provide an early warning of a recurrence of this or another virus.

4.62.5 Other Information

This virus is the only known virus that has the author's name and address in the original copy. It was written as a demonstration, so that people could safely "experiment" with it – hence the fact that it avoids infecting drives other than A or B.

4.62.6 Technical Details

The "Infected!" message is checksummed, and if the checksum is incorrect, the infected program halts. The virus tests to see what drive it is running from, and only infects if it is A or B.

The code of the virus is an exercise in obfuscation. Additional bytes are inserted in the code, with jumps around them, so that disassembler programs become confused. Interrupt 3s are scattered throughout the code; without any function, but again adding to the work of disassembly. Elsewhere, interrupt 3 is used to call interrupt 21h, which would hinder the use of Debug. Where any normal program would move a value into AX before calling an interrupt 21h, this virus frequently relies on a previous value in AX, and adds or subtracts from that to give the necessary value.

It checks to see if an active monitor program is installed in memory, by testing the location of interrupt 21h compared with interrupt 13h. Addresses are calculated in an obscure way, too. The virus uses the fact that addresses will "wrap around" when the offset exceeds 64 k.

The virus self-identification code for disk files is a value of 62 in the seconds field of the date/time.

Most viruses that suppress the DOS critical error message do so by defining their own simple handler. This virus uses the interrupt 4 handler, and revectors interrupt 24h to point to that.

4.63 Zapper

Other names: none
Infects: the partition sector of hard disks, the boot sector of floppies in drive A
Classification: partition sector virus

4.63.1 Recognition and Detection

You might find that the directories of 1.2 Mb diskettes are being corrupted.

4.63.2 How the Virus Copies Itself

When you boot from an infected diskette, the virus goes memory-resident; this is true whether the diskette is a boot disk or not. So the usual thing is for someone to have an infected data diskette, which they leave in drive A when they shut down. Next day when they start up the computer, it attempts to boot from that diskette; if it isn't a system diskette, you see the message. "Not a system disk. Please insert a system disk and retry" or a similar message. If that diskette was infected the virus is now in memory, and when you continue the boot, it remains there. It is also written immediately to the partition sector of the hard disk, if one is present.

While the virus is in memory, any disk that you access is liable to be infected. If you access the diskette (whether read or write) and the diskette is write-enabled then Zapper will replace the boot sector with its own code and move the boot sector further up the disk.

4.63.3 What the Virus Does

Randomly (using the system clock), one infection in 256 triggers the trojan. This consists of overwriting the first 16 tracks of the disk, followed by a screen message "I ZAPPED YOU!"

Because the place that Zapper stores the original boot sector does not change according to the kind of diskette it infects, it causes problems on 1.2 Mb floppies if they have more than 32 files, by overwriting the directory entries for files 33 to 48, and would also cause problems on 3½-inch diskettes. On a small percentage of hard disks it over-writes part of the FAT, because it assumes that cylinder zero, head zero has nothing on it after the partition sector, whereas there are some disks that begin the DOS partition immediately after the partition sector.

4.63.4 How To Get Rid of It

You can use FindVirus to detect Zapper, and a disk sector editor will confirm it, since the partition sector (boot sector on diskettes) has the distinctive message.

Boot from a clean DOS disk; this is a DOS diskette that has come from the manufacturer, and has never been write-enabled. This ensures that there is nothing unwanted installed in memory. Use FindVirus to determine which diskettes are infected.

Treatment consists of simply copying all the files off an infected diskette (using "COPY *.*"; do not use Diskcopy or any image copier), and reformatting the diskette (see below for details). Alternatively, you can use UnVirus or any virus removal program to remove the infection from a diskette; UnVirus is a lot faster.

In the case of a hard disk, you could use a disk sector editor. Find the original partition sector (it will be at cylinder 0, head 0, sector 7, although there is another version which puts it at 0, 0, 2) and copy it back to the place where it should be, at Physical Sector Number zero. I would recommend that you take a full backup before doing this, as if you get it wrong, you could make your disk inaccessible.

If the hard disk is the kind that has the boot sector immediately after the partition sector, Zapper will have overwritten one sector of the first copy of the FAT. In order to recover the data from the hard disk, it will be necessary to copy the genuine partition sector back to cylinder 0, head 0, sector 1, and to make a copy of the relevant sector from the second copy of the FAT, onto the sector that Zapper has corrupted.

An alternative, and much easier (but more long winded) method, is as follows. First boot from a clean DOS disk. Then make two backups of the hard disk (the second backup is in case you find that you have a problem restoring the first backup). Then do a low level format of the hard disk, remembering to mark any bad tracks on the bad track map. Many hard disk controllers will trigger a low level format if you load up Debug, and type "G=C800:5" (some controllers might want 6, or CCC instead of 5). Even better, you might have a low level formatting utility (which might be called HDFMT, HDPREP or something like that) that came with your computer, or possibly the diagnostics diskette would have this on. There are also programs available that allow low level formatting, such as Disk Manager and Speedstor.

When the disk is formatted, it must be partitioned, using FDISK (some hard disk formatters do this as part of the formatting process). After partitioning the disk, it must be high level formatted using "FORMAT /S/V". Check the disk again with FindVirus, and then restore the backup.

You can also inoculate against this virus, using Inoculate or any other inoculator program; this can help deal with a widespread outbreak of the virus.

If a large number of diskettes are potentially infected, then you should consider borrowing a hopper-fed diskette cleaning machine, which can handle up to 700 diskettes per hour, sorting them into clean and contaminated bins.

4.63.5 Other Information

The virus is quite small – only about 500 bytes of code. It has been found in the field in the UK.

4.63.6 Technical Details

Zapper virus is a partition sector virus, and works in a very similar way to Stoned virus. On hard disks, it hides itself by existing in a place that most people don't even know exists. It puts the displaced partition sector at cylinder 0, head 0, sector 7 on the hard disk. On most hard disks this is safely before the start of the DOS partition, but on some (between 1 and 5 per cent) hard disks, this is in the middle of the FAT, and will therefore make a mess of the disk.

On floppy disks it is a boot sector virus, as floppies don't have a partition sector. On floppy disks, it puts the original boot sector at cylinder 0, head 1, sector 3. On a 360 k floppy, this puts it on the last sector of the directory, and will only cause trouble if there are more than 96 files on the diskette. On a 1.2 Mb floppy this is the third sector of the directory, and will give big problems if there are more than 32 files on the diskette. Other diskettes can likewise suffer.

4.64 Prudents

Other names: 1210
Infects: any EXE file on any writable DOS device
Classification: direct action file virus

4.64.1 Recognition and Detection

EXE files grow by approximately 1210 bytes. Date and time are preserved.

4.64.2 How the Virus Copies Itself

When you run an infected file, the virus infects another file. It searches through the directory tree on the disk to do so. If a diskette is write-protected, you will not see the "Write-protect error" when it tries to infect; the virus suppresses this.

4.64.3 What the Virus Does

When the year is not 1989, and the month is May to December, and the day is the first, second or the third of the month, the disk trojan is installed. This converts every write of the disk to a verify, so that it appears as if the write has been successful, whereas actually it hasn't happened. This applies to floppy and hard disks.

If it can't open a file, or if an EXE file doesn't have the "MZ" at the start, then it deletes the file.

There is another trojan in the virus, but it is never called. This is code to do a low level format of the hard disk. It is concealed from programs that search for such code by using a runtime patch to complete the interrupt code.

4.64.4 How To Get Rid of It

Boot from a clean DOS disk; this is a DOS diskette that has come from the manufacturer, and has never been write-enabled. You can then remove the virus by using FindVirus to search for all instances of the virus. Every infected file that you find, you can delete, and copy a

good file in its place. Run FindVirus again when you are finished, to make sure that all instances have been found.

Finally, you should install ChkVirus or any other cryptographic checksummer on all machines that are potentially infectable, to provide an early warning of a recurrence of this or another virus.

4.64.5 Other Information

There is a message in the file, encrypted. When the virus runs, it is decrypted, but not displayed. The message says "£ Prudents virus. Barcelona 2028289 £".

4.64.6 Technical Details

The virus does an are-you-there call, by putting 0ff0fh into AX and doing an interrupt 21h. If 101h comes back in AX, it refrains from infecting a file. Please see also Eight Tunes virus, which does a similar thing. Prudents also does the same thing again, putting 0ff0eh into AX and calling interrupt 21h; if 1234h comes back in AX, it refrains from infecting (see also Sunday virus).

Only subdirectories with an empty extension are searched for files to infect. The virus self-recognition code is 1372h at offset 12h from the start of the file.

4.65 Kennedy

Other names: none
Infects: any COM file on any writable DOS device
Classification: direct action file virus

4.65.1 Recognition and Detection

COM files grow by 333 bytes. Attribute, date and time are preserved.

4.65.2 How the Virus Copies Itself

When you run an infected file, the virus infects all COM files in the current subdirectory. If a diskette is write-protected, you will see the

"Write-protect error" when it tries to infect; the virus does not suppress this.

4.65.3 What the Virus Does

When the date is 6 June, 18 November or 24 November, it displays "Kennedy er dd - lnge leve The Dead Kennedys" and then runs the infected program.

4.65.4 How To Get Rid of It

Boot from a clean DOS disk; this is a DOS diskette that has come from the manufacturer, and has never been write-enabled. You can then remove the virus by using FindVirus to search for all instances of the virus. Every infected file that you find, you can delete, and copy a good file in its place. Run FindVirus again when you are finished, to make sure that all instances have been found.

Finally, you should install ChkVirus or any other cryptographic checksummer on all machines that are potentially infectable, to provide an early warning of a recurrence of this or another virus.

4.65.5 Other Information

The three dates are the anniversaries of deaths of members of the Kennedy family.

4.65.6 Technical Details

Files greater than 65 000 bytes are not infected. Only COM files that start with 0e9h as the first byte are infected. This means that the COM file must start with a jump that is at least 128 bytes. The purpose of this is unclear. Perhaps it is meant to avoid infecting small files.

The virus recognises itself in files by looking for 65h, 64h at offset -3 relative to the start of the virus code

4.66 Solano

Other names: none
Infects: any COM or EXE file on any writable DOS device
Classification: indirect action file virus

4.66.1 Recognition and Detection

COM files grow by 2000 bytes without changing their date and time or read/write/hidden attributes. COMMAND.COM does not become infected, probably to help the virus avoid detection. The virus suppresses the "Abort, Retry, Ignore" message if it is run on a write-protected diskette.

4.66.2 How the Virus Copies Itself

When an infected COM or EXE file is executed, the virus goes memory-resident. Each time an EXE program or uninfected COM program is executed thereafter, the virus infects that program.

4.66.3 What the Virus Does

Minutes after the virus goes memory-resident, it picks a random position on the screen. If there is a figure there, and a figure in the position to the right, it swaps the two figures. It then does the same thing every 73 seconds.

4.66.4 How To Get Rid of It

Boot from a clean DOS disk; this is a DOS diskette that has come from the manufacturer, and has never been write-enabled. This ensures that the virus is not installed in memory. You can then remove the virus by using FindVirus to search for all instances of it. Every infected file that you find, you can delete, and copy a good file in its place. Run FindVirus again when you are finished, to make sure that all instances have been found.

Finally, you should install ChkVirus or any other cryptographic checksummer on all machines that are potentially infectable, to provide an early warning of a recurrence of this or another virus.

4.66.5 Other Information

The virus was named after the place in the USA where it was first found. It may be aimed at spreadsheet users.

4.66.6 Technical Details

Solano works rather like Jerusalem. It traps interrupt 21h and makes a modification to function 4bh, load and execute a program. Files larger than 60 k are not infected.

The virus goes TSR by using the normal means, interrupt 21h function 31h, and so is one of the few that will be trapped by memory-resident active monitor programs.

It detects itself in memory by doing interrupt 21h, function 0c0h; if it gets back 1234h in AX, the virus is in memory. On disk it recognises itself by a nine-byte string at the end of the file.

It avoids infecting COMMAND.COM by checking that the filename is not COMMAND. It does so in an unusual way – it checks the letters A, C, D, M, M, N, O in that order.

It hooks interrupt 8 to do the digit swapping trick, and uses the system clock to choose the random position on the screen. It works for mono and colour screens, but not when in graphics mode.

The virus traps the DOS critical error handler, so that if it tries to infect a file on write-protected media, there is no give-away "Write-protect error".

4.67 Vbasic

Other names: none
Infects: any COM or EXE file on any writable DOS device
Classification: direct action file virus

4.67.1 Recognition and Detection

COM and EXE files grow by approximately 5 k. Attribute, date and time are preserved. COM files don't work any more. When you run an infected file, you will see a lot of disk activity as it searches for more files to infect.

4.67.2 How the Virus Copies Itself

When you run an infected file, the virus infects another four files. It searches through the directory tree on the disk to do so, starting with the current subdirectory. It infects EXE files before infecting the COM files in each subdirectory.

4.67.3 What the Virus Does

After 1 April 1992, when you try to run an infected program, it infects all other programs on the disk, and then puts "Access denied" on the screen as an error message.

4.67.4 How To Get Rid of It

Boot from a clean DOS disk; this is a DOS diskette that has come from the manufacturer, and has never been write-enabled. You can then remove the virus by using FindVirus to search for all instances of the virus. Every infected file that you find, you can delete, and copy a good file in its place. Run FindVirus again when you are finished, to make sure that all instances have been found.

Finally, you should install ChkVirus or any other cryptographic checksummer on all machines that are potentially infectable, to provide an early warning of a recurrence of this or another virus.

4.67.5 Other Information

BASRUN.EXE, BRUN.EXE, IBMBIO.COM, IBMDOS.COM and COMMAND.COM are not infected. The virus looks as if it has been written in a higher level language than assembler, because of the way every subroutine call is done.

4.67.6 Technical Details

The virus recognises a file as infected by looking for the hex string "78h, 56h, 34h, 12h" in the file. It looks for this signature 13e4h bytes before the end of file. When a COM or EXE file is infected, the number of bytes it grows to is calculated by rounding the file size up so that it is a multiple of 16, and then adding 5120 bytes. This makes it one of the largest viruses around. COM files are not infected if doing so would make them larger than 64 k (the limit for a COM file).

COM files are not, however, infected correctly, and they do not work any more.

The virus is written as a large number of subroutines. Each routine starts off with "Push BP 2 Mov BP,SP 2 Sub SP,10h" and ends with "Mov SP,BP 2 Pop BP 2 Ret" which makes it look as if a compiler has been used to create the code. Also, everything is passed to these subroutines by using the stack.

4.68 Casper

Other names: none
Infects: any COM file on any writable DOS device
Classification: direct action file virus

4.68.1 Recognition and Detection

COM files are infected, growing by 1200 bytes. Attribute, date and time are preserved. If it tries to infect on a write-protected diskette, you'll see the "Write-protect error" message from DOS.

4.68.2 How the Virus Copies Itself

When you run an infected file, the virus searches the directory for an uninfected file, and infects it. It stores the attribute of the file and sets it to read/write; this is so that it can restore the attribute after infection. Likewise, date and time are preserved in the usual way.

4.68.3 What the Virus Does

On 1 April, it formats track zero of the floppy diskette in drive A.

4.68.4 How To Get Rid of It

Boot from a clean DOS disk; this is a DOS diskette that has come from the manufacturer, and has never been write-enabled. You can then remove it by using FindVirus to search for all instances of the virus. Every infected file that you find, you can delete, and copy a good file in its place. Run FindVirus again when you are finished, to make sure that all instances have been found. I would suggest that you use the option in FindVirus to check all files, not just executable ones.

Finally, you should install ChkVirus or any other cryptographic checksummer on all machines that are potentially infectable, to provide an early warning of a recurrence of this or another virus.

4.68.5 Other Information

This virus has not been seen in the field. There is a message in the virus: "Hi! I'm Casper The Virus, And On April The 1st I'm Gonna Fuck Up Your Hard Disk REAL BAD! In Fact It Might Just Be Impossible To Recover! How's That Grab Ya! GRIN".

This message is part of the encrypted code, so won't be visible in the virus. I checked by setting the date to 1 April and running an infected program, and it did format track zero, head zero of the floppy drive; the hard disk was untouched, but because the registers were pointed to a non-legal track buffer, the diskette was unreadable.

However, this code could be changed to point to the hard disk with a one-byte change, so I wouldn't rely on the original virus being harmless.

4.68.6 Technical Details

This virus is based entirely on Chameleon or 1260 (see description). But the second layer of encryption using interrupt 3s is not present.

It is not possible to use the standard search-string technique to locate instances of the virus, as the longest reliable search-string is just two bytes long. The virus uses a different key to do its encryption each time it copies itself, so only the decryptor/loader part is clear, just like 1701 virus. But it has another trick – the decryptor code is variable; as the virus copies itself, it uses a random number generator to intersperse the parts of the decryptor with instructions that do nothing useful (and do nothing to prevent the decryption). It also makes the code appear in random order, again, subject to the needs of making the decryption actually work.

The decryptor is divided into three parts. First is the setup code; this consists of three instructions to load the registers. These instructions can appear in any order, and can be interspersed with five other instructions that have no effect. The virus picks from these eight instructions until it has all of the necessary three.

The second part of the decryptor is the two XORs. Again, there are five unnecessary instructions, and the virus picks at random from these seven (and a NOP) until the three instructions that are needed are in place. The third part of the decryptor increments the registers before doing the next iteration of the loop. Again, there are two necessary instructions plus a NOP, and five unnecessary instructions, and all of these can appear in any order.

It uses the same virus self-recognition code as Vienna (62 seconds in the date/time field). It also tries to avoid infecting files that are too large or too small, but there is a bug in the code, and it just avoids infecting files that are exactly 0ah or 0f800h bytes long.

It has been necessary to rewrite a number of anti-virus programs that depend on using search-strings, in order to deal with this virus.

4.69 Luz Virus

Other names: Amstrad
Infects: any COM file on any writable DOS device
Classification: direct action file virus

4.69.1 Recognition and Detection

COM files are infected, growing by 847 bytes. Attribute, date and time are not preserved.

4.69.2 How the Virus Copies Itself

When you run an infected file, the virus searches the disk for an uninfected file, and infects it. It only looks at the current subdirectory, and it infects all the files in it. If a diskette is write-protected, it will not suppress the "Write-protect error" when it tries to infect.

4.69.3 What the Virus Does

There is a counter that keeps track of the generation number of the virus. After the fifth generation, when you run an infected file there is a 50 per cent probability of getting the following message: "Hello, John Mcafee,please uprade me.Bests regards,Jean Luz".

4.69.4 How To Get Rid of It

Boot from a clean DOS disk; this is a DOS diskette that has come from the manufacturer, and has never been write-enabled. You can then remove the virus by using FindVirus to search for all instances of the virus. Every infected file that you find, you can delete, and copy a good file in its place. Run FindVirus again when you are finished, to make sure that all instances have been found.

Finally, you should install ChkVirus or any other cryptographic checksummer on all machines that are potentially infectable, to provide an early warning of a recurrence of this or another virus. You can use Inoculate or any other inoculator to prevent files from getting this virus in future.

4.69.5 Other Information

This virus is Pixel virus, with a couple of bugs added, and a different message. It is completely unclear why this virus should be called the Amstrad virus, but this is what it was called on the copy I received.

4.69.6 Technical Details

The virus self-recognition code is "IV" in bytes 3 and 4 in the file. If a file is read-only, it will not infect it.

The added bugs consist of a failure to close files because the wrong byte is loaded into BX as the file handle, and a difference in the attribute mask when searching for a file to infect.

4.70 Anarkia Virus

Other names: none
Infects: any COM or EXE file on any writable DOS device
Classification: indirect action file virus

4.70.1 Recognition and Detection

COM files grow by 1813 bytes (EXE files usually by 1808 bytes, but always by an amount between 1792 and 1808 bytes) without changing their date and time or read/write/hidden attributes. COM files just grow once; EXE files grow each time they are executed. Eventually, an EXE file could get too large to load into memory.

Some EXE files are not infected correctly by the virus, and fail to run as soon as they are infected. COMMAND.COM does not become infected, probably to help the virus avoid detection. You might also spot the slowdown (see below).

4.70.2 How the Virus Copies Itself

When an infected COM or EXE file is executed, the virus goes memory-resident. Each time an EXE program or uninfected COM program is executed thereafter, the virus infects that program.

4.70.3 What the Virus Does

On every Friday 13th, any program that you try to run is deleted. On all dates, 60 minutes after the virus being installed, a standard PC system slows down to a fraction of normal speed; on faster machines the slowdown will not be so noticeable.

4.70.4 How To Get Rid of It

Boot from a clean DOS disk; this is a DOS diskette that has come from the manufacturer, and has never been write-enabled. This ensures that Anarkia is not installed in memory. You can then remove Anarkia by using FindVirus to search for all instances of the virus. Every infected file that you find, you can delete, and copy a good file in its place. Run FindVirus again when you are finished, to make sure that all instances have been found.

Finally, you should install ChkVirus or any other cryptographic checksummer on all machines that are potentially infectable, to provide an early warning of a recurrence of this or another virus.

4.70.5 Other Information

This virus is almost identical to Jerusalem (see Section 4.12). The differences are minor. The once-off scroll of Jerusalem virus has been removed, the slowdown happens after one hour instead of 30 minutes, and the slowdown loop is twice as long, so the slowdown effect is worse.

4.70.6 Technical Details

The technical details for this virus are the same as for Jerusalem. One difference is the use of the string ARKIA as the self-recognition, with the string ANARKIA at the start of the virus. Another is the test for the virus in memory. It makes an interrupt 21h call with 0e4h in AH, and if the virus is in memory, 4 is returned in the AH register. The scrolling instructions are left in place except for interrupt 10h, which is replaced with NOP instructions.

4.71 Thanksgiving

Other names: 1253
Infects: any COM file on any writable DOS device, hard disk partition records, floppy diskette boot sectors
Classification: combination indirect action file and boot sector virus

4.71.1 Recognition and Detection

COM files grow by 1253 bytes; date and time are changed to the current system time. Attributes are not preserved. The virus does not suppress the "Abort, Retry, Ignore" message if it is run on a write-protected diskette. You might notice the floppy diskette drive seeking to the last track when it infects a diskette.

The most likely way to notice it is by the fact that when the virus is installed by booting from an infected disk or diskette, 64 k of memory is no longer available.

4.71.2 How the Virus Copies Itself

When an infected COM file is executed, the virus goes memory-resident. Booting from an infected hard or floppy diskette also installs the virus in memory. Each time an uninfected COM program is executed thereafter, the virus infects that program. Every floppy disk put into a diskette drive gets infected as well. This makes this one of the most infectious viruses so far, as it has the infectivity of Stoned and Jerusalem combined, and those are the commonest viruses as of mid-1990.

4.71.3 What the Virus Does

On 23 November 1990, and any day thereafter, the trojan is triggered (22 November 1990 is Thanksgiving Day in the US). The trojan overwrites 17 sectors on heads 0 and 1 of the hard disk, stepping through the cylinders starting from cylinder 0. There is no stopping point, so the virus will go as far as cylinder 255, then cycle back to zero and round and round again.

The hard disk will then be unreadable, and the best way to recover will be to run FDISK, FORMAT and restore the backups.

4.71.4 How To Get Rid of It

Boot from a clean DOS disk; this is a DOS diskette that has come from the manufacturer, and has never been write-enabled. This ensures that the virus is not installed in memory. Then you will need to take two backups, because the most reliable way to remove it from the partition record is to low level format the hard disk, and then FDISK and FORMAT it. Then you can restore the backup, which will of course include infected files. You can then remove the virus from files by using FindVirus to search for all instances it. Every infected file that you find, you can delete, and copy a good file in its place. Run FindVirus again when you are finished, to make sure that all instances have been found.

Finally, you should install ChkVirus or any other cryptographic checksummer on all machines that are potentially infectable, to provide an early warning of a recurrence of this or another virus.

4.71.5 Other Information

The virus was found in Austria. It is the first known combination boot sector and file virus.

4.71.6 Technical Details

If you run an infected file, the virus first checks to see if it is in memory already, by looking for the characters "V-1L" at location 184h (where interrupt vector 61h should be). If it is not there, then it goes memory-resident by using interrupt 27h, taking up 2 k of memory. It defines a new interrupt 60h, calls that interrupt, and then runs the program that it had infected.

If you boot from an infected disk or diskette, the virus subtracts 2 k from memory, and if that leaves at least 256 k it subtracts another 62 k, so almost every system will lose 64 k. The rest of the virus is loaded in from wherever it is stored on the disk; on a hard disk it is at cylinder 0, head 0, sectors 4–7. On a floppy disk it is on the track beyond the last one (so on a 40-track disk, it is on track 41 and on an 80-track disk, it is on track 81) and on the last head (on a double-sided diskette, head 1). Again, the code is stored on sectors 4–7. When this code is in memory interrupt 60h is defined, and then interrupt 60h is called.

So, irrespective of whether the virus is installed by running a COM file or by booting from an infected disk or diskette, interrupt 60h is installed, with the same functionality in either case.

Interrupt 60h This checks to see if the virus is in memory. If it is not, it hooks into interrupt 8 (the timer tick) and redefines the function of that. It then sets the "in memory" bytes to "V-1L" and exits.

Interrupt 8 This is executed 18.2 times per second. 10 seconds after it is first installed, it installs new interrupts 13h and 21h, hooking them into the existing interrupt chain.

Interrupt 13h This is used to infect partition sectors and boot sectors, and to do the trojan damage. The new interrupt 13h checks to see if the trojan flag is set. If it is, it writes whatever happens to be in the ES:BX buffer onto 17 sectors of track 0 head 0, track 0 head 1, track 1 head 0, track 1 head 1, and so on down the hard disk; there is no stopping condition, so it will go to cylinder 255, then cycle back to zero again until it is stopped. The hard disk light stays on, and you can hear the heads stepping.

If the trojan flag is not set (i.e., it is before 23-11-1990) then the virus will attempt to infect the boot sector of the floppy (or partition sector of the hard disk). It reads the boot sector, and checks to see if it is infected (looking for the usual "V-1L", and if the disk is clean, it writes its own code into place. On a hard disk this is put at cylinder 0, head 0, sectors 4–7. On nearly every hard disk this is between the partition and the boot sector, but on a small percentage this will overwrite part of the FAT.

On a floppy disk it will calculate the position of the last track, then format one more track (putting nine sectors on the track), and write itself to head 1, sectors 4–7 of that track (unless the disk has only one head, in which case it will write itself to head 0). Finally, the patched boot sector (or partition sector) is written into place, and control is passed back to the original interrupt 13h.

Interrupt 21h The other interrupt that is installed by interrupt 8 is interrupt 21h. This interrupt is used by the virus to infect files. It passes every function except 4bh (load and execute a program) on to the original interrupt 21h handler. If 4bh is called, it checks to see if the program being loaded has a COM extension, and if so, it attempts to infect it. It then checks for a date of 23-11-1990 (the day after Thanksgiving in the US) and if that is the date, or any day after that date, the trojan flag is set (see above for what happens after that).

If the file has "V-1L" at bytes 3–6, then it is infected, so the virus leaves it alone. Otherwise it infects it, adding 1253 bytes to the file.

The COM infection is very straightforward. First, it checks to see if the file is greater than 60 k or less than 8 bytes; if so, it doesn't infect it. It doesn't change the attribute (so read-only files will not be infected), and it doesn't preserve the date and time of the file. While it is infecting, it doesn't suppress the DOS critical error handler, so that if it tries to infect a file on write-protected media, there is the give-away "Write-protect error".

4.72 Joshi

Other names: Joshua
Infects: the partition sector of hard disks, the boot sector of floppies
Classification: partition sector virus

4.72.1 Recognition and Detection

You lose 6 k of memory (Chkdsk will notice this). Also, see below for the effect on 5 January. 720 k 3½- inch diskettes have track 40 overwritten, destroying any data that was there.

4.72.2 How the Virus Copies Itself

When you boot from an infected diskette, the virus goes memory-resident; this is true whether the diskette is a boot disk or not. So the usual thing is for someone to have an infected data diskette, which they leave in drive A when they shut down. Next day when they start up the computer, it attempts to boot from that diskette; if it isn't a system diskette, you see the message "Not a system disk. Please insert a system disk and retry." or a similar message. If that diskette was infected, the virus is now in memory, and when you continue the boot it remains there.

While the virus is in memory, any disk that you access is liable to be infected. If you access the diskette (whether read, write or verify) and the diskette is write-enabled, and the access is to the boot sector (if a floppy) or the partition record (if a hard disk) then Joshi will replace the boot (or partition if a hard disk) sector with its own code and move the boot sector further up the disk.

4.72.3 What the Virus Does

On 5 January it saves the screen that is currently displayed to memory, and replaces it with a display in 40 column mode that is large type, on a blue background, with a double-line border around it. The display says "Type 'Happy Birthday Joshi' !". This remains in place until the user types "Happy Birthday Joshi", and then the original screen is restored.

4.72.4 How To Get Rid of It

You can use FindVirus to detect Joshi, and any disk sector editor will confirm it, since the partition sector (boot sector on diskettes) is different from any normal one.

Switch the computer off; this is to clear the virus from memory. Joshi will survive a warm reboot (Ctrl-Alt-Del) by doing some faking. Boot from a clean DOS disk; this is a DOS diskette that has come from the manufacturer, and has never been write-enabled. This ensures that there is nothing unwanted installed in memory. Use FindVirus to determine which diskettes are infected.

Treatment consists of simply copying all the files off an infected diskette (using "COPY *.*"; do not use Diskcopy or any image copier), and reformatting the diskette (see below for details). Alternatively, you can use UnVirus or any virus removal program to remove the infection from a diskette; UnVirus is a lot faster.

In the case of a hard disk, you could use a disk sector editor. Find the original partition sector (it will be at cylinder 0, head 0, sector 9) and copy it back to the place where it should be, at Physical Sector Number zero. I would recommend that you take a full backup before doing this, as if you get it wrong you could make your disk inaccessible.

If the hard disk is the kind that has the boot sector immediately after the partition sector, Joshi will have overwritten the boot and some sectors of the first copy of the FAT. In order to recover the data from the hard disk it will be necessary to copy the genuine partition sector back to cylinder 0, head 0, sector 1, and to make a copy of the relevant sector from the second copy of the FAT, onto the sector that Joshi has corrupted.

An alternative, and much easier (but more long winded) method, is as follows. First boot from a clean DOS disk. Then make two backups of the hard disk (the second backup is in case you find that you have a problem restoring the first backup). Then do a low level format of the hard disk, remembering to mark any bad tracks on the bad track map. Many hard disk controllers will trigger a low level format if you load up Debug, and type "G=C800:5" (some controllers might want 6, or CCC instead of 5). Even better, you might have a low level formatting utility (which might be called HDFMT, HDPREP or something like that) that came with your computer, or possibly the diagnostics diskette would have this on. There are also programs available that allow low level formatting, such as Disk Manager.

When the disk is formatted it must be partitioned, using FDISK (some hard disk formatters do this as part of the formatting process). After partitioning the disk, it must be high level formatted using "FORMAT /S/V". Check the disk again with FindVirus, and then restore the backup.

If a large number of diskettes are potentially infected, then you should consider borrowing a hopper-fed diskette cleaning machine, which can handle up to 700 diskettes per hour, sorting them into clean and contaminated bins.

4.72.5 Other Information

The virus was first seen in India, where it is one of the commonest. It has since been found in the field all over the world.

4.72.6 Technical Details

Joshi is a partition sector virus, and works in a very similar way to Stoned virus. On hard disks it hides itself in the partition sector. It puts the displaced partition sector at cylinder 0, head 0, sector 9 on the hard disk. On most hard disks this is safely before the start of the DOS partition, but on some (between 1 and 5 per cent) hard disks, this is in the middle of the FAT, and will therefore make a mess of the disk.

On floppy disks it is a boot sector virus, as floppies don't have a partition sector. On floppy disks it creates a new track for the body of the virus.

On a 360 k floppy the virus formats a new track 40 (normal disks use 0 to 39) and stores the body of the virus on that. On 1.2 Mb and 1.44 Mb diskettes it does the same thing, but uses track 80 for the purpose. But the virus uses a test that gives the wrong answer for 720 k diskettes, and it writes the body of the virus onto track 40 (it should have used track 80).

On hard disks it stores the body of the virus at cylinder 0, head 0, sectors 2 to 6. In memory the virus stores itself in the top 6 k.

The virus traps interrupts 8, 9, 13h and 21h. It uses interrupt 8 to install interrupt 21h. Interrupt 21h is used to trigger the screen display. It traps functions 48h, 49h, 4ah (allocate, release and resize memory) and 2ah, 2bh, 2ch, and 2dh (get and set date and time). If any of these functions are called, and it is 5 January, and it has not already done the popup, it does it. It allocates a 16 k block of memory to save the screen, and puts up its screen. It then traps each keystroke, looking for "Happy Birthday Joshi". If you mistype, it starts scanning again from the start. If the message is typed in correctly, the original screen is restored, the memory is released, and the computer can continue. It is entirely likely that the machine will hang at this point, however.

Interrupt 8 is used to install interrupt 21h. It checks to see if the virus's interrupt 21h is installed, and if not, it installs it. Interrupt 9 is used for two purposes. It is used to keep track of the user's typing "Happy Birthday Joshi", and it is also used to trap and attempt to warm reboot using Ctrl-Alt-Del. If it detects that key combination, it restores the interrupt vector table to what it had been just after booting (see below), then clears the screen, beeps, and triggers an interrupt 19h.

The reboot code at interrupt 19h checks to see if the virus' interrupts 8, 9 and 13h are in, and if not, it installs them, before running the genuine DOS boot. Before it does this, it copies the interrupt vector table (locations 0:0 to 0:3ff) to higher memory (to cs:1000, for use as above). Whenever the virus' interrupt 8 gets control, it restores the interrupt 21h vector if necessary.

Interrupt 13h is used for copying the virus. Any read, write or verify on any device, if it accesses cylinder 0, head 0, sector 1, triggers an infection. Then Joshi checks the whole sector to see if it is already installed (this makes inoculation impracticable) and if it isn't, it installs itself.

4.73 VP Virus

Other names: none
Infects: any COM file on any writable DOS device
Classification: direct action file virus

4.73.1 Recognition and Detection

COM files grow by a number of bytes that is calculated as follows. Round up the file size to a multiple of 16, then add 909. Date and time are preserved. If the virus tries to infect a write-protected diskette, DOS will display "Write-protect error".

4.73.2 How the Virus Copies Itself

When you run an infected file, the virus infects another file. It searches through the drives on the disk to do so, excluding drive B. Files that are less than 16 bytes are not infected; nor are files that are greater than 63 k. On each drive, it searches through the subdirectories recursively.

4.73.3 What the Virus Does

After doing an infection (which it attempts to do every time an infected file is run), it looks at the system time. If this is in the first five seconds of the minute, it clears the screen and writes a message to the middle of it. In the specimen I saw first, the message had been zeroed out. It then waits for a keystroke, clears the screen again and exits.

4.73.4 How To Get Rid of It

Boot from a clean DOS disk; this is a DOS diskette that has come from the manufacturer, and has never been write-enabled. You can then remove the virus by using FindVirus to search for all instances of the virus. Every infected file that you find, you can delete, and copy a

good file in its place. Run FindVirus again when you are finished, to make sure that all instances have been found.

Finally, you should install ChkVirus or any other cryptographic checksummer on all machines that are potentially infectable, to provide an early warning of a recurrence of this or another virus.

4.73.5 Other Information

This virus was first sent to me from Holland. The specimen I was sent was slightly corrupted, and would not replicate, but it is fairly clear which bytes have become corrupted, and what they used to be. Also, the message has been overwritten with nulls.

4.73.6 Technical Details

The virus's self-recognition code is VP. It marks disks this way on the boot sector at byte offset 3 and 4, and it marks files with a VP at the start of the file, at offset 0fh and 10h. If a floppy is already marked with the VP on the boot sector, then it doesn't get infected.

VP tries to infect all drives, except the B drive. The reason for avoiding the B drive is probably because many computers emulate a B drive by telling the user to switch floppies and press any key, which would be very noticeable.

4.74 Zerotime Virus

Other names: V1721, Slow
Infects: any COM or EXE file on any writable DOS device
Classification: indirect action file virus

4.74.1 Recognition and Detection

COM files grow by 1721 bytes without changing their date and time or read/write/hidden attributes. EXE files are rounded up to the next multiple of 16, and then 1716 bytes are added.

Some EXE files are not infected correctly by the virus, and fail to run as soon as they are infected. COMMAND.COM does not become infected, probably to help the virus avoid detection. You might also spot the file time change (see below).

4.74.2 How the Virus Copies Itself

When an infected COM or EXE file is executed, the virus goes memory-resident. Each time an EXE program or uninfected COM program is executed thereafter, the virus infects that program.

4.74.3 What the Virus Does

On every Friday in 1991 and thereafter, whenever you close any file, the file time is set to zero. It looks as if the author had intended that the date be set to zero also, but it is set to whatever happened to be in the DX register at the time – most often that means that the date is zeroed also, but not always.

4.74.4 How To Get Rid of It

Boot from a clean DOS disk; this is a DOS diskette that has come from the manufacturer, and has never been write-enabled. This ensures that Zerotime is not installed in memory. You can then remove the virus by using FindVirus to search for all instances of the virus. Every infected file that you find, you can delete, and copy a good file in its place. Run FindVirus again when you are finished, to make sure that all instances have been found.

Finally, you should install ChkVirus or any other cryptographic checksummer on all machines that are potentially infectable, to provide an early warning of a recurrence of this or another virus.

4.74.5 Other Information

This virus is yet another rewrite of Jerusalem virus.

4.74.6 Technical Details

Although this virus is based on Jerusalem, there are substantial differences. For a start, this virus is encrypted using a variable encryption key, and the virus data area is encrypted a second time. The encryption keys are based on the system time.

The virus makes files read/write before infecting them, and restores the attribute afterwards. Likewise, it preserves the date and time of the file. The interrupt 24h critical error handler is suppressed during an infection. COM files larger than 63 819 bytes are not infected.

Zerotime traps interrupt 21h and makes a modification to function 4bh, load and execute a program. The virus defines a couple of new functions for interrupt 21h. With 0c0h in AH, it returns the version number of the virus (currently version 3). 0c2h is a subroutine that is called by the virus to load and execute the original program.

The virus distinguishes between COM and EXE files on the basis of the file name; if it ends in M, it is treated as a COM file, otherwise it is assumed to be an EXE. This will result in a tiny number of mis-infections, as it is entirely possible to have a misnamed file, since DOS distinguishes on the basis of the "MZ" signature at the beginning of EXE files.

The virus uses five bytes at the end of the file as its self- recognition code, just like Jerusalem. But these bytes are variable. On the specimen that I have, they are 55h, 89h, e5h, cdh, 09h, but every 150 days the virus chooses a new self- recognition code (VSC) by using the system timer. It remembers the previous one, though, so it will not re-infect files with the current or the previous codes. Thus, it is not possible to reliably inoculate against this virus.

The VSC is only changed if the time of day is between noon and 4 p.m. On Fridays in 1991 and thereafter, any time a file is closed, the time is set to zero. It looks as if the author meant to set the date to zero also, with a MOV DX,CX instruction, but there is actually a MOV DX,DX instruction, so the date will be set to whatever value happened to be in DX. This will quite often be zero. A file with a zero date or time shows no date/time entry against that file when you do a DIR.

The virus traps the DOS critical error handler, so that if it tries to infect a file on write-protected media, there is no give-away "Write-protect error".

4.75 Virus-101

Other names: none
Infects: any COM file on drives A or B
Classification: direct action file virus

4.75.1 Recognition and Detection

Files grow by 2560 bytes. Attribute, date and time are preserved. If the diskette is write-protected, the "Write-protect error" is suppressed.

4.75.2 How the Virus Copies Itself

Every time you run a program, it infects another program.

4.75.3 What the Virus Does

When an infected file is run on the 9th, 18th or 27th of the month, a display is triggered. The display consists of white bars moving down the screen from the top; after a period of this, the computer is rebooted. If the day of month is anything else, the virus patches the boot sector of the diskette. If the letters "No" (as in "Not a system diskette" appear in the boot sector, it replaces everything from there onwards with the message:

> This file has been safely infected by
> VIRUS101 - the safe, educational virus utility.
> This copy furnished to John McAfee.

4.75.4 How To Get Rid of It

Boot from a clean DOS disk; this is a DOS diskette that has come from the manufacturer, and has never been write-enabled. You can then remove the virus by using FindVirus to search for all instances of the virus. Every infected file that you find, you can delete, and copy a good file in its place. Run FindVirus again when you are finished, to make sure that all instances have been found.

Finally, you should install ChkVirus or any other cryptographic checksummer on all machines that are potentially infectable, to provide an early warning of a recurrence of this or another virus.

4.75.5 Other Information

This virus appears to have been written for "educational purposes". It was written as a demonstration, so that people could safely "experiment" with it – hence the fact that it avoids infecting drives other than A or B. It looks very like Virus-90, with more obfuscation and features added.

4.75.6 Technical Details

First, the virus decrypts itself. Interspersed between the instructions that do the decryption, there are random instructions that serve no purpose other than to make it impossible to search for this virus with a simple scanning program. There is a message in the code that says:

> This file has been safely infected by
> VIRUS101 - the safe, educational virus utility.
> This copy furnished to John McAfee.

The virus checksums this message, and if the checksum is incorrect, the infected program halts. If not, that message is displayed. Next, the system timer is read, and based on this there is a 50 per cent chance that an infection is attempted. Next, it checks to see if the code segment of interrupt 21h is less than or equal to that of interrupt 13h. If that is the case, there is a good chance that this is an anti-virus active monitor in action, so no infection is attempted.

The DOS critical error handler is suppressed (interrupt 24h) by setting its vector to that of interrupt 4, and interrupt 3 is given the same vector as interrupt 21h; the virus uses interrupt 3 for all the things that would normally be done by interrupt 21h.

The virus tests to see what drive it is running from, and only infects if it is A or B; this is presumably the reason for the claim that it is "safe" and "educational". It does a recursive directory search to find a COM file, then an EXE.

The code of the virus is an exercise in obfuscation. Additional bytes are inserted in the code, with jumps around them, so that disassembler programs become confused. Interrupt 3s are scattered throughout the code; without any function, but again adding to the work of disassembly. Elsewhere, interrupt 3 is used to call interrupt 21h, which would hinder the use of Debug. Where any normal program would move a value into AX before calling an interrupt 21h, this virus frequently relies on a previous value in AX, and adds or subtracts from that to give the necessary value.

Addresses are calculated in an obscure way, too. The virus uses the fact that addresses will "wrap around" when the offset exceeds 64 k.

The virus self-identification code for disk files is a value of 62 in the seconds field of the date/time.

Most viruses that suppress the DOS critical error message, do so by defining their own simple handler. This virus uses the interrupt 4 handler, and revectors interrupt 24h to point to that.

4.76 XA1 Virus

Other names: Tannenbaum
Infects: any COM file
Classification: direct action file virus

4.76.1 Recognition and Detection

Files grow by 1539 bytes. Attribute, date and time are preserved. If the diskette is write-protected, the "Write-protect error" is suppressed.

4.76.2 How the Virus Copies Itself

Every time you run a program, it infects another program. It searches the current subdirectory for a COM file that is between 7 and 63 487 bytes long, and if it finds one uninfected, it infects it. It avoids IBMBIO.COM and IBMDOS.COM.

4.76.3 What the Virus Does

On 1st April of any year, it replaces the partition sector of the hard disk with its own version. Thereafter, when the computer is started up, it displays "April, April ...", beeps and hangs.

Between the 24th and the 31st of December, it displays a Christmas tree, and the message:

Und er lebt doch noch : Der Tannenbaum! Frohe Weihnachten ...

4.76.4 How To Get Rid of It

Boot from a clean DOS disk; this is a DOS diskette that has come from the manufacturer, and has never been write-enabled. You can then remove the virus by using FindVirus to search for all instances of the virus. Every infected file that you find, you can delete, and copy a good file in its place. Run FindVirus again when you are finished, to make sure that all instances have been found.

Finally, you should install ChkVirus or any other cryptographic checksummer on all machines that are potentially infectable, to provide an early warning of a recurrence of this or another virus.

If the virus has done the partition sector replacement, the disk will be inaccessible. But the virus moves the original partition to cylinder 0, head 0, sector 17, so it is possible to replace it using a disk sector editor.

4.76.5 Other Information

This virus was found in Germany, and the messages are in German. The "April, April ..." message is the equivalent of "April Fool!", and the "Christmas tree And it lives still" might be a reference to the Christmas exec worm that went through the IBM network at the end of December 1987.

4.76.6 Technical Details

The virus's self-recognition code is the first seven bytes of the file; if these are ebh, 07h, 56h, 0ah, 03h, 59h, 00h then it assumes that the file is infected. If the file is less than 1539 bytes, it is padded to that length before it is infected. When it is infected, it randomly chooses one of nine sets of instructions to go at the start of the file. Infecting adds 1539 bytes to the file. All but the first 35h bytes are encrypted, and those first 35h bytes are variable, making the virus harder to find if a program is using constant search-strings.

Before infecting, it checks the system date. On 1st April it drops a replacement partition sector in place (it puts the same code onto the boot sector on drives A and B as well) and on the 24th to the 31st December, it does the Christmas tree display.

4.77 Hallochen

Other names: none
Infects: any executable file
Classification: indirect action file virus

4.77.1 Recognition and Detection

COM and EXE files grow by the following amount. Round the file size up to the nearest multiple of 16, and add 16 if it was already. Then add 2011 bytes, so files grow between 2012 and 2027 bytes. Attribute, date and time are preserved. If the diskette is write-protected, the "Write-protect error" is suppressed.

4.77.2 How the Virus Copies Itself

When an infected COM or EXE file is executed, the virus goes memory-resident. Each time an EXE program or uninfected COM program is executed thereafter, the virus infects that program. Files that are dated in the current month are not infected. COM files less than 5000 bytes, or more than 63 510 bytes, are not infected. There is also a test for EXE files, but it tests for a file being less than 64 k or more than 5000, which will always be true.

4.77.3 What the Virus Does

After 50 infections, the machine gradually but increasingly slows down. After 70 infections, the keyboard increasingly gives wrong characters. See below for the exact algorithm that is used for this.

4.77.4 How To Get Rid of It

Boot from a clean DOS disk; this is a DOS diskette that has come from the manufacturer, and has never been write-enabled. You can then remove the virus by using FindVirus to search for all instances of the virus. Every infected file that you find, you can delete, and copy a

good file in its place. Run FindVirus again when you are finished, to make sure that all instances have been found.

Finally, you should install ChkVirus or any other cryptographic checksummer on all machines that are potentially infectable, to provide an early warning of a recurrence of this or another virus.

4.77.5 Other Information

This virus was found in Germany, and the messages are in German. The virus contains the text strings:

    Hallochen !!!!!!, Here I'm
    Acrivate Level 1

These are not displayed.

4.77.6 Technical Details

The virus installs an interrupt 01 handler, and every eighth time it is called, it patches the interrupt vector 01 back to the original one, and replaces the interrupt 21h handler.

It installs a time-wasting loop into interrupt 8, the timer tick. This wastes between 1264th and 1 of the CPU time, depending on the number of infections. If the number is less than 50, the time waster is not installed. If it is greater than 50, then 50 is subtracted, and that becomes the number of 1264ths of processor speed that is wasted.

If the number of infections is greater than 70, it also adds a keyboard handler. The infection count has 70 subtracted from it, it is divided by 2, and that is the number of chances out of 256 for any given keystroke to be corrupted. The corruption consists of one being added to the ASCII value (for values over 32), so A becomes B, B becomes C and so on.

It also patches a far jump into the interrupt 21h handler that DOS installed, to jump into its own handler, and patches this back and forth as necessary. The virus self-recognition code in EXE files is 55h, 55h at byte 12h in the file, in COM files it is 55h, 55h at byte 4 in the file.

4.78 Jojo

Other names: none
Infects: any COM file on any writable DOS device
Classification: indirect action file virus

4.78.1 Recognition and Detection

COM files grow by 1701 bytes. If an infected program is run after 7 p.m., it triggers a kaleidoscopic display, if run on a colour screen. If the virus tries to infect a write-protected diskette, DOS gives the "Abort, Retry, Ignore" message.

4.78.2 How the Virus Copies Itself

If you run an infected COM program, the virus installs itself into memory. Once it is installed in memory, it will infect any program that is run as a COM file, including COMMAND.COM. The virus does not go memory-resident via the DOS interrupts, so some programs which try to detect viruses going memory- resident may not detect it.

4.78.3 What the Virus Does

The kaleidoscopic display is the only effect. The virus takes up 2 k of memory when it goes memory-resident.

4.78.4 How To Get Rid of It

Boot from a clean DOS disk; this is a DOS diskette that has come from the manufacturer, and has never been write-enabled. You can then remove the virus by using FindVirus to search for all instances of it. Every infected file that you find, you can delete, and copy a good file in its place. Run FindVirus again when you are finished, to make sure that all instances have been found.

Finally, you should install ChkVirus or any other cryptographic checksummer on all machines that are potentially infectable, to provide an early warning of a recurrence of this or another virus.

4.78.5 Other Information

Jojo is just a version of Cascade (the 1701 version), extensively hacked. It contains the message "Welcome to the JOJO virus." near the beginning, and "Fuck the system (c) - 1990 xxxxxxxxxxxxxx zzz" near the end. The letterfall code has been replaced by the kaleidoscope effect. Another difference is that the encryption and decryption routines are not called.

4.78.6 Technical Details

Jojo checks the BIOS copyright message to see if it is running on an IBM copyright BIOS – if it is, the code seems to quit without doing anything. But there is a bug in the code, and the virus has exactly the same effect on IBMs as on non-IBMs.

Interrupt 21h is hooked, and function 4bh is replaced; all other functions are passed through to the original 21h. A new subfunction is defined – 0FFh. This subfunction is used to return the message that the virus is already installed, and so need not be re-installed. This stops a repeated re- installation of the virus from clogging up all of memory, which would soon be noticed by the user.

Subfunction 0 of function 4bh is replaced. The job of this function is to load and execute a program. The virus changes this, so that before a program is loaded, it is infected if it is a COM file and has not previously been infected. The attribute of the file and the date and time are preserved.

When the virus installs itself, it doesn't use the DOS services to run the host program and install itself in memory. Instead, it manipulates the Memory Control Blocks and Program Segment Prefixes, and this makes the virus appear to have been installed by a different program. It also means that a program that intercepts the interrupts to detect programs going memory-resident will not trap Jojo. The virus assumes that it is running on a colour monitor, without checking to see.

The DOS critical error is not trapped, and so if the virus tries to infect on write-protected media, the DOS critical error message ("Write-protect error") is displayed.

4.79 Victor

Other names: none
Infects: any COM or EXE file on any writable DOS device
Classification: indirect action file virus

4.79.1 Recognition and Detection

Files grow by 2442 to 2458 bytes, depending on rounding. Date, time, and attribute are preserved. The DOS critical error handler is suppressed.

4.79.2 How the Virus Copies Itself

When an infected COM or EXE file is executed, the virus goes memory-resident. Each time one of several DOS functions is used thereafter, the virus tries to infect another program.

4.79.3 What the Virus Does

On Wednesdays, when the hours are between 9 a.m. and 10 a.m., 11 a.m. and 12 a.m., 1 p.m. and 2 p.m., or 3 p.m. and 4 p.m., it deletes files in the current subdirectory.

4.79.4 How To Get Rid of It

Boot from a clean DOS disk; this is a DOS diskette that has come from the manufacturer, and has never been write-enabled. This ensures that Victor is not installed in memory. You can then remove it by using FindVirus to search for all instances of the virus. Every infected file that you find, you can delete, and copy a good file in its place. Run FindVirus again when you are finished, to make sure that all instances have been found.

Finally, you should install ChkVirus or any other cryptographic checksummer on all machines that are potentially infectable, to provide an early warning of a recurrence of this or another virus.

4.79.5 Other Information

This virus has a message in the code, which says:

> Victor V1.0 The Incredible high Performance Virus
> Enhanced versions available soon.
> This program was imported from USSR.
> Thanks to Ivan.

4.79.6 Technical Details

The virus self-recognition codes are: to detect itself in memory, it puts 0ffffh into AX, 0ff0h into BX and does an interrupt 21h. If CX comes back with 0fec1, the virus was in memory. It goes memory-resident using interrupt 21h, function 31h, so will be detected by memory-resident anti-virus programs.

On files, the virus clears the last three bits of the seconds field of the file's date/time. It uses this to search for uninfected files, but this is for performance. To verify that the file is infected, it looks at the last six bytes, which should be eah, 80h, 49h, 25h, 02h, 2eh.

Infection is attempted whenever any program uses DOS functions: 3eh, 41h, 3ch, 42h, 43h, 4bh, 4eh, 4fh, 5bh, 39h, 3ah, 3bh, 3dh, 3fh, 40f. The virus checks the time of day, and if it is less than 30 seconds since it last did anything, it skips the attempt to do anything. Otherwise, it makes a random number of between 1 and 4 attempts. If the day is Wednesday, and the hour of day is 9, 11, 13 or 15, the virus does a delete instead of an infect. The delete has a 75 per cent probability for each time it is attempted.

At all other times the virus tries to infect another file. It searches down the current directory for an uninfected file, looking for COM and EXE extensions. If it finds one, it sets a flag according to whether it is COM or EXE, then checks the last three bits of the time field. If these are not all clear, the file is uninfected, and it proceeds. If they are all clear, this might be because the file is infected, but it may be just that the file was created at a time where the seconds were divisible by 16. So with a 12.5 per cent probability, the virus looks at the file anyway, and checks the last six bytes for its string.

Files that are less than 2442 bytes, and COM files greater than 62 198 bytes are not infected.

The virus traps the DOS critical error handler, so that if it tries to infect a file on write-protected media, there is no give-away "Write-protect error".

4.80 PSQR Virus

Other names: 1720
Infects: any COM or EXE file on any writable DOS device
Classification: indirect action file virus

4.80.1 Recognition and Detection

COM files grow by 1720 bytes (EXE files by an amount between 1719 and 1734 bytes) without changing their date and time or read/write/hidden attributes. To get the EXE size increase, round the file size up to the next multiple of 16, then add 1719.

4.80.2 How the Virus Copies Itself

When an infected COM or EXE file is executed, the virus goes memory-resident, unless it is January or December. Each time an EXE program or uninfected COM program is executed thereafter, the virus infects that program. COMMAND.COM is not infected.

4.80.3 What the Virus Does

On every thirteenth of the month, any program that you try to run is deleted. In addition, junk is written to the hard disk partition sector, and to the nine sectors after that. When the virus goes memory-resident, it takes up 2064 bytes of memory.

4.80.4 How To Get Rid of It

Boot from a clean DOS disk; this is a DOS diskette that has come from the manufacturer, and has never been write-enabled. This ensures that the virus is not installed in memory. You can then remove it by using FindVirus to search for all instances of the virus. Every infected file that you find, you can delete, and copy a good file in its place.

Run FindVirus again when you are finished, to make sure that all instances have been found.

Finally, you should install ChkVirus or any other cryptographic checksummer on all machines that are potentially infectable, to provide an early warning of a recurrence of this or another virus.

4.80.5 Other Information

This virus is similar to Jerusalem, but with substantial differences. It is called PSQR because that is the self-recognition code. PSQR is also the ASCII equivalent of a very common sequence of assembler instructions: Push AX, Push BX, Push CX, Push DX.

4.80.6 Technical Details

PSQR traps interrupt 21h and makes a modification to function 4bh, load and execute a program. The virus defines a couple of new functions for interrupt 21h. With 0e1h in AH, it returns 3 in AH (Jerusalem does the same if you put 0e1h into AH). 0ddh is a routine that is called by the virus to run the infected program.

PSQR also puts 0ff0fh into AX and does an interrupt 21h, and if 101h is returned, it doesn't install itself in memory. Similarly, it looks at the segment part of the address of interrupt 0f1h (address 3c6h) and if this is 1234h, it doesn't install in memory. The next test is for January or December; in either of these months, it doesn't install. Finally, it calls interrupt 21h, function e1h, and if the result returned in AH is between 3 and 0e0h, it installs itself into memory.

The installation procedure into memory is just like Jerusalem; it drops some code onto 3fch to copy itself into high memory, and uses interrupt 21h function 31h to remain resident. At the same time, it sets a flag if the day of the month is 13. This flag is tested when a program is loaded (via interrupt 21h, function 4bh) and if set the file is deleted and the partition record and the nine subsequent sectors are overwritten. Overwriting the partition record will make the hard disk inaccessible, although this condition could be cured fairly easily using one of a number of disk-fixing utilities. It is not clear what overwriting the other nine sectors is meant to accomplish, but hard disks partitioned by Disk Manager will find that this is a nuisance, and Disk Manager keeps important information about the disk in this area.

The virus avoids infecting COMMAND.COM by using an explicit test for it, but (presumably to escape notice) the string "COM-MAND.COM" in the virus is encrypted.

The virus self-recognition code is "PSQR"; four bytes compared with the five that Jerusalem uses.

The virus distinguishes between COM and EXE files on the basis of the file name; if it ends in M, it is treated as a COM file, otherwise it is assumed to be an EXE. This will result in a tiny number of mis-infections, as it is entirely possible to have a misnamed file, since DOS distinguishes on the basis of the "MZ" signature at the beginning of EXE files.

The virus traps the DOS critical error handler, so that if it tries to infect a file on write-protected media, there is no give-away "Write-protect error".

4.81 Tiny Virus

Other names: none
Infects: any COM file on any writable DOS device
Classification: direct action file virus

4.81.1 Recognition and Detection

COM files grow by 163 bytes. Date/time is set to the current system value.

4.81.2 How the Virus Copies Itself

When an infected COM file is executed, the virus searches in the current directory for the first uninfected file, and infects it.

4.81.3 What the Virus Does

Nothing.

4.81.4 How To Get Rid of It

You can remove the virus by using FindVirus to search for all instances of the virus. Every infected file that you find, you can delete, and copy a good file in its place. Run FindVirus again when you are finished, to make sure that all instances have been found.

Finally, you should install ChkVirus or any other cryptographic checksummer on all machines that are potentially infectable, to provide an early warning of a recurrence of this or another virus.

4.81.5 Other Information

This virus is unlikely to spread, because the infection mechanism is so feeble. It looks as if it has been written as an exercise to see how small a virus could be.

4.81.6 Technical Details

The virus self-recognition in the file consists of the bytes 07h, 08h just after the end of the host program.

Only files that are less than 65 024 bytes are infected, and only files that start with an 0e9h (most COM files start with this).

The DOS critical error handler is not disabled, and the date/time is not preserved. If a file is read-only, it will not be infected.

4.82 The Swedish Disaster

Other names: none
Infects: partition sectors on hard disks, boot sectors on floppies
Classification: partition sector virus

4.82.1 Recognition and Detection

One in eight infective boot-ups, the virus displays "The Swedish Disaster I". Some 1.2 Mb diskettes may have garbage on directories.

4.82.2 How the Virus Copies Itself

When you boot from an infected diskette, the virus goes memory-resident; this is true whether the diskette is a boot disk or not. So the usual thing is for someone to have an infected data diskette, which they leave in drive A when they shut down. Next day when they start up the computer, it attempts to boot from that diskette; if it isn't a system diskette, you see the message "Not a system disk. Please insert a system disk and retry" or a similar message. If that diskette was infected, the virus is now in memory, and when you continue the boot, it remains there. It is also written immediately to the partition sector of the hard disk, if one is present.

While the virus is in memory, any disk that you access is liable to be infected. If you access the diskette (whether read or write) and the diskette is write-enabled then the virus will replace the boot sector with its own code, and move the boot sector further up the disk.

4.82.3 What the Virus Does

No intentional damage is done. But because the place that Swedish Disaster stores the original boot sector does not change according to the kind of diskette it infects it causes problems on 1.2 Mb floppies if they have more than 32 files, by overwriting the directory entries for files 33 to 48, and would also cause problems on 3½-inch diskettes. On a small percentage of hard disks, it overwrites part of the FAT, because it assumes that cylinder 0, head 0 has nothing on it after the partition sector, whereas there are some disks that begin the DOS partition immediately after the partition sector.

4.82.4 How To Get Rid of It

You can use FindVirus to detect this virus, and any disk sector editor will confirm it, since the partition sector (boot sector on diskettes) has the distinctive message "The Swedish Disaster I".

Boot from a clean DOS disk; this is a DOS diskette that has come from the manufacturer, and has never been write-enabled. This ensures that there is nothing unwanted installed in memory. Use FindVirus to determine which diskettes are infected.

Treatment consists of simply copying all the files off an infected diskette (using "COPY *.*"; do not use Diskcopy or any image copier), and reformatting the diskette (see below for details). Alternatively, you can use UnVirus or any virus removal program to remove the infection from a diskette; UnVirus is a lot faster.

In the case of a hard disk, you could use a disk sector editor. Find the original partition sector (it will be at cylinder 0, head 0, sector 7, although there is another version which puts it at 0, 0, 2) and copy it back to the place where it should be, at Physical Sector Number zero. I would recommend that you take a full backup before doing this, as if you get it wrong, you could make your disk inaccessible.

If the hard disk is the kind that has the boot sector immediately after the partition sector, the virus will have overwritten one sector of the first copy of the FAT. In order to recover the data from the hard disk, it will be necessary to copy the genuine partition sector back to cylinder 0, head 0, sector 1, and to make a copy of the relevant sector from the second copy of the FAT, onto the sector that the virus has corrupted.

An alternative, and much easier (but more long winded) method, is as follows. First boot from a clean DOS disk. Then make two backups of the hard disk (the second backup is in case you find that you have a problem restoring the first backup). Then do a low level format of the hard disk, remembering to mark any bad tracks on the bad track map. Many hard disk controllers will trigger a low level format if you load up Debug, and type "G=C800:5" (some controllers might want 6, or CCC instead of 5). Even better, you might have a low level formatting utility (which might be called HDFMT, HDPREP or something like that) that came with your computer, or possibly the diagnostics diskette would have this on. There are also programs available that allow low level formatting, such as Disk Manager and Speedstor.

When the disk is formatted it must be partitioned, using FDISK (some hard disk formatters do this as part of the formatting process). After partitioning the disk it must be high level formatted using "FORMAT /S/V". Check the disk again with FindVirus, and then restore the backup.

If a large number of diskettes are potentially infected, then you should consider borrowing a hopper-fed diskette cleaning machine, which can handle up to 700 diskettes per hour, sorting them into clean and contaminated bins.

4.82.5 Other Information

The virus was discovered in Sweden. It is functionally equivalent to Stoned virus described in this manual, but it is not simply that virus with changed strings. It looks as if the virus author tried to do a substantial rewrite, but retained exactly the same functional specification.

4.82.6 Technical Details

Swedish Disaster virus is a partition sector virus. On hard disks it hides itself by existing in a place that many programs cannot access. It puts the displaced partition sector at cylinder 0, head 0, sector 7 on the hard disk. On most hard disks, this is safely before the start of the DOS partition, but on some (between 1 and 5 per cent) hard disks, this is in the middle of the FAT, and will therefore make a mess of the disk.

On floppy disks it is a boot sector virus, as floppies don't have a partition sector. On floppy disks it puts the original boot sector at cylinder 0, head 1, sector 3. On a 360 k floppy, this puts it on the last sector of the directory, and will only cause trouble if there are more than 96 files on the diskette. On a 1.2 Mb floppy, this is the third sector of the directory, and will give big problems if there are more than 32 files on the diskette. Other diskettes can likewise suffer.

4.83 V1024 Virus

Other names: Diamond
Infects: any COM or EXE file on any writable DOS device
Classification: indirect action file virus

4.83.1 Recognition and Detection

COM files grow by 1024 bytes. Date/time is preserved. The growth in the file size is hidden from DIR commands if the virus is in memory.

4.83.2 How the Virus Copies Itself

When an infected program is executed, the virus goes memory-resident. Thereafter, any uninfected program that is run is infected.

4.83.3 What the Virus Does

If you have a colour monitor and you are using it in text mode, then when the time is on the hour, a display triggers. This starts off as a multi-coloured diamond (made up of four by four smaller diamonds) in the centre of the screen. After a brief pause, the smaller diamonds scatter, and bounce independently around the screen. Every time they pass over a character they blank it out, so the screen is gradually cleared, apart from the bouncing diamonds.

4.83.4 How To Get Rid of It

Boot from a clean DOS disk; this is a DOS diskette that has come from the manufacturer, and has never been write-enabled. This ensures that the virus is not installed in memory. You can then remove it by using FindVirus to search for all instances of the virus. Every infected file that you find, you can delete, and copy a good file in its place. Run FindVirus again when you are finished, to make sure that all instances have been found.

Finally, you should install ChkVirus or any other cryptographic checksummer on all machines that are potentially infectable, to provide an early warning of a recurrence of this or another virus.

4.83.5 Other Information

It is rather unlikely that this virus will be seen very much, as it is so obvious that you have it, and it will be eradicated before it has any chance to spread.

4.83.6 Technical Details

The virus puts 0d5aah into AX, and calls interrupt 21h. If the virus is already in memory, it returns 2a55h in AX, and if that happens the virus simply runs the host program. If the virus is not already in memory, it uses the MCB chain to install itself there. It then runs the host program. Two interrupts are revectored, 21h (the DOS function) and 8, the timer tick.

Interrupt 21h is mostly used for infecting more programs. Only files that are more than 1024 bytes are infected; they must also be less than 64 000 bytes if they are COM files. The infection is done by the usual procedure of trapping interrupt 24h to suppress the "Abort, Retry,

Ignore", save the file attribute and date/time, set the file to read/write, infect, and restore the date/time and attributes. The virus sets the time field to indicate 60 seconds (an impossible value for DOS to use).

The virus checks the first two bytes of the file to see if it is a COM or EXE file; the bytes "MZ" or "ZM" mean EXE file. The test for ZM is a characteristic of the Bulgarian team of virus authors.

Interrupt 21h is also used to hide the increase in file size. If the DOS directory functions 11h or 12h (find first file, find next file) are called, the file time is checked, and if the seconds field is set to 60, the virus makes it appear to be zero and the file size is made to look 1024 bytes smaller than it really is, which is exactly the size of the virus. The file, therefore, looks normal to a DIR.

Interrupt 8 is used to trigger, and control, the display.

4.84 Amoeba Virus

Other names: 1392, Khetapunk
Infects: any COM or EXE file on any writable DOS device
Classification: indirect action file virus

4.84.1 Recognition and Detection

COM and EXE files grow by 1392 bytes. Date and time are not preserved; nor are read/write/hidden attributes.

4.84.2 How the Virus Copies Itself

When an infected COM or EXE file is executed, the virus goes memory-resident. Each time an uninfected EXE or COM program is executed thereafter, the virus infects that program. COM files less than 512 bytes or greater than 60 k are not infected.

4.84.3 What the Virus Does

Nothing noticeable; there are many bugs in the code.

4.84.4 How To Get Rid of It

Boot from a clean DOS disk; this is a DOS diskette that has come from the manufacturer, and has never been write-enabled. This ensures that the virus is not installed in memory. You can then remove it by using FindVirus to search for all instances of the virus. Every infected file that you find, you can delete, and copy a good file in its place. Run FindVirus again when you are finished, to make sure that all instances have been found.

Finally, you should install ChkVirus or any other cryptographic checksummer on all machines that are potentially infectable, to provide an early warning of a recurrence of this or another virus.

4.84.5 Other Information

The virus has the following text in it, in an encrypted form:

SMA KHETAPUNK - NOUVEL Band A.M.O.E.B.A. by PrimeS-oft Inc

4.84.6 Technical Details

Amoeba first checks to see if it is already in memory, by looking at location 0:3cch (which is where the vector for interrupt 0f3h would be). If it finds 0cdcdh there, it assumes it is already in memory.

Otherwise it reserves 3 k of memory at the top of memory by subtracting 3 from 0:413h, copies itself to there, and puts 0cdcdh at 0:3cc. Finally, the virus copies 1089 bytes back to the start of the host program in memory, and loads and executes it.

Amoeba traps interrupt 21h and makes a modification to function 4bh, load and execute a program, in order to copy itself to the program being loaded. It also traps function 36h (get drive information) and 4ch (terminate process), and infects on those; on the last two, it infects COMMAND.COM.

To infect, it first checks to see if there is plenty of space left in the drive (10 free clusters, which would be 20 k on most hard disks). It installs a replacement interrupt 24h to suppress DOS critical error messages, which is more sophisticated than the replacement installed by most viruses. It distinguishes between disk errors (non-disk errors are handled by the original handler) and non-disk errors. With disk errors, if the error is a write-protect error, the error message is suppressed; for all other errors, it calls the old interrupt

10h (this last is presumably a bug; the author intended to call the old interrupt 24h). There is also a bug in the installation of this routine; it attempts to store the address of the original interrupt 24h so that it can use it as above, but an instruction has been omitted, and what is stored is not the correct address.

After the faulty installation of a faulty interrupt 24h, the virus clears the read/write attribute of the file it is infecting, and reads the first 512 bytes. If the first two are "MZ", it treats it as an EXE file, otherwise as a COM file. If it is an EXE file, it looks for 542h at offset 14h (the load point) in the header and if it finds that there, it exits without infecting. For COM files, it checks to see that the size is less than 512 bytes or greater than 60 k; if so, it doesn't infect. If it does infect, it reads the first 1089 bytes, or the whole file. It sets its COM-file flag (0cch at offset 0bh in the file) and checks its self-recognition flag (0cdcdh at offset 5), and if the file has not already been infected, it infects it. It writes 1089 bytes of virus, then the original file (with the first 1089 bytes written after the rest of the file), then 303 bytes of virus.

For EXE files, it patches the first 512 bytes to change the load point, and adds the whole 1392 bytes of the virus to the end of the file.

Two other interrupts are hooked, 1ch and 10h. 1ch is the timer tick; this counts up to 1000h (34 minutes) and then, if the video is colour and in text mode, the display is triggered. The other way the display is triggered is when any program tries to change the video mode.

The main reason to hook interrupt 10h is to interfere with the scrolling. Where row 25 should be the lowest row to scroll, it changes it to 24. This is a bug; since rows are counted from 0, the bottom row in the screen is row 24, not 25. There is another bug in this routine; it was intending to trap the scroll up and the scroll down routines, but only the scroll up is trapped.

The display consists of writing the message (see above) to the screen, except that it will not be written to the visible screen, but to an area of video memory that is not displayed.

4.85 Shake Virus

Other names: none
Infects: any COM file on any writable DOS device
Classification: indirect action file virus

4.85.1 Recognition and Detection

COM and EXE files grow by 476 bytes, but this is concealed if the virus is in memory. Date and time are preserved, and any attempt to write to write-protected media does not give an error message. The most likely way to notice the virus is the "Shake well before use !" message.

4.85.2 How the Virus Copies Itself

When an infected COM file is executed, the virus goes memory-resident. Each time any program calls interrupt 21h, function 36h (get drive information), the virus infects the next uninfected file in the current subdirectory. COM files greater than 60 k are not infected.

4.85.3 What the Virus Does

There is a 1 in 16 chance that instead of running the program, it beeps and displays "Shake well before use !". After doing this once, it patches itself so that it doesn't do it again, until the next time it goes memory-resident.

4.85.4 How To Get Rid of It

Boot from a clean DOS disk; this is a DOS diskette that has come from the manufacturer, and has never been write-enabled. This ensures that the virus is not installed in memory. You can then remove it by using FindVirus to search for all instances of the virus. Every infected file that you find, you can delete, and copy a good file in its place. Run FindVirus again when you are finished, to make sure that all instances have been found.

Finally, you should install ChkVirus or any other cryptographic checksummer on all machines that are potentially infectable, to provide an early warning of a recurrence of this or another virus.

4.85.5 Other Information

This virus contains some ideas that have not appeared in other viruses.

4.85.6 Technical Details

Shake first checks to see if it is already in memory, by calling interrupt 21h with 4203h in AX. If 1234h comes back in AX, it assumes that it is already in memory, and runs the host program.

Otherwise, it reserves 480 bytes of memory at the top of memory by calling interrupt 21h, function 48h, and then copies itself to there. It patches the interrupt vector table (interrupt 21h) to point to itself, and then runs the host program.

Whenever interrupt 21h is called, it first traps functions 11h and 12h (find file and find next). These are used by the DOS DIR command. It looks at the time stamp on the file, and if the value in the seconds field is 60 (DOS programs will only set values between 0 and 59) then it knows that an infected file is being looked at, so it subtracts 476 from the file size before passing the information on to DOS. Thus, if the virus is in memory, the file size looks unchanged.

The other function it traps is 4bh, load and execute a program. It uses the system time as a random number generator, so that there is a 1 in 16 chance that instead of running the program, it beeps and displays "Shake well before use !". After doing this once, it patches itself so that it doesn't do it again, until the next time it goes memory-resident.

The infection process is called for any call to interrupt 21h function 36h, get drive information. It looks for the first uninfected COM file in the current subdirectory, by checking the time field for a value of 60 seconds. It suppresses the DOS critical error handler, opens the file and reads the first three bytes, and stores them. If the file is greater than 60 k, it ignores it. It appends the virus to the end of the file, patches the first three bytes of the file to a jump to the virus, sets the seconds field of the file time to 60, and closes the file.

4.86 Mendoza Virus

Other names: none
Infects: any COM or EXE file on any writable DOS device
Classification: indirect action file virus

4.86.1 Recognition and Detection

COM files grow by 1813 bytes (EXE files usually by 1808 bytes, but always by an amount between 1792 and 1808 bytes) without changing their date and time or read/write/hidden attributes. COM files just grow once; EXE files grow each time they are executed. Eventually an EXE file could get too large to load into memory.

Some EXE files are not infected correctly by the virus, and fail to run as soon as they are infected. COMMAND.COM does not become infected, probably to help the virus avoid detection.

You might notice the cursor becoming a block, the lock keys being toggled to off, or the deletion of files.

4.86.2 How the Virus Copies Itself

When an infected COM or EXE file is executed, the virus goes memory-resident. Each time an EXE program or uninfected COM program is executed thereafter, the virus infects that program.

4.86.3 What the Virus Does

If the year is 1980 or 1989, it does nothing. Otherwise, when the virus goes memory-resident, then if the floppy disk drive motor count is 25, it sets a flag (this will happen if the program is run from a diskette drive). If that flag is set, every program that you try to run is deleted.

On years other than 1980 and 1989, if the delete flag is not set, then 30 minutes after the virus is installed, the cursor is changed from whatever it is currently to a block.

After an hour, it switches Insert, Caps lock, Num lock and Scroll lock to off.

4.86.4 How To Get Rid of It

Boot from a clean DOS disk; this is a DOS diskette that has come from the manufacturer, and has never been write-enabled. This ensures that the virus is not installed in memory. You can then remove it by using FindVirus to search for all instances of the virus. Every infected file that you find, you can delete, and copy a good file in its place. Run FindVirus again when you are finished, to make sure that all instances have been found.

Finally, you should install ChkVirus or any other cryptographic checksummer on all machines that are potentially infectable, to provide an early warning of a recurrence of this or another virus.

4.86.5 Other Information

This virus is a modification of Jerusalem virus.

4.86.6 Technical Details

The differences from Jerusalem virus are as follows:

The memory self-recognition is done by putting 0e1h in AH and doing an interrupt 21h; the virus returns 3 in AH. With Jerusalem, this is 0e0h.

The file self-recognition is done by looking for 0a2h, 0f4h, 44h, 94h, 0e4h at the end of COM files, where Jerusalem puts "MsDos".

There is a minor bug in the virus; the starting jump is to the wrong location, but this should not affect its operation.

The data area used by the virus is encrypted, probably to cause problems for anti-virus programs.

4.87 Jerspain Virus

Other names: none
Infects: any COM or EXE file on any writable DOS device
Classification: indirect action file virus

4.87.1 Recognition and Detection

COM files grow by 1813 bytes (EXE files usually by 1808 bytes, but always by an amount between 1792 and 1808 bytes) without changing their date and time or read/write/hidden attributes. COM files just grow once; EXE files grow each time they are executed. Eventually, an EXE file could get too large to load into memory.

Some EXE files are not infected correctly by the virus, and fail to run as soon as they are infected. COMMAND.COM does not become infected, probably to help the virus avoid detection.

File deletes are triggered on the 26th of each month.

4.87.2 How the Virus Copies Itself

When an infected COM or EXE file is executed, the virus goes memory-resident. Each time an EXE program or uninfected COM program is executed thereafter, the virus infects that program.

4.87.3 What the Virus Does

If the year is 1987 it does nothing. Otherwise, if the date is the 26th then when the virus goes memory-resident, it sets a flag. If that flag is set, every program that you try to run is deleted.

On days other than the 26th, it installs a routine into the timer tick, so that after half an hour a box on the left of the screen is scrolled up, and a time-wasting loop slows the computer down. But there is a bug in the scroll routine, and it is likely to hang the machine.

4.87.4 How To Get Rid of It

Boot from a clean DOS disk; this is a DOS diskette that has come from the manufacturer, and has never been write-enabled. This ensures

that the virus is not installed in memory. You can then remove by using FindVirus to search for all instances of the virus. Every infected file that you find, you can delete, and copy a good file in its place. Run FindVirus again when you are finished, to make sure that all instances have been found.

Finally, you should install ChkVirus or any other cryptographic checksummer on all machines that are potentially infectable, to provide an early warning of a recurrence of this or another virus.

4.87.5 Other Information

This virus is yet another modification of Jerusalem virus.

4.87.6 Technical Details

The differences from Jerusalem are as follows:

There is a minor change to the installation code, probably to escape detection by one of the virus scanners.

The file self-recognition is done by looking for 00h, "prog" at the end of COM files, where Jerusalem puts "MsDos".

There is a bug in the virus; as soon as the timer count gets down to 2 (about 30 minutes after the virus goes memory- resident, it does a sequence of register pushes (AX, BX, CX, DX) which should be assembled to the bytes "PSQR". Instead, the bytes at that point are "pSQR", which is a completely different thing, and the computer is likely to halt soon after reaching this.

4.88 Frere Virus

Other names: none
Infects: any COM or EXE file on any writable DOS device
Classification: indirect action file virus

4.88.1 Recognition and Detection

COM files grow by 1813 bytes (EXE files usually by 1808 bytes, but always by an amount between 1792 and 1808 bytes) without changing their date and time or read/write/hidden attributes.

Some EXE files are not infected correctly by the virus, and fail to run as soon as they are infected. COMMAND.COM does not become infected, probably to help the virus avoid detection.

The most likely way to notice it is by the way the virus plays "Frere Jacques" on Fridays and on the 13th.

4.88.2 How the Virus Copies Itself

When an infected COM or EXE file is executed, the virus goes memory-resident. Each time an EXE program or uninfected COM program is executed thereafter, the virus infects that program.

4.88.3 What the Virus Does

If the year is 1987 it does nothing. Otherwise, if the date is the 13th, or a Friday, then when the virus goes memory- resident it installs a routine on to the timer tick, so that 34 minutes later it plays "Frere Jacques", badly. It repeats this every 34 minutes.

4.88.4 How To Get Rid of It

Boot from a clean DOS disk; this is a DOS diskette that has come from the manufacturer, and has never been write-enabled. This ensures that the virus is not installed in memory. You can then remove by using FindVirus to search for all instances of the virus. Every infected file that you find, you can delete, and copy a good file in its place. Run FindVirus again when you are finished, to make sure that all instances have been found.

Finally, you should install ChkVirus or any other cryptographic checksummer on all machines that are potentially infectable, to provide an early warning of a recurrence of this or another virus.

4.88.5 Other Information

This virus is yet another modification of Jerusalem virus. It is much too obvious to ever spread.

4.88.6 Technical Details

The differences from Jerusalem virus are as follows:

The memory self-recognition is done by putting 0f0h in AH and doing an interrupt 21h; the virus returns 3 in AH. With Jerusalem, this is 0e0h. Frere also gives the "in memory" signal for Jerusalem.

The file self-recognition is done by looking for 029h, 09eh, e9h, 72h, 099h at the end of COM files, where Jerusalem puts "MsDos".

The bug in Jerusalem that leads to multiple infection of EXE files has been corrected.

4.89 More Pixel Viruses

Other names: none
Infects: any COM file on any writable DOS device
Classification: direct action file virus

4.89.1 Recognition and Detection

COM files are infected, growing by a number of bytes that depends on the version. Attribute, date and time are preserved in some versions, not in others.

4.89.2 How the Virus Copies Itself

When you run an infected file, the virus searches the disk for an uninfected file, and infects it. It only looks at the current subdirectory, and it infects all the files in it. If a diskette is write-protected, it will not suppress the "Write-protect error" when it tries to infect.

4.89.3 What the Virus Does

There is a counter that keeps track of the generation number of the virus. After the fifth generation, when you run an infected file there is a 50 per cent probability of getting the following message: "Program sick error:Call doctor or buy PIXEL for cure description".

4.89.4 How To Get Rid of It

Boot from a clean DOS disk; this is a DOS diskette that has come from the manufacturer, and has never been write-enabled. You can then remove the virus by using FindVirus to search for all instances of the virus. Every infected file that you find, you can delete, and copy a good file in its place. Run FindVirus again when you are finished, to make sure that all instances have been found.

Finally, you should install ChkVirus or any other cryptographic checksummer on all machines that are potentially infectable, to provide an early warning of a recurrence of this or another virus. You can use Inoculate or any other inoculator to prevent files from getting this virus in future.

4.89.5 Other Information

This is a very short and simple virus, so therefore easily modified. I doubt if it will ever appear in the field.

4.89.6 Technical Details

Two more variants: the first is 277 bytes long, and is also called V-277. The message is absent and is replaced by a beep, but that never happens as there is a bug in the code that tests for a 50 per cent chance to do it. The virus self-recognition is "UM" in bytes 2 and 3.

Nocargar is like Pixel-847, except that the message is different. It has been changed to "En tu PC hay un virus RV1, yesta es su quinta generacion".

4.90 Form

Other names: none
Infects: the boot sector of disks and diskettes
Classification: boot sector virus

4.90.1 Recognition and Detection

On the 24th of each month, each key beeps when you type it. Infected floppy disks have 1 k in bad sectors.

4.90.2 How the Virus Copies Itself

When you boot from an infected diskette, the virus goes memory-resident; this is true whether the diskette is a boot disk or not. So the usual thing is for someone to have an infected data diskette, which they leave in drive A when they shut down. Next day when they start up the computer, it attempts to boot from that diskette; if it isn't a system diskette, you see the message "Not a system disk. Please insert a system disk and retry" or a similar message. If that diskette was infected, the virus is now in memory, and when you continue the boot, it remains there. It is also written immediately to the hard disk, if one is present.

While the virus is in memory, any disk that you access is liable to be infected. If you access the diskette (whether read or write) and the diskette is write-enabled then Form will infect it.

Similarly, if you boot from an infected hard disk, the virus goes memory-resident, and is ready to infect any diskette that you read from in any drive.

4.90.3 What the Virus Does

On the 18th of each month, on AT machines, each key should beep when you type it. But the speaker has not been set up correctly, so this does not work.

4.90.4 How To Get Rid of It

You can use FindVirus to detect the virus. Boot from a clean DOS disk; this is a DOS diskette that has come from the manufacturer, and has never been write-enabled. This ensures that there is nothing unwanted installed in memory. Use FindVirus to determine which diskettes are infected.

Treatment consists of simply copying all the files off an infected diskette (using "COPY *.*"; do not use Diskcopy or any image copier), and reformatting the diskette. Alternatively, you can use UnVirus or any virus removal program to remove the infection from a diskette; UnVirus is a lot faster.

In the case of a hard disk, you boot from a clean DOS disk, and then do a full backup (just in case – you shouldn't need it). Then SYS the disk, by typing "SYS C:". SYS is fully documented in your DOS manual.

If a large number of diskettes are potentially infected, then you should consider borrowing a hopper-fed diskette cleaning machine, which can handle up to 700 diskettes per hour, sorting them into clean and contaminated bins.

4.90.5 Other Information

There is a message in the virus that never gets displayed. It says:

> The FORM-Virus sends greetings to everyone who's reading this text. FORM doesn't destroy data! Don't panic! Fuckings go to Corinne.

The specimen that came to me, via another virus researcher, was in a very interesting form. First of all, it arrived as a COM file, and of course in that form it could not run. When I looked at that COM file it looked as if those parts of the virus that were not on the boot were on the last two directory sectors. If the necessary sectors are put in that place, the virus works, but it could never have got that way by copying itself, as this virus stores that code in bad sectors, and directory sectors can never be bad. So, either someone has done this deliberately, or else this is yet another of the viruses that have been written and sent to a virus researcher, rather than existing in the field.

4.90.6 Technical Details

Form virus is a boot sector virus. On hard disks, it hides itself at the end of the logical volume; on floppies, in sectors that it marks as bad.

When you boot from an infected diskette, the virus code runs. It first reserves 2 k from the top of memory, then moves 510 bytes of itself to there, and then loads the rest of the virus, which is in the last directory sector but one, to high memory. The original boot sector is then read in, so that when the virus has infected the hard disk and redefined interrupts 13h and 9, it can run the old boot sector.

To infect the hard disk, the virus calls interrupt 13h, function 8 to determine the geometry of the hard disk. It then reads the partition sector, and searches the data area for a bootable partition. If it finds one, it reads the boot sector. It checks the sector at offset 3fh for the value 0fe01h; if it finds that, it assumes that the disk is already infected, so leaves it alone. It also refrains from infecting if the number of bytes per sector is anything other than 512. It assumes that the bootable partition is DOS.

If the infection does proceed, it writes the original boot sector to the last sector of the hard disk, and the second sector of the virus to the last sector on the hard disk but one (without checking to see whether there is anything already there, or whether it is a writable area of disk). It doesn't do anything to protect what it has put there.

If it is the 18th of the month, interrupt 9 is redefined, so that an AT will beep every time a key is pressed; this code does not work. Interrupt 13h is redefined; if it is a reference to a hard disk, or if it is not a read, or it is not an access to cylinder zero, it is ignored. Otherwise (it is therefore a floppy read to cylinder zero of a floppy diskette), the virus attempts to infect the diskette.

The diskette infection works as follows. The boot sector is read, and tested (0fe01h at offset 3fh) to see if it is already infected. It looks to see if the sector size is 512, and exits if it is not. It calculates where the data area starts and ends, and searches the FAT for an unused cluster; when it finds one, it marks it as bad by changing the zero to 0ff7h. It creates a second bad cluster if clusters are only one sector in size, and copies the body of the virus to the first sector, and the original boot sector to the second. The two sectors do not have to be contiguous. Finally, the virus puts its own boot sector into place.

4.91 SVIR Virus

Other names: none
Infects: any EXE file on any writable DOS device
Classification: direct action file virus

4.91.1 Recognition and Detection

EXE files grow by 512 to 527 bytes. The date/time is changed to the current system time. After using an infected file for a while, you'll see a lot of unanticipated accesses to drive A.

4.91.2 How the Virus Copies Itself

When an infected EXE file is executed, the virus infects the next file in the current subdirectory.

4.91.3 What the Virus Does

When the infection counter gets to zero, it tries to access drive A each time the infected program is run; if there is no diskette in drive A, you will get the normal DOS error message.

4.91.4 How To Get Rid of It

Boot from a clean DOS disk; this is a DOS diskette that has come from the manufacturer, and has never been write-enabled. This ensures that the virus is not installed in memory. You can then remove it by using FindVirus to search for all instances of the virus. Every infected file that you find, you can delete, and copy a good file in its place. Run FindVirus again when you are finished, to make sure that all instances have been found.

Finally, you should install ChkVirus or any other cryptographic checksummer on all machines that are potentially infectable, to provide an early warning of a recurrence of this or another virus.

4.91.5 Other Information

This virus is not likely to become common, as the infective mechanism is weak.

4.91.6 Technical Details

This is a very simple EXE infector. It adds 512 bytes to the file, then rounds it up to a multiple of 16. It contains a counter, which starts at 55. Each time an infected program is run, the counter is decremented, and when it reaches zero, floppy drive A is accessed each time that program is run. It does not preserve the date and time of the infected file, or the attribute. It does not suppress the DOS critical error message, so that if it tries to infect on a write-protected floppy, you'll see "Write-protect error".

4.92 Subliminal Virus

Other names: Subli110
Infects: any COM file on any writable DOS device
Classification: indirect action file virus

4.92.1 Recognition and Detection

COM files grow by 1496 bytes, without changing their date and time or read/write/hidden attributes.

4.92.2 How the Virus Copies Itself

When an infected COM file is executed, the virus goes memory-resident. Each time an uninfected COM program is executed thereafter, the virus infects that program. COMMAND.COM is not infected.

4.92.3 What the Virus Does

Occasionally, the virus flashes a message at the bottom right of the screen, too fast to be able to read it. The message says "LOVE, REMEMBER?".

4.92.4 How To Get Rid of It

Boot from a clean DOS disk; this is a DOS diskette that has come from the manufacturer, and has never been write-enabled. This ensures that the virus is not installed in memory. You can then remove it by using FindVirus to search for all instances of the virus. Every infected file that you find, you can delete, and copy a good file in its place. Run FindVirus again when you are finished, to make sure that all instances have been found.

Finally, you should install ChkVirus or any other cryptographic checksummer on all machines that are potentially infectable, to provide an early warning of a recurrence of this or another virus.

4.92.5 Other Information

This virus is similar to Jerusalem and Solano, but with substantial differences.

4.92.6 Technical Details

The virus first looks to see if it is in memory, by putting 0c0h in AH, and doing an interrupt 21h. It looks for 1234h on return. If it sees this, it calls interrupt 21h, function 0c1h to run the host program. If it was not already in memory, it defines a new interrupt 21h. It sets a timer count to 241 minutes, and determines whether it is running on a mono or colour screen. If it is 1989, it exits without doing anything.

Otherwise, it defines a new interrupt 8 (timer tick), and uses interrupt 21h, function 31h to terminate and remain resident.

Interrupt 21h, function 0c0h returns 1234h in AX, to let the world know that the virus is already in memory. Function 0c1h is used to run the host program, and 4bh (load and execute) is used to infect. The virus checks the disk free space, and checks that the file that is being loaded is not COMMAND.COM (it does this by checking for the letters A, C, D, M, M, N, O, in the order COMMAND). If this is OK, it stores the file attribute. It checks the last nine bytes of the file for the self-recognition code of 05h, 17h, 16h, 19h, 0ah, 01h, 10h, 0fh, 64h. If it finds that, it doesn't infect the file.

Interrupt 8 decrements the counter, which is originally set for 241 minutes, and thereafter when it is reset, it is set for 12 minutes. Whenever it triggers, it looks at the last line on the screen, column 65. If there isn't a space character there, it waits for another 20 seconds. If there is a space there, it does its subliminal display, and resets the counter for 12 minutes again.

The subliminal display decrypts and displays "LOVE, REMEMBER?". The display is on the bottom line, starting at column 60, and the attribute used is 07h. The display is left there as long as it takes the machine to do an empty loop of 4000h iterations, and on a 4.77 Mhz PC, this would be about 0.06 seconds. Then the original display is restored.

4.93 Liberty Virus

Other names: none
Infects: any COM or EXE file on any writable DOS device
Classification: indirect action file virus

4.93.1 Recognition and Detection

COM files grow by 2858 bytes without changing their date and time or read/write/hidden attributes.

4.93.2 How the Virus Copies Itself

When an infected COM or EXE file is executed, the virus goes memory-resident. Each time an uninfected COM or EXE program is executed thereafter, the virus infects that program.

4.93.3 What the Virus Does

Nothing.

4.93.4 How To Get Rid of It

Boot from a clean DOS disk; this is a DOS diskette that has come from the manufacturer, and has never been write-enabled. This ensures that the virus is not installed in memory. You can then remove it by using FindVirus to search for all instances of the virus. Every infected file that you find, you can delete, and copy a good file in its place. Run FindVirus again when you are finished, to make sure that all instances have been found.

Finally, you should install ChkVirus or any other cryptographic checksummer on all machines that are potentially infectable, to provide an early warning of a recurrence of this or another virus.

4.93.5 Other Information

The virus contains the text:

4.93.6 Technical Details

The virus first checks to see if it is already in memory, by looking at the vector for interrupt 62h; if it finds 0ffffh, it assumes that it is already installed. It patches the Memory Control Block chain to make space, moves itself into place, redefines interrupt 21h, sets the in-memory flag, decrypts and replaces the 120 bytes of the host program, and runs it. The new interrupt 21h is looking for function 4bh, load and execute a program. When it sees one, it starts the infect procedure. This traps and replaces interrupt 23h (the Ctrl-C routine) and interrupt 24h, the DOS critical error handler. It tries to open the file for read/write, and if it succeeds, it reads the first 120 bytes of the file. If the first two bytes are MZ, it treats it as an EXE file, otherwise as a COM file.

It checks the virus self-recognition, which is the word "Liberty", decrypts the first 120 bytes of the host program that it has stored in the virus, and then checks the file size. If the file is less than 1280 or greater than 60 k, it refrains from infecting. It appends the virus bytes to the end of the file, but if when doing this write, it actually writes fewer bytes than it should have, a special routine is triggered (see below).

Otherwise, it writes the 120 bytes of the virus to the beginning of the file, closes the file and tidies up, restoring the interrupts. The special routine consists of replacing interrupt 13h with its own code. But the routine put in place looks nothing like a replacement for interrupt 13h.

There is a lot of unused code in this virus; either I have some kind of corrupted version, or else this virus isn't complete. For example, there is code in the middle of the virus, which is an interrupt 13h service routine. What this would do if called, is if anything is trying to write to the floppy disk, it would read the first nine sectors of cylinder zero, reformat that track in a peculiar way, and then write the data back. The peculiar format is to number the sectors as 31h to 39h, instead of the normal 1 to 9. This would leave the diskette such that DOS wouldn't be able to read it. However, this routine is not installed.

4.94 Fish Virus

Other names: Fish6
Infects: any COM or EXE file on any writable DOS device.
Needs DOS 3 or later
Classification: indirect action file virus

4.94.1 Recognition and Detection

Files grow by 3584 bytes, but the virus conceals the change in file size when it is resident. The virus slows down any access to DOS when it is resident, because of the large number of things it does at every interrupt 21h call. This is very noticeable when the screen is written to as a DOS device. Screen access of some programs (such as the DOSEDIT utility) becomes very slow.

When the year is 1991 by the DOS system calendar, the virus announces itself, but it is more complicated than just changing the date, so this is not a simple check (see below).

4.94.2 How the Virus Copies Itself

When an infected COM or EXE file is executed, the virus goes memory-resident. Thereafter, almost any disk access involving an executable file will cause the virus to try to infect it. The virus can change the attribute of files, so it will infect files with read-only attribute set. The original attribute is preserved and restored, and so (apparently, but see below) are the original date and time.

This virus traps rather a lot of DOS functions, and it is very infectious. It will infect any program that is copied or run. If a program (such as a virus scanner) examines other programs on a disk when the virus is resident, all the programs examined will be infected. A feature of this virus is that it immediately seeks out and infects COMMAND.COM when it first goes resident.

4.94.3 What the Virus Does

When the DOS date is in the year 1991 or later, and an infected COM program is run, Fish prints a message and then hangs the computer with a HALT instruction. This will be the second infected program run, as Fish must be resident when the COM program is run (so the first infected program run, probably COMMAND.COM, just gets Fish into memory). If the COM program is not infected, Fish will infect it rather than print the message. If the program is infected, but is an EXE program, Fish will ignore the date. Only an infected COM file will trigger the virus.

The message is: "FISH VIRUS 6 - EACH DIFF - BONN 2290 '~knzyvo}'". The significance of the nonsense string in single quotes is not known. But if you subtract 10 from each character, you get "tadpoles". Someone apparently wishes us to believe that there are at least five other Fish variants, but only one has been seen so far. The fish names that can be seen in the decrypted virus are: Cod, Shark, Carp, Bass, Trout, Fin, Sole, Pike, Mackerel, Fish and Tuna.

Fish does not deliberately damage data on disk, other than infecting executable files, but it can "infect" data files if they have peculiarly unfortunate names (see below). When Fish is resident, the infection" will be concealed, but when you have purged the virus, you could be left with a corrupted data file. Fish spends a lot of time concealing itself, so it makes the computer run slowly.

4.94.4 How To Get Rid of It

Boot from a clean DOS disk; this is a DOS diskette that has come direct from the manufacturer and never been write-enabled. This ensures that Fish is not installed in memory. This is especially important because of the efforts Fish makes to conceal itself. You can then remove Fish by using FindVirus to search for all instances of the virus. Every infected file you find, you can delete, and copy a good file in its place. Run FindVirus again when you are finished, to make sure that all instances have been found.

Finally, you should install ChkVirus or any other cryptographic checksummer on all machines that are potentially infectable, to provide an early warning of a recurrence of this or another virus.

4.94.5 Other Information

One of the methods Fish uses to identify files already infected is to add 100 years to the directory file date. This is outside the range of years that DOS will display, so you only see the original file date in the directory. When resident, Fish conceals the extra hundred years from other programs that look at the date, and will even let you change the file date and then adds the hundred years back on again afterwards.

4.94.6 Technical Details

This virus spends most of its time trying to disappear up its own entrails. Its code consists mostly of tricks to conceal itself and make investigation by virus researchers very hard work indeed. The infection and payload routines take little space compared to the code devoted to obfuscation. The single-step and breakpoint interrupts (01h and 03h) are revectored to incorporate routines essential to the operation of the virus, the only object being to make the investigation of Fish by debugger impossible. Nonsense bytes and the names of various fish are sprinkled liberally through the code to trip up disassemblers and put them out-of-step with the execution thread.

Fish virus is encrypted, not once but many times. Each infection is encrypted differently, by XORing the virus code with a different key each time, and when it is memory-resident it encrypts itself in between DOS calls, using a different key each time. The idea is to defeat attempts to detect the virus by scanning files or memory, but part of the virus (the decryption routine) must remain unencrypted if it is to work, so scanners still have a piece of code they can look for.

Fish replaces the critical error interrupt 24h and disk interrupt 13h with its own routines, to suppress the "Abort, Retry, Ignore" message when it tries to infect a file on a write-protected disk. It replaces the DOS general purpose interrupt 21h in an unusual way that is very unlikely to be spotted by any monitoring software. The virus interrupt 21h traps DOS functions for the purposes of infecting files, but it also traps many more functions to make the virus code appended to infected files "invisible", by falsifying directory file sizes and showing only innocent parts of the infected program when the file is read, perhaps by a virus scanner program.

As every DOS call has to go through the decryption and re- encryption routines even if not trapped, and so many are trapped, DOS runs very slowly.

The routine that determines if a file is an executable program, and hence infectable, is poorly written. It adds up the ASCII codes of the last three letters of the file specification (assuming them to be a three-letter extent) and decides that the file is a program if the codes add up the same as EXE or COM. This will cause data files with names like TELECOM, SPANDEXE, PHOTOCLP, or CLOTHDYE to become infected uselessly. Such files may appear corrupted once your Fish infestation has been eradicated.

Fish goes resident at the top of available memory. This removes the resident portion of COMMAND.COM from the computer's memory, which means that when the infected program that first brings Fish into the computer finishes running and hands control back to the system prompt, COMMAND.COM is automatically reloaded. This has the effect of causing COMMAND.COM to be the first thing infected when Fish gets on to a new computer. After that, Fish will always be resident from boot-up. This is just a side-effect of the way that the virus goes resident, but it is so useful to the virus that it is possible that the memory-residence routine was chosen primarily for the side-effect.

4.95 Murphy Virus

Other names: Murphy-1, Murphy-2, 10 AM
Infects: any non-tiny COM or EXE file on any writable DOS device
Classification: indirect action file virus

4.95.1 Recognition and Detection

Variant 1 grows files by 1277 bytes. Variant 2 grows files by 1521 bytes. Murphy makes no attempt to conceal the file size changes.

Between 10 a.m. and 11 a.m. (by the DOS clock), variant 1 causes the speaker to whistle and crackle, while variant 2 initiates a bouncing ball screen display.

Earlier versions of FindVirus may report this virus as Dark Avenger, which appears to be from the same author(s).

The virus disables disk error messages, but due to bugs, there are some circumstances in which the "Abort, Retry, Ignore" message will be displayed several times if the virus tries to write to a write-protected disk.

4.95.2 How the Virus Copies Itself

When an infected COM or EXE file is executed, the virus goes memory-resident. Thereafter, whenever a COM or EXE file is opened as a read-only file, or whenever a program is run, the virus tries to infect it. Neither variant will infect files smaller than the virus' own size (1277 or 1521 bytes). The virus does not try to change the attribute of files, so cannot infect files with read-only attribute set. Date and time of infected files are preserved.

Although this virus traps very few DOS functions, it is very infectious. It will infect any program that is copied or run. If a program (such as a virus scanner) examines other programs on a disk when the virus is resident, all the programs examined will be infected. A feature of this virus is that it immediately seeks out and infects COMMAND.COM when it first goes resident.

4.95.3 What the Virus Does

Both variants trigger when the system clock reads any time between about 10 a.m. and 11 a.m. Variant 1 causes the speaker to whistle at a high frequency, and crackle when keys are pressed or a program run. The crackle will stop if you change the system time to another hour or if the computer is left running until after 11:00, but the whistle continues.

Variant 2 causes a dot (character 07, the smaller diamond shape) to bounce around the screen. The dot bounces off the edge of the screen and any other characters present. It does not usually corrupt the text, but occasionally leaves a trail of dots on screen and moves a few existing characters when the screen scrolls. The dot continues to bounce after the hour changes.

Neither variant deliberately damages data on disk, other than infecting executable files.

4.95.4 How To Get Rid of It

Boot from a clean DOS disk; this is a DOS diskette that has come direct from the manufacturer and has never been write-enabled. This ensures that Murphy is not installed in memory. You can then remove Murphy by using FindVirus to search for all instances of the virus. Every infected file you find, you can delete, and copy a good file in its place. Run FindVirus again when you are finished, to make sure that all instances have been found.

4.95.5 Other Information

Variant 1 contains the message: "Hello, I'm Murphy. Nice to meet you friend. I'm written since Nov/Dec. Copywrite (c)1989 by Lubo & Ian, Sofia, USM Laboratory". Variant 2 contains: "It's me -

Murphy. Copywrite (c)1990 by Lubo & Ian, Sofia, USM Laboratory". These messages are not used or displayed by the virus.

4.95.6 Technical Details

In some aspects, this virus seems a simplified and less destructive version of Dark Avenger. Like Dark Avenger, it looks for particular disk controller ROMs and tries to replace interrupts 13h and 40h with jumps going directly to the ROM routines. It also replaces the critical error interrupt 24h with its own routine, to suppress the "Abort, Retry, Ignore" message when it tries to infect a file on a write-protected disk. This doesn't work properly, and you can get several of these messages in a row when diskettes are write-protected. The DOS general purpose interrupt 21h is the only other interrupt changed. Dark Avenger tries to stop other programs using interrupt 27h to go memory-resident, or redirecting interrupts 21h and 27h, but Murphy doesn't bother.

No attempt is made to alter a file's attribute, so files marked read-only will not be infected. Files are only infected when run, or when opened as read-only files. Files opened for reading *and* writing are not infected, so that renaming a file, for instance, will not infect it. When copying a file, the file is infected when it is opened for reading, then the infected file is read, and a copy of it, already infected, is written, so this mechanism is quite effective despite trapping so few DOS functions.

Murphy goes resident at the top of available memory. This removes the resident portion of COMMAND.COM from the computer's memory, which means that when the infected program that brings Murphy into the computer finishes running and hands control back to the system prompt, COMMAND.COM is automatically reloaded. This has the effect of causing COMMAND.COM to be the first thing infected when Murphy gets on to a new computer. After that, Murphy will always be resident from boot-up. This is just a side-effect of the way that the virus goes resident, but it is so useful to the virus that it is possible that the memory-residence routine was chosen primarily for the side-effect.

4.96 The "Legendary" Agiplan

Some two years ago, a virus was reported at a company called Agiplan, and this was named the Agiplan virus. No specimen of the virus appeared to have survived, as there was nothing that resembled the description that it was given in the library of viruses that circulates amongst the virus research community.

In November 1990, this legendary virus seems to have turned up. At the end of October, Mr Skulason, an Icelandic virus researcher, received a phone call from someone claiming to have this virus, and promising to send it. We all receive such calls, and generally suspend judgement until the virus arrives, and in this case, nothing turned up. Then, at a South African show, the distributor of an anti-virus product was approached by a person asking that a diskette be scanned at the show. The vendor refused, explaining that a show is not an appropriate venue for such things, but that he would look at the diskette later. The diskette contained a file AGIPLAN.COM, which was submitted to me, and which I have examined.

It is a memory-resident virus that infects COM files apart from COMMAND.COM. It avoids this file by name, but it is very odd that the file AGIPLAN.COM is a copy of an infected COMMAND.COM, the one file that cannot be infected, unless it is renamed in order to do this. It matches the legendary Agiplan, in the infective length, and in the first 17 bytes, which were published as an aid to detection.

Another very significant fact is that I was not able to run the file that I was sent, as it stood. But after making the virus go memory-resident by single stepping it, I was then able to infect other files with Agiplan. But there is a bug in the memory handling, and often when I try to run an infected file, the virus runs, then passes control to the host, and then when the host returns to DOS, there is a "Memory allocation error", COMMAND.COM cannot be reloaded, and the system halts.

4.96.1 Agiplan Structure

There are a number of interesting features to this virus. The most important of these is the damage routine – if a file is run six months after it is infected, the virus attacks physical drives 0, 1, 80h and 81h (these are the first two floppy drives, and the first two hard disks). In each case, the first nine sectors, on each head, on the first five tracks, are overwritten with garbage; this will destroy the FAT and root directory of the first logical volume on the drive. But, if there is no drive B, then only drive A is overwritten, and so it would seem that the hard disk will not usually suffer, as many hard disk machines do not have a drive B. There is also a routine that goes live four months after infection; see below.

The virus installs an especially complex interrupt 24h handler, so as to conceal an attempt to write to write-protected media. Only the virus's own writes have critical errors suppressed, otherwise the original critical error handler is chained to. But the interrupt 24h is permanently replaced, and this is different from the normal method used in most viruses, where the interrupt 24h replacement is done temporarily, while the infection process happens.

The virus also traps interrupt 21h and it is looking for four functions. It looks for 4eh (find first file), 4bh (load and execute a program), 0eh (select a disk) and 40h (write to a file). But having trapped those calls, it then does nothing about 0eh and 4eh, apart from passing them on to the original interrupt 21h handler.

If the function is a write to disk, then it looks at the trojan byte. If this is set for minor damage (four months), it checks to see that a file is being written to (as opposed to a standard device handle). If that is so, it looks at the system time, and uses that as a random number to decide whether to interfere with the stack before doing the write. With each write operation, the probability gradually increases.

If the flag is set for major damage (six months), the routine described above is triggered, which aims at making volumes A, B, C and D inaccessible.

If the DOS function being intercepted is 4bh (load and execute), then the file being loaded is infected. The file must be a COM file, but not COMMAND.COM. If the drive letter is in the range "A" to "Z" or "a" to "p", then it is converted from a drive letter to a device number correctly, but if it is the range "q" to "z", then this is done wrongly; this would appear to be a bug.

The file attribute is stored, and it is set to read/write and opened. The flags on the open are for a read/write open, using the DOS 3 "deny none" sharing mode. This is rather unusual in a virus; they usually use the non-sharing open calls ("Compatibility mode").

Then it tries to read 0ffffh bytes, and reads whatever is actually in the file. It adds 600h to the size that it has read, and tests to see if this is less than 4 k, or more than 52 k. The test for less than 4 k has a bug. It checks the first 16 bytes of the file to see if it is already infected with Agiplan, and if not, the infection proceeds.

If the file to be infected is COMMAND.COM, then the virus patches some code, but the code it is looking for is not in the virus. It seems to be looking for the sequence: Mov DX, xxyy Xor CX,CX Mov AX,4200 and it adds 600h to the xxyy word. This sequence looks like a seek into the file. If this means that seeks into files are displaced by 600h bytes, then anything that has this happen while reading the file will see a normal uninfected file; however, this does not seem to work.

It looks for this sequence in the 12 k bytes just above the virus, and does the patch if it finds it. If it fails to find it, it does an interrupt 7eh (which will call the old interrupt 21h) using whatever was left in the registers; presumably this is another bug. Date and time of the file are preserved, the infected version of the file is written back, and the file is closed with the old date and attribute.

When an infected application is run, it first checks the last location in Cmos (3fh). If this is greater than 0f0h, it displays "load error" and runs the host program. If the Cmos at 3fh is less than or equal to 0f0h, it looks at interrupt 7fh, to see if the virus is already installed; a value of 0ffffh means that it is. If it was not already in memory, it sets that flag, and then traps interrupt 21h, putting the old address of interrupt 21h onto interrupt 7eh, which it uses instead of interrupt 21h. It also sets interrupt 24h to its own handler, and checks for the trigger dates.

To set the trojan byte, it looks at the dates that have been preset; if the minor damage date has been reached, it sets the byte to 0f0. If the major damage date has been reached, it sets the byte to 0ffh. Next, it sets the minor and major damage dates for the file it is infecting to be 4 and 6 months in the future. There seems to be a bug here; if the month is 12 or more, then 11 is subtracted from the month number, and one added to the year. This should probably have said that if the month number is 13 or more, then 12 is subtracted from the month number and one added to the year.

The virus also increments a generation counter; the specimen that I saw was number 13h (I cannot, of course, be sure that the counter was started from zero). Memory allocations are modified, and the host program is then run. There seems to be a bug here, which means that the system halts with a memory allocation error when the host has run. The virus is actually 4eeh bytes long, it is only built up to 600h bytes by some padding.

So, there are a number of mysteries about this virus. Is it indeed the "lost" Agiplan virus? That virus had the same first 17 bytes as this one, and the same characteristic length (except that this one is only 600h because of the padding). There are a lot of bugs in the virus; perhaps even more than usual. Why are the functions 0eh and 04eh trapped, but then passed on to the old interrupt 21h without any action? Why did the virus arrive in a renamed COMMAND.COM, which it could not have infected under its real name? There are a lot of NOP instructions in the virus; are these covering up something that used to be there; if not, what are they there for? What is it looking for, and trying to patch in memory? Why does it look at 3fh in Cmos – it doesn't make any corresponding change in Cmos? And above all – is this really the "lost" Agiplan, or is a virus that has been written to resemble it, and if so, what on earth is the point?

4.97 The Anticad Series of Viruses

Other names: Plastique, Taiwan, ABT
Infects: COM and EXE files, and boot sectors
Classification: indirect action file virus and boot sector virus

4.97.1 Recognition and Detection

These viruses all have a few things in common. They all cause a slowdown of the computer, and that slowdown is an incremental effect. Secondly, they look for anyone running a program, or opening a file, called ACAD.EXE, and aim to do damage. The damage that these viruses do when they trigger is severe. They all have music included; three of them are an unrecognisable tune, and the fourth is "Blue Danube".

4.97.2 How the Viruses Copy Themselves

When an infected application is run, the viruses go memory-resident. Thereafter, they infect when a program is loaded, or a file is copied. In addition, Anticad 1 and 4 go memory-resident when you boot from an infected floppy or hard disk (if the boot sector is infected). In the case of those two, the boot sector of the hard disk or floppy disk is infected.

4.97.3 What the Viruses Do

When these viruses trigger, they aim to totally trash all hard disks and floppies on the system, and then overwrite the Cmos on ATs.

4.97.4 How To Get Rid of Them

Cold-boot from a clean Dos diskette. Identify each infected file, and delete it. Replace the boot sector by using "SYS C:", and then replace all infected files. This is preferable to using the virus removal facility of FindVirus, but in an emergency (for example, it might take a long time to get a clean executable) the remover could be used. If you do, you must still use SYS to put on a boot sector that is appropriate for your DOS.

4.97.5 Other Information

These viruses appear to have come from Taiwan, and were first isolated by Roger Riordan, in Australia. Mr Riordan did the first disassembly of these viruses, which has been very helpful in countering them. His names ABT1, ABT2 and ABT3 correspond to my Anticad 2, Anticad 3b and Anticad 1.

4.97.6 Technical Details

The Anticad family consists of, currently, a series of five viruses which have a lot in common – in particular, they trigger when anyone runs a program with the filename ACAD.EXE. I have called the viruses ANTICAD 1, 2, 3, 4 and 3b, in the order in which they have turned up; possibly there are others previous, subsequent or in between these. They also get called Plastique, after the text in them, or Taiwan, which is where they were written.

Anticad 2 and 3 infect COM and EXE files; Anticad 1 and 4 infect those, and also boot sectors of hard and floppy diskettes. There is a strong family relationship to Jerusalem in these viruses, as if the author had examined Jerusalem carefully in order to write them.

The infective lengths are:

- Anticad 2: 2900
- Anticad 3: 3012
- Anticad 3b: 3004
- Anticad 1: 4096
- Anticad 4: 4096

The order in which they were written is, of course, a guess, but they might have been 2, 3, 1, 4. I might have named them in that order, but if another one turned up in between two of the above, that would have meant renaming, amid much confusion. The trojan in all cases is similar – the virus aims to hit the two floppy drives, and the two hard disks, and when those are completely overwritten, it overwrites the Cmos in an AT.

The in-memory virus self-recognition codes are similar. For versions 1, 2 and 3, the virus puts 4b40 into AX, and calls interrupt 21h. The virus returns 5678h if it is there. In the case of Anticad 4, it puts 0ffh into BL, and 4243 into AX before calling interrupt 21h, and back comes 5678h.

Each of the viruses contains text, encrypted using an XOR. Anticad 2 contains "Copyright (C) 1988, 1989 by ABT Group". Anticad 3 contains "Program: Plastique 4.51 (plastic bomb), Copyright (C) 1988,1989 by ABT Group. Thanks to: Mr. Lin (IECS 762??), Mr. Cheng (FCU Inf-Center)". Anticad 1 contains "PLASTIQUE 5.21 (plastic bomb) Copyright (C) 1988-1990 by ABT Group (in association with Hammer LAB.) WARNING: DON'T RUN ACAD.EXE!" Anticad 4 contains "by Invader, Feng Chia U., Warning: Don't run ACAD.EXE!"

Anticad 2, 3 and 1 play a tune which I do not recognise – it is perhaps a Chinese tune. Anticad 4 plays "Blue Danube".

The two versions that infect boot sectors do so on hard and floppy disks. On hard disks, the body of the virus is written in the sectors before the DOS boot sector. On floppy disks, the body is written on the first track beyond the normal tracks; track 80 if the media byte is less than or equal to 0fbh, otherwise track 40.

Another trojan that all these viruses have in common is that they gradually cause the computer to slow down, by introducing a time-wasting loop into the timer tick, and gradually increasing the length of that loop. All of them avoid infecting COMMAND.COM. All of them trap the critical error handler, so that on write-protected media, the "Abort, Retry, Ignore" message is suppressed.

Anticad 2 installs the timer routine if a program is run more than 30 days since it was infected; Anticad 3 reduces this to 7 days, and the other Anticads don't have a delay.

Each virus chains into interrupts 8, 9, 13h, 21h and 24h. Interrupt 8 is the timer tick. In Anticad 1 and 4, this is always intercepted, and used to introduce a delay loop into the timer tick, which will have the effect of slowing the computer down. The delay loop is gradually made longer, up to a limit which is determined at the time that the virus installs itself in memory. In Anticad 2, the slowdown trojan is installed if you run a program 30 days after it is infected; in Anticad 3, this is 7 days.

Anticad 2 This virus has a characteristic length of 2900 bytes, and infects COM and EXE files. It has two possible interrupt 8 handlers. The non-fatal one is installed if the system time has an even number of seconds when the virus goes TSR. This handler gives the increasing delay. If the time was odd, it installs the fatal handler instead, which counts up to 5000 (about 4½ minutes) before triggering the song – there is no slowdown. In Anticad 1 and 4, the refresh timer is used to generate a random number, giving a probability of approximately ⅞ that the fatal trojan will be triggered. Then, just one handler is used, and the delay is 30 minutes. When the timer ticks trigger, the song is played, and the delays are reset. The tune is "Blue Danube" in Anticad 4, and an unknown melody in the others.

Interrupt 9 is the keyboard handler. In Anticad 2, it looks for Ctrl-Alt-Del, and if that combination has not been pressed, it increments a counter – when that counter reaches 4000, the Muddle flag is set (see interrupt 13h for the effect of this). Muddle is cleared if a disk write is performed.

If a Ctrl-Alt-Del is done, and the counter has reached 5000, then if the fatal flag is set, it trashes the Cmos of an AT. If the fatal flag is not set, it does the full trojan (described below). This reversal is probably a bug.

The full trojan works as follows. First the keyboard is cleared, sound is switched off, the video mode is set to graphics (which clears the screen). It then reads the boot sector of the floppy in drive A, to get the drive statistics, and writes random data to head zero, all tracks, however many sectors are on the diskette. It then does the same to drive B.

On device 128 (drive C), it writes to all heads on cylinder 0, then works its way down the disk, incrementing the cylinder number by an amount that is incremented each time. Then it does the same to device 129 (drive D) and then overwrites all bytes of the Cmos RAM with 0ffh, and finally hangs the system by going into an infinite loop.

The replacement interrupt 13h checks for writes, and if there have been 4000 keypresses since the last one, the write is disabled.

The new interrupt 21h is used to infect on load and execute (function 4bh) or open file (3dh). If the file in question is COMMAND.COM, it is ignored; if it is ACAD.EXE, the full trojan is triggered.

The virus self-recognition code is the two bytes at offset 12h from the beginning of the file being 89h, 19h. In memory, interrupt 21 function 4b40h returns 5678h.

When the virus seeks to the end of the file to determine the length, it goes to eof - 5, just like Jerusalem does; it does not, however, read the five bytes there, but simply adds five to what it finds. Another similarity to Jerusalem is the way that it relocates itself in memory, by using a three-byte instruction that it puts at 0:3fc to 0:3fe.

Anticad 3 This virus has two variants. One has a characteristic length of 3012 bytes; the other (Anticad 3b) has a length of 3004 bytes. It is very similar to Anticad 2, but there are some differences.

In Anticad 3, the time after an infected program installs the slow-down routine is reduced from 30 to 7 days.

If the fatal flag is set, and a Ctrl-Alt-Del is done while the tune is playing, then the full trojan is called. If the fatal flag is not set and Ctrl-Alt-Del is done while the tune is playing, it just overwrites the Cmos. If you run ACAD.EXE, the full trojan is called, except that the screen is not cleared, or sound switched off, and the hard disks are not touched. Likewise if you open a file called ACAD.EXE.

If the trojan is run, the bytes used to do the overwriting start with the message given above ("Program: Plastique 4.51" etc.).

In the interrupt 8 code, there are one-byte interrupts (0cch) which are possibly meant as a debug trap.

When the virus infects a file, it also increments the delay counter before using it to generate the encryption key; Anticad 2 and 3b don't do that.

Anticad 1 This is the next in the series – it is called Anticad 1 because it was the first in the series to be isolated. Its characteristic length is 4096 bytes.

The main difference is that it infects boot sectors on floppy and hard disks, as well as files. On floppy disks, it goes to the boot sector, and on to the track beyond the last track on the floppy, on head 0. On hard disks, it goes to the DOS boot sector, and to cylinder 0, head 0, sectors 7 to 14.

The fatal flag is set using a random number generator that gives it a $7/8$ chance of being set. The slowdown is still implemented, but it gets worse more gradually; instead of the loop incrementing by one each timer tick, it does so about one tick in three. If the fatal flag is set, instead of the slowdown, there is a delay of 30 minutes, at which point the tune is triggered.

If the tune is playing, and the user does a Ctrl-Alt-Del, then the full trojan is triggered. This is slightly different from the trojan of Anticads 2 and 3. The screen is cleared, and the computer beeps. Then the drive parameters of the physical devices 128, 129, 0 and 1 are discovered, with the hard disk by using interrupt 13, function 8, and on the floppy by reading the boot sector. It builds up a table for these devices, showing whether the device is present, and if so, the number of cylinders, heads and sectors. Then, it loops round the devices (C, D, A, B), writing data that begins "Plastique 5.21" as given above. It writes this on all heads of track zero of all devices, then to track 1, track 2 and so on. When this is complete, it tests to see whether it is running on an AT, and if it is, it overwrites the Cmos with 0ffh, and then halts the processor.

This damage routine is worse than for the Anticad 2 and 3 viruses, as it will hit all drives before it is possible to react, whereas those viruses complete one drive before going on to the next.

Anticad 1 also intercepts interrupt 13h, in order to infect boot sectors. It passes everything except reads on to the old handler. If the drive is device 0, 1 or 2, it is looking for a read of track 0, head 0, sector 2; this is the first FAT sector. If it is device 80, it is looking for cylinder 0, head 1 (where the FAT is). It ignores two out of three accesses to the FAT, but on the other, it infect the boot sector, and writes the body of the virus to track 40 on a 360 k floppy, track 80 on other floppies, and to sectors 0, 0, 7 to 0, 0, 14 on a hard disk.

Interrupt 21h is used to infect files, exactly as Anticad 2 and 3. If a file called ACAD.EXE is opened or run, it displays "Plastique …", including the "WARNING: DON'T RUN ACAD.EXE!". It sets the fatal flag, and jumps into the middle of the trojan, omitting the hard disk check, and so it only trashes the floppies.

If the virus is installed by booting from an infected disk or diskette, then the timer tick is used to install interrupt 21h. The virus occupies 8 k of high memory, and sets 0:84, the offset of interrupt 21h, to 0ffffh. It then counts 128 timer ticks before installing the replacement interrupt 21h (7 seconds). Also, the value at location 0:84, is checked to see if it is still 0ffffh. If so, the replacement interrupt 21h is not installed.

Anticad 4 The most noticeable difference between Anticad 4 and Anticad 1 is that the tune for Anticad 4 is "Blue Danube". Its characteristic length is 4096 bytes.

Also, the slowdown is made worse on every timer tick, instead of only on a proportion of them.

The bytes used in overwriting start with "by Invader …" as given above.

The in-memory self-recognition is done by an interrupt 21h, function 4243h, and 5678h comes back in AX, and 0ffh in BL. If you install the virus by booting from an infected disk, it goes memory-resident in the top 5 k.

If you open or run ACAD.EXE, and the fatal flag is not set, it just increases the maximum delay. If the fatal flag is set, it adds 400h to the counter that triggers the tune when it reaches 8000h. It also increments the ACAD-counter.

If you hit Ctrl-Alt-Del, there is a probability that the full trojan is triggered. This probability is calculated as follows: take the low byte of the slowdown counter, which is equally likely to be anywhere in the range 0 to 255. Compare that with the ACAD-counter, but divide the ACAD-counter by: (i) 2 if the tune is playing; (ii) 16 if the fatal flag is set; or (iii) 32 if the fatal flag is not set.

If that low byte is less than or equal to the ACAD-counter after division, trigger the trojan. The ACAD counter is cumulative; each instance of the virus inherits the counter from the parent virus. On the instance of the virus that I examined, the ACAD counter was 94h. So, if the fatal flag is not set, there is a probability of 1 in 64 of triggering the trojan, but if the tune is playing, the probability is 74 in 256; slightly more than 1 in 4.

Chapter 5
Action Plans

5.1 Precautions

The advice that I give people is to make a backup. This isn't an anti-virus precaution at all. It's just that when I look at most people's systems, they don't have an adequate backup, and you are much more likely to lose data from a hardware failure, a software crash or from "user error" than from a virus. I have seen too many people lose too much data that is too important. So if you, or your users, have some spare energy, put it into making a good, reliable, restorable backup.

But let's suppose that you've already got good, restorable backups. What can you do about viruses?

The first thing you could do is run a virus finder, such as FindVirus. Remember, this doesn't find all viruses, only the ones I know about.

If you think (or are willing to assume) that you are clean, and if it is important to you to stay clean, you should install a cryptographic checksummer, such as ChkVirus. ChkVirus, if used in accordance with the instructions, will tell you as soon as your computer is hit by a virus. It works by using the one weakness that every virus has – it has to alter executable code in order to propagate, and very few other programs will alter executable code.

You could inoculate your diskettes against boot sector viruses (BSVs) using Inoculate or any other inoculator, or even buy pre-inoculated diskettes. Again, this is a precaution that costs very little.

Another thing to do is to make sure that you have a clean copy of DOS – you'll need it if you have to go virus-hunting. Next, make a clean copy of all your executables, and write-protect the diskettes. Write-protect all your boot diskettes, and indeed any diskette that you aren't expecting to have to write to.

Write-protect tabs are wonderful, and although the diskette drive write-inhibit isn't quite 100 per cent, it is nearly so. I know it isn't quite 100 per cent, because I have some unmodified diskette drives, and some un-notched diskettes, and I can write to the diskettes in those drives. But that is because the diskette jackets are transparent to the light that the drives are using to detect the notch – normally, a write-protect tab will prevent any writes. I prefer the black ones, as they stick to the diskette much better than the silvery ones. Actually, any gummed paper will do fine, provided it is opaque.

If you accidentally boot from a non-bootable diskette, switch off instead of continuing the boot as DOS advises. This costs nothing, and will interfere with the infection process of some BSVs.

Get all your software from a reputable source. That doesn't mean that you must stop using Shareware and Public Domain software, it just means that you should use a reputable source. What is a reputable source? Well, Joe-in-the-next- office is not a reputable source, whereas Lotus Development (for example) is a reputable source. Somewhere in between Joe-in-the-next-office and Lotus are the great swarm of software vendors, most of whom are reputable and reliable, and some of whom may not be.

Obviously, you shouldn't pirate software; but the virus threat means that even a temporary copy is something to be concerned about. I would add this – suppose you have a legal copy of XYZ, and you are temporarily at another place without your diskettes, and without it on your hard disk. You might argue that taking a copy from someone else isn't piracy, since you have a licence to use the program. I won't argue about the legitimacy, but remember that copying executable files around is one way to spread viruses.

Some companies have issued a ban on the use of bulletin boards. That is actually a bad idea. For example, I run a free bulletin board (0494 724946, or +44 494 724946 outside the UK), on which you will find the most up-to-date information on the latest viruses – other bulletin boards offer similar information. The writers of these edicts have probably confused the act of downloading software (not all bulletin boards are run by reputable people) with the messaging function of a BBS, which is much more important, and quite safe.

Some companies have issued a blanket ban on games. This is also a bad idea, as a ban on playing games, coupled with threats of dismissal, is just not credible or enforceable. A much better idea is to ensure that the games that are played come from a reputable source. This means that they should have their original packaging (in the case of commercial games) or be obtained from a reputable User Group or supplier of Shareware. Probably the best thing to do is to channel games via the information centre, or at least through a responsible user (who is perhaps an enthusiastic games player). The problem of games being played in company time is the same as the problem of crosswords being done in company time, and is a simple management problem.

5.2 What To Do If You Are Hit: General Advice

Firstly, DON'T PANIC. That does more damage than anything else. Don't just start deleting and formatting – at least keep a specimen so that I can disassemble it. The flame thrower approach tends to destroy the evidence of how it got in (which could help the unfortunate person that inadvertently gave it to you) and without even fixing the problem. It can do even more damage: if you low level format a hard disk, you'd better have backups which actually restore. It is surprising how often they don't.

Even worse – I was once called in to a case of Italian virus in which there was one hard disk machine infected. The engineer had been, and he'd low level formatted the hard disk, and FDISK and FORMATed it. When I got there, all that was on the hard disk was IBMBIO.COM, IBMDOS.COM, COMMAND.COM … and the virus. All he'd succeeded in doing was to destroy the information that would have told me when the virus had installed, which would probably have told us where it had come from.

DON'T PANIC includes stopping other people from panicking. Senior management, as soon as they understand what has happened, want to do something immediately. Before you do anything, think through the consequences of what you are about to do.

Secondly, make sure that everyone who knows about it is told to keep quiet for now. An immense amount of damage could be done to the company's name. If the company decides to tell the world, that's fine, but the decision must be made at the appropriate level in the company.

Next, seek expert advice, unless you have in-house expertise. Do not attempt to deal with it yourself unless you are sure that you know what you are doing. You have to be a bit twisted and devious; the virus is not a naturally occurring bit of fluff with no brains. It was written by someone who is pretty twisted, and probably quite devious, and you may think that you understand the virus when you don't. In particular, if it looks and behaves like the XYZ virus, don't assume that it is. It might be version two of the virus, with a couple of extra surprises thrown in, or it might be a completely different virus, written to resemble one of the less harmful viruses. For example, Brain doesn't infect hard disks. So if you are twisted and devious, and you want to surprise people with a new boot sector virus, you make it look like Brain, but you have differences.

One of the biggest problems is in dealing with the diskettes. Every PC is accompanied by a vast cloud of diskettes, and at least some of these must be infected. Usually, less than 1 per cent are infected, but the problem is finding them. If you leave even one infected diskette – well, it was almost certainly just one diskette that brought the problem in. One approach is to use a hopper-fed machine that can check 700 floppy diskettes per hour; the main alternative is to train sufficient operators to do it manually.

How you treat infected disks and diskettes depends on the virus and its *modus operandi*. I haven't yet seen a situation where it was necessary for anyone to lose any data.

5.3 Procedures for Eradicating a Virus

5.3.1 Academic Institutions

In the special instance of an academic institution becoming infected with Brain or Italian, there is a particular problem with students having disks at home, not handing disks in, and so on. One technical college that I know of had Italian in May 1988, and still had it in June 1989.

I've devised a procedure for these cases. As well as doing a clean-up operation, you should start systematically inoculating every diskette. So, from a population where 100 per cent of diskettes are susceptible, you get down to only 10 per cent, then 1 per cent, then 0.1 per cent susceptible diskettes, and the virus is unable to reproduce, and is choked by the inoculation process. In order to help this along, you need to give a copy of a reliable inoculator program to a large number of people.

5.3.2 Major Companies

It's really quite easy to remove a virus from a disk. First, and always, boot from a DOS diskette that you *know* is uninfected. In the case of a file virus, all you have to do is delete all infected files, and replace them with clean copies. In the case of a BSV or partition sector virus (PSV), the simplest and most reliable way is to copy everything off the disk onto other media, and reformat the disk (if it's a PSV, then it'll have to be a low level format).

The problem is in finding the infected instances. You really ought to find them all, because if you leave one instance behind, that's how it got started in the first place.

I have organised a number of virus-hunts, and so have extensive experience in this. Essentially, what you have to do is examine every diskette and hard disk, plus other data storage media, to check for that virus. To do that, you must go round the user areas and check them there, or else organise all the diskettes into a central checking location, in which case you have to ensure that all the diskettes get back to the user they came from. This is not a trivial problem when a large number of computers are involved.

First, estimate the size of the problem. You should assume that every user in the company knows about the virus, and is worried that they might have it. Obviously, only a tiny percentage will, but they'll all want to be checked, and will complain and feel insecure if they aren't. So you should expect to check every machine and its diskettes within the building, and any associated building.

You must get the willing co-operation of the users, otherwise they won't turn in all their disks and backups. Make it clear that we aren't looking for a scapegoat, just viruses. You should also consider allowing users to send in their private, home PCs and diskettes.

Choose a large room for the operation, and make sure that there are plenty of tables, chairs, power leads, sticky labels, felt-tip pens, Sellotape, envelopes and assorted stationery. One person should be nominated as Diskette Control; all diskettes are his responsibility, and must pass via him, or one of his staff.

Each user should parcel up his diskettes in a box provided, including his name, location and telephone extension. The box should be easy to open and close. They should send that box to Diskette Control on the Friday evening.

You should expect about 100 floppies per computer, on average. It could be as high as 200, or as low as 50. You should aim to complete the operation over a weekend. If you think that you have 100 computers, then you probably have 120 or even 150. One company had twice as many as they originally thought. For a company with 200 computers, and 20 000 floppies, you'll need the following staff:

- Operations controller/technical advisor: 1 plus assistant
- Diskette Control: 2 plus assistant
- Hard disk team: 3
- Diskette checkers: 12

For a company with 20 computers, you will need:

- Operations controller: 1
- Diskette Control: 1
- Hard disk team: 1
- Diskette checkers: 3

For smaller companies, the staffing can be reduced slightly; for larger ones, there can be more economies of scale.

The main objective is to get the first hopper-fed machine started as soon as possible, and keep it going continuously. Everything else is secondary to keeping diskettes flowing through that machine as fast as possible.

Start early on Saturday morning, and get the first machine into action as soon as possible. Diskette Control should have a large box of diskettes ready to start feeding through, all from one user. When that is started, the rest of the operation can be set up.

Diskette Control's job is to issue diskettes to the checkers and receive them back, checking that there are the same number, and that they have all been checked. In a larger hunt there will be two Controllers, one for Diskettes Out, and one for Diskettes In.

One person will man the hopper-fed machine, keeping it fed with floppies and restarting it if it gets empty or jammed. That person will be relieved for meals, but the machine keeps going.

Any diskettes that are failed by the primary machine are marked with the user's phone number, and passed to a second workstation for further checking, as are any 3½-inch floppies (there are not usually enough 3½-inch floppies to warrant a dedicated 3½-inch drive machine – your company might be different). This workstation must, of course, first be certified as virus-free. The 3½-inch floppies are checked using the same software as is used in the primary computer, and any that fail are passed down the line.

The next machine in line should have a 1.2 Mb drive (and a 1.44 Mb, if possible) and must also, of course, be certified as virus-free. This should use Peeka, or some similar sector-reading software, to examine the floppies; if they are unreadable, then they should be considered candidates for reformatting, unless there is some good reason (for example, they might be Fastback backups). In any case, they should be marked as "NOT CHECKED" and the user advised to reformat them as soon as possible. If the floppies are readable, then the boot sector should be inspected if a BSV is being hunted; if a file virus, then FindVirus should be used to verify that the virus is on that diskette. If there is any uncertainty, the diskette should be put aside for a final check by the Operations Control.

Diskettes that pass the final check should be returned to Diskette Control, for return to the user. All checked diskettes should have a write-protect tab put on them, marked in green to show that they are clean. This is mainly to give the users confidence that their diskettes have been checked.

In the case of BSVs, the diskettes should be inoculated as they pass through the system, to make it very difficult for an outbreak to re-occur.

Once the diskette production line is working, you can start on the computers sent in from home. If they need unpacking and assembling, set up a production line to do so. Ideally, the home users will only have sent in the system box, and the same keyboard, power cables and screen can be used for each machine.

For each machine, boot from a clean DOS diskette, then type "DIR C:". If you see anything unusual, stop and call technical support, otherwise run Findvirus. If nothing is found, reboot from the hard disk and check to see if there are any other drives. If so, run Findvirus on them.

Next install ChkVirus or some other cryptographic checksummer. There are two reasons for installing ChkVirus. The first is to give a very early warning of any re-infestation, but the second is equally important – it gives the user a visible assurance that his computer is virus-free, which will reduce the number of support calls. Strictly speaking, ChkVirus (or other cryptographic checksummer) should be installed after booting from a clean DOS disk, and run from a floppy.

Exactly the same procedure can be used for the hard disk machines in the user areas, except that while the software is running, you should search for floppies in all the likely hiding places. Users might think that many floppies "don't count" as they are only backups, or haven't been written to for a very long time, or are only blank and formatted, or whatever. Any floppies found should be enveloped up, labelled with the user's phone number, and sent to Diskette Control.

Round about 5 p.m. on Saturday, you should estimate how well the job is going. If necessary, you should ask staff to work till midnight, and make whatever meal and transport arrangements are needed.

By the end of the second day (or the end of the first, if the company is small or there are fewer diskettes than expected) you should be left with a relatively small number of infected diskettes. These are most easily dealt with by doing a file-by-file copy from one diskette to another, in the case of BSVs, or by deleting the file in the case of file viruses.

On the Monday you should have a clean building. Inform the users how it went over the weekend, and explain the precautions that you've installed to prevent a re-occurrence.

Chapter 6
General Advice

6.1 Some General Advice

There are a number of things you can do, most of which cost nothing and which will tend to slow down the spread of viruses.

Use write-protect tabs on diskettes that do not need to be written to. Diskettes are the greatest carrier of viruses, and just doing a DIR on a data diskette can infect it with a boot sector virus.

Don't pirate software, and don't even copy software around that you are entitled to copy. If you have a site licence to a program, issue the copies from a central source, rather than allow users to copy each other's software.

If you see the "Not a system disk" message, then you've tried to boot from a non-bootable diskette. DOS recommends that you make sure that you have a system disk, then press any key. I recommend that you switch off and on again, as this will interfere with the spread of some of the boot sector viruses (but not Stoned).

If users want to play games, don't try to stop them, as you won't succeed. Instead, make sure that they get their games from a clean source. This could mean shrink-wrapped software, or Shareware from a reputable source, such as a User Group, or via a central source in the company.

Make sure that every engineer that goes round the company has write-protect tabs on all his diskettes. If he needs a scratch diskette for testing, provide him with one. If the engineer is external, and the diskettes were not write-protected, check his diskettes using Find-Virus for the various viruses before allowing him access to any computers. The same is true for PC Support staff.

If you receive software regularly from a particular source, ask that source what anti-virus precautions they are taking. If they trot out the usual "No games, no pirating" and nothing else, ask for them to do something more positive.

Watch out for anything from a university or college. These institutions have public access computers, and are almost helpless against viruses. Check any diskette from an educational institution using FindVirus. If you use students in sandwich courses, do not allow them to bring diskettes in without testing them.

Install anti-virus software on every computer that you can (site licences for such programs are usually available). Use it to check the partition sector, the boot sector and a selection of files.

Try to stay informed about the latest viruses. Newspapers and computer magazines tend to give a partial and distorted picture. The best up-to-date information will be in the IBM PC User Group magazine (phone 081-863 1191 for membership information) and on my bulletin board (0494 724946) and on Connect (081-863 6686) or subscribe to *Virus News International*.

Whenever you get new software, write-protect the diskette it came on before even putting it into your diskette drive. This will mean that you will never accidentally infect the distribution diskette.

6.2 The Anti-virus Service

A number of companies specialise in ridding companies of viruses. Usually, only one consultant is sufficient, working alongside some of the affected company's staff. These staff should be trained fully in the ins and outs of this particular virus, and help to plan the clean-out operation.

6.3 Inoculated Blank Diskettes

It is possible to get blank, formatted diskettes that are inoculated against Brain, Italian and Stoned virus (and other known boot sector viruses), which means that even though they are write-enabled, they will not get infected by those viruses.

6.4 Update Service

This book covers many of the PC viruses. Unfortunately, I can be quite sure that new viruses will appear. If you want to subscribe to an update service, please contact a reputable company – like S&S International. I'll be disassembling and reverse engineering any viruses that appear – this is quite a lot of work, and will take quite a lot of effort. I don't know how many new viruses will appear over that period, so I don't know how many new inoculators I'll be bringing out, or how many times I'll be adding new viruses to the documented list, or how many I'll be adding to FindVirus. But I do know that I'll be keeping up with what is going on in the field.

6.5 Further Reading

The Computer Virus Crisis (Fites, Johnson and Kranz). This book is a good general introduction to viruses. It explains what a virus is, and how it behaves on PCs and other types of computer. It covers a variety of ways to protect yourself from viruses, including a discussion of "safe" computing practices. It doesn't cover most of the common PC viruses; it touches on Brain and the Israeli virus (1813) but doesn't cover many others.

The Complete Computer Virus Handbook. This explains what a virus is, and lists many viruses. It is mostly summaries of other research, plus an evaluation of some anti- virus products. It is available from Price Waterhouse, price £20.

Virus Telex. This is a newsletter giving current information in the virus field. It is only available in German.

Virus News International. In order to get the most up-to-date information possible about the virus situation, you can subscribe to *Virus News International*. This will be sent to you in the middle of each month, and there may be extra supplements in between these if the situation calls for it. These will be faxed out, as a response to some virus or trojan emergency. The advantage of a faxed newsletter over traditional media is that the lead time between the completion of an issue and its arrival at your desk is a matter of hours instead of weeks. A diskette with the latest anti-virus software is included each month.

6.6 How It All Got Started In The UK

I run a Data Recovery Centre; people come to us when they have lost all the data from their hard disks, and I get it back for them. Usually, the problem is caused by erasing the wrong files, or data corruption; sometimes the disk is totally dead and has to be resuscitated. Late in 1987 we started getting people coming to us with dead disks that they claimed had been infected with a computer virus, so I decided to make some investigations. Nearly all of these weren't viruses at all – they were the old trio of data-killers, consisting of hardware problems, software problems and user errors.

One day, a disk arrived through the post marked "Danger Virus Infected". I didn't take it too seriously, and put it aside for later examination. It turned out to be the real McCoy.

I set up an examination room. I set up a two-floppy machine, and cleared out all unneeded diskettes. I took in a few copies of DOS, a few blank disks and my toolbox disks. The "infected" disk was a bootable disk, so I booted off it; it seemed normal. I had a look at it with Norton, and it looked quite ordinary. So I put in my DOS disk with FORMAT on it, formatted one of the blank disks; again I looked at it and it looked normal. I tried copying files to and from disks, I checked through COMMAND.COM and other system files using Debug and saw nothing unusual. Then I realised that I'd been using a potentially suspect version of DOS, so I rebooted from my DOS disk, and had another look around. Everything looked tickety-boo.

I had another look at the original contaminated disk, and noticed something unusual. There were a few bad sectors on the disk – this is fairly normal, except there didn't seem to be very many bad sectors. I ran Chkdsk and it reported 3 k in bad sectors, and I knew something fishy was going on.

When FORMAT formats a diskette, if it finds a defect on a track it marks the entire track as bad. So the minimum amount of bad sectors is 5 k, and bad sectors are usually a multiple of that. DOS FORMAT doesn't format a disk with 3 k of bad sectors.

DOS marks a cluster as bad by putting hexadecimal FF7 in the corresponding entry in the File Allocation Table (FAT). This marker tells DOS not to use that piece of disk for data, and normally you won't be able to read it because it will not even have been formatted.

I had a look at those bad clusters using Peeka. Sure enough, it was readable and full of code. This disk was infected! I had another look at the boot sector and it was normal, so I was completely baffled. The virus was somehow copying itself onto the disk, but it wasn't affecting any executable file; I had a look at a blank disk, and that also had the code in the 3 k of bad clusters, and definitely no executable file. So how could the virus spread itself? I had another look at the boot sector, and that was still normal.

At that point, I sat down and had a good think – I often find that thinking is a good substitute for flailing around at random. There had to be some copying mechanism, otherwise how could the virus spread itself? And if the copier wasn't a patched executable file, it had to be the boot sector, but the boot sector was clean. Then it hit me – how did I know that the boot sector was clean?

I went and got a clean copy of DOS, on a diskette with a write-protect tab. I booted off this disk, and had a look at the boot sector of the infected disk. What I saw was fearsome. I looked at the other diskettes, and saw the same thing on each boot sector. I had managed to infect just about every diskette that I'd taken into that room with me, including some of my toolbox disks. The contents of the boot sector, reproduced exactly as seen, were:

```
Welcome to the Dungeon
(c) 1986 Brain & Amjads (pvt) Ltd
VIRUS__SHOE RECORD v9.0
Dedicated to the dynamic memories
of millions of virus who are no longer with us
today - Thanks GOODNESS!!
BEWARE OF THE er..VIRUS : this program is catching
program follows after these messeges….. $#@%$@!!
```

This was not, of course, a disaster. I had taken only a limited number of disks into the room, and now all I had to do was assume that they were all infected. I could kill the virus by formatting them, but only if the computer had been booted from an uninfected diskette.

The real worry was that even an experienced disk expert like myself had nearly fallen for the virus's method of camouflage; the ordinary user wouldn't stand a chance.

Now that I understood what was going on, I could really begin to investigate. I worked from a machine that had been booted from a clean DOS disk. I captured the 3 k of bad sectors into a file, and disassembled the code. Every time a diskette is accessed (whether to do a DIR, or even to log on to the drive) the virus's code is copied onto that diskette. Every time a computer is booted from an infected diskette, the computer is infected with the virus and will infect other diskettes. Even if the diskette is not a boot disk, then trying to boot from it will infect the computer, and when you do put in a boot disk and boot from it, the computer remains infected and that boot disk becomes infected.

So how was the virus hiding its boot sector from me? Well, it needed a copy of the genuine boot sector in order to complete the boot process and load DOS, after it finished loading itself. So it stores a copy of the original boot sector on one of those bad clusters. When you ask to see sector zero (the boot sector), it simply shows you that sector instead and you are fooled into thinking all is well.

Since my first brush with Brain, I have disassembled many other viruses. Viruses use all sorts of techniques to hide themselves and to reproduce, and it is never safe to make assumptions about the way an unknown virus works, or to make assumptions about what is or is not possible.

Perhaps the biggest problem I had in those days was that I didn't have any idea what to expect – I'd read third-hand reports about viruses, and I believed many of the folk tales. Even worse, I didn't have proper anti-virus tools. Since then, of course, I've done a lot of research into real viruses, specimens from the field, and written some useful anti-virus tools, and so there's no need for anyone to be in that position in future.

Glossary

Assembly language A language that translates directly to machine code, giving total access to the hardware

Assembler A program that makes the translation from Assembly Langauge to machine code

Backup A copy of your data in another place, made because of the possibility of losing your working copy

BBS Bulletin board system; accessed via a modem

BIOS Basic input/output system

Boot To start up the computer by loading in the operating software (e.g. DOS)

Boot sector A sector on every disk and diskette, containing a program that is read in and executed by the computer at boot time

Boot sector virus (BSV) A virus that replaces the code in the boot sector

Bug Unintentional fault in a program

Clean DOS disk DOS diskette supplied by vendor, either notchless or write-protected from Day 1, known not to be infected with a virus

Cluster A group of sectors that is allocated to a file as a group, or else is all available for use

Cmos A technology for manufacturing chips, used for the permanent memory in an AT computer

COM file An executable program

COMMAND.COM The part of DOS that carries out commands like COPY

Cryptographic checksummer A program for calculating the checksum of the bytes of an executable, after encrypting each byte

Cylinder All the tracks on the disk that are the same distance out from the centre

Diagnostics Programs for testing (usually) the hardware of the computer

Direct action file virus (DAF) A file virus that infects without needing to be memory-resident

Directory An area that DOS uses to store file names and other information about files

EXE file An executable program

Executable Anything that the computer may run as a program; includes COM, EXE, overlay, BIN, SYS, boot sectors and partition sectors

FCB File control block

File allocation table (FAT) The area on the disk that tells DOS which clusters belong to which file

File virus A virus that infects a file

Format Initialise a disk ready for use

Head One of the read/write coils in the disk drive

Hexadecimal Arithmetic in base 16, represented by the digits "0123456789abcdef". Hexadecimal numbers are often suffixed with a letter "h", so "10h" is equivalent to 16 in normal decimal notation

Indirect action file virus (IAFV) A file virus that goes memory-resident and infects from memory

Infected file A file with one or more instances of a virus

Inoculate To fool a virus into thinking that it is already present, by using its self-recognition code

Interrupt The way that programs ask DOS and the BIOS to perform a task

LAN Local area network

Low level format (Factory format) A more final and lower level erasure of the contents of the disk than an ordinary format

Mace A popular disk sector editor, with other facilities

Memory-resident program A program that leaves part of itself in memory after it is run

MCB Memory control block

MBR Master boot record

NOP No operation; an assembler instruction

Norton Utilities A popular disk sector editor, with other facilities

Panic Doing something before you've planned what you ought to do

Partition sector The first sector on a hard disk to be read in at boot time

Partition sector virus (PSV) A virus that replaces the partition sector

Patch the disk To make a small change in a file or sector of the disk

PC Tools A popular disk sector editor with other facilities

PD software Public domain software, which you can legally copy

RAM Random access memory

Reboot, cold Starting a computer by switching the power off and on again

Reboot, warm IBM and similar computers can be restarted by holding down CTRL and ALT, and pressing DEL – this is called a warm reboot

Root directory (root) The area of the disk where the top level of files is catalogued

Sector A part of the disk, usually 512 bytes long

Shareware Software that you can legally copy, but must usually pay for if you decide to use it

Sheep-dip A computer used for testing incoming disks and files for possible viruses

Subdirectory An area of disk where the lower level of files is catalogued

Track All the sectors around the disk that can be read by one head

Trojan Program that deliberately does something (often harmful) in addition to what is expected

TSR A memory-resident program

Virus Program that copies itself

Worm A "chain letter" that propagates through a network

Write-protect On a 5¼-inch diskette a sticky tab over the write-protect notch makes a diskette unwritable. On a 3½-inch, you change the position of a plastic slider

How to claim your HALF PRICE copy of

Having purchased this book, you are entitled to claim 50% off the price of Dr. Solomon's Anti-Virus Toolkit, the leading anti-virus software for IBM and compatible PCs, which includes the ChkVirus and FindVirus programs described in this book. In the first instance, please contact one of the following offices for the Toolkit price details. Then, to receive your copy, simply complete the coupon below and return it with the appropriate remittance.

In the USA, Canada, and Mexico:
Ontrack Computer Systems, Inc, Suites 15–19, 6321 Bury Drive, Eden Prairie, MN 55346, USA. Tel: (612) 937 1107

In Australia and New Zealand:
Loadplan Australasia Pty Ltd, Suite 5, 17 Pakington Street, St Kilda, Melbourne, NSW 3182, Australia. Tel: 3/525 4088

In all other countries:
S&S International Ltd, Berkley Court, Mill Street, Berkhamsted, Hertfordshire HP4 2HB, England. Tel: 0442 877877 (International +44 442 877877)

This offer is limited to one copy per purchaser. Please send original form; photocopies not accepted.

Dr. Solomon's Anti-Virus Toolkit is a registered trademark of S&S International Ltd
IBM is a registered trademark of International Business Machines Corporation.

Name ....

Address...

....

Postal Code:.................................... Country...